Electronic Literature

For my parents, Paul and Barbara, my children, Jessica, Benjamin, and Aurora, and most of all for my wife, partner, and first reader, Jill.

Electronic Literature

SCOTT RETTBERG

polity

First published in 2019 by Polity Press

Polity Press
65 Bridge Street
Cambridge CB2 1UR, UK

Polity Press
101 Station Landing
Suite 300
Medford, MA 02155, USA

ISBN-13: 978-1-5095-1677-3 (hardback)
ISBN-13: 978-1-5095-1678-0 (paperback)

A catalogue record for this book is available from the British Library.

Library of Congress Cataloging-in-Publication Data

Names: Rettberg, Scott, author.
Title: Electronic literature / Scott Rettberg.
Description: Cambridge, UK ; Medford, MA, USA : Polity Press, 2018. |
   Includes bibliographical references and index.
Identifiers: LCCN 2018019604 (print) | LCCN 2018025325 (ebook) | ISBN
   9781509516810 (Epub) | ISBN 9781509516773 (hardback) | ISBN 9781509516780
   (pbk.)
Subjects: LCSH: Hypertext literature. | Electronic publications. |
   Interactive multimedia. | Literature and the Internet. | Literature and
   technology.
Classification: LCC PN56.I64 (ebook) | LCC PN56.I64 R48 2018 (print) | DDC
   802.85--dc23
LC record available at https://lccn.loc.gov/2018019604

Typeset in 11 on 13pt Adobe Garamond Pro by
Servis Filmsetting Ltd, Stockport, Cheshire
Printed and bound by CPI Group (UK) Ltd, Croydon

For further information on Polity, visit our website: politybooks.com

Contents

Acknowledgments

Segments of Chapter 2, "Combinatory Poetics," were adapted from "Dada Redux: Elements of Dadaist Practice in Contemporary Electronic Literature" by Scott Rettberg in *Fibreculture* 11 (2008).

Segments of Chapter 3, "Hypertext Fiction," were adapted from *Destination Unknown: Experiments in the Network Novel* by Scott Rettberg, PhD dissertation, University of Cincinnati, 2002; "Narrative and Digital Media" by Scott Rettberg and Jill Walker Rettberg in *Teaching Narrative Theory*, David Herman, Brian McHale, James Phelan, eds, Modern Language Association, 2010; "The American Hypertext Novel and Whatever Became of It?" and "Post-Hyperfiction: Practices in Digital Textuality" by Scott Rettberg in *Interactive Digital Narrative: History, Theory, and Practice*, Hartmut Koenitz, Gabriele Ferri, Mads Haahr, Diğdem Sezen, Tonguç İbrahim Sezen, eds, Routledge, 2015.

Segments of Chapter 5, "Kinetic Poetry," were adapted from "Bokstaver i begevelser" ["Letters in Space, At Play"] by Scott Rettberg, published in Norwegian in *Vagant* 2011:1.

Segments of Chapter 6, "Network Writing" were adapted from "All Together Now: Hypertext, Collective Narratives, and Online Collective Knowledge Communities" in *New Narratives: Stories and Storytelling in the Digital Age*, Ruth Page, and Browen Thomas, eds, University of Nebraska Press, 2011.

A short segment of Chapter 7 was adapted from the interview "Cavewriting" by Scott Rettberg, Jill Walker, Noah Wardrip-Fruin, Robert Coover, and Josh Carroll in *The Iowa Review Web* (July 2006).

I gratefully acknowledge the support of the Meltzer Research Fund, the University of Bergen, Brown University, and the Massachusetts Institute of Technology, and particularly John Cayley and Nick Montfort, my hosts at Brown and MIT during my 2017 sabbatical when the bulk of this book was written.

Thanks to all my friends, collaborators, and colleagues in the Electronic Literature Organization and in the field of electronic literature, who are too many to name individually. It is fair to say that during the past two decades, my professional and social lives have become indistinguishable. I could never have hoped to find more creative, supportive, dedicated, intelligent, funny, and talented people in my life. The best way I can thank them is to note that most of their names can found in the pages of this book. Finally, thanks to my students and colleagues in the University of Bergen Digital Culture program and the Bergen Electronic Literature Research Group.

1   Genres of Electronic Literature

Imagine a book. That should be easy enough, you're holding one now. The book is a particular reading technology, and it's a good one. It took a long time to develop. The codex book is portable and can be easily lugged from place to place. It is addressable. It has page numbers so I can easily communicate with you exactly where any piece of information is within its volume: we can get on the same page and read the same words. The book has a complex and multifunctional navigational apparatus. There is a table of contents, there is an index, and so the book can be navigated nonlinearly. The book is verifiable. It has a copyright page with a publisher and a place and a year and an author. The book is fixed. If I put it on the shelf now and come back and pull it out ten years later, the same words will be on the same pages as when I last opened the book. While the book could be destroyed in a fire or flood or might slowly decay, there is a sense of permanence to it. One of its main functionalities is to get thoughts down in print and carry them through time.

Imagine that the book were different. Imagine it offered other affordances (see Norman, 1999) and material properties. Imagine that instead of turning pages you could make any word in the book a link to some other part of the book, or even some other book. Imagine it were bound on a spool, so that you could enter and exit anywhere; a book without beginning or end. Imagine what you would do with that as a storyteller. Imagine what it would mean if every time you put the book up on the shelf, the words in the book shifted order and rearranged themselves. Would it still be the same book? What would you do with that as a poet? Imagine if, when you pulled the book down from the shelf and opened up the first page, the book asked you in what direction you wanted to go, and would not begin to tell a story until you responded. Imagine if the book were a conversation, a novel that you had to talk to. Imagine that, as you read a poem on the page of the book, the words jumped off the page into three-dimensional space and began flying around the room, shifting form and regrouping in the physical environment. Imagine that when you opened the book, it was filled with threads connecting it to all of the other books in your library, which would make it possible to pull part of another book right into the text of the one you were reading. Imagine if the book could read the newspaper and change its content depending on the time of the day, or the weather, or the season. Imagine if you opened the book and found all those of your friends who were reading the book at the same time leaving their comments in the margins. Imagine that when you opened the book, those same friends were all writing the book simultaneously. Imagine the book as a network, always on, always connected, and always changing. Imagine what you could do as a reader. Imagine what you could do as a writer. Imagine the book as a networked computer.

People imagined all of these things, both before the computer and the Internet came along and after. The difference between the way that we imagine the book before and after the digital turn is that now the affordances of the computer and the Internet are readily available to us. We can actualize these affordances. But how can we figure out how to best use these capabilities effectively to develop new kinds of poetry, new types of stories? We need to experiment to find out. Those experiments are what the field of electronic literature is all about.

Electronic literature is most simply described as new forms and genres of writing that explore the specific capabilities of the computer and network – literature that would not be possible without the contemporary digital context.

Electronic literature is an area that has rapidly developed as a field of creative practice, academic research, and pedagogy over the past half-century, most intensively from the 1990s until the present. Computers and the network have radically affected many aspects of life for a significant proportion of people on the planet. Textuality and communication are now digitally mediated. This book examines literature that reflects our new situation through the work of writers and artists who consciously explore the potential of new media for new modes of storytelling and poetic practice.

The first question asked by beginning readers of electronic literature – and even experienced readers encountering a new text – is "how do I read this?" For electronic literature, this question is not only hermeneutic – it refers not simply to how readers might encounter the meaning, style, themes, and language of the work but also to how readers can operate the text-machine itself. As Espen Aarseth established in *Cybertext: Perspectives on Ergodic Literature* (1997), non-trivial effort is required from the reader of a cybertext in order to *traverse* the text – and this understanding of how to move through the text must happen before any kind of interpretative reading can take place (p. 1). One reason to consider genre in electronic literature is to simplify that aspect of the process, to give readers a set of tools to enable them to understand "how to read" as they encounter the new forms of digital writing that electronic literature comprises.

This book is intended to address a significant lack in the literature of the field: so far few books have attempted to constitute electronic literature in a broad sense *as a subject* in totality. *Electronic Literature* attempts to place the most significant genres of electronic literature in historical, technological, and cultural contexts to make the subject more readily accessible. *Electronic Literature* provides a genre-driven approach to the corpus of electronic literature, albeit one that calls for a reconsideration of what qualities distinguish a creative genre in contemporary networked culture, as this may differ from traditional notions of genre in literature, art, and media studies. Genre in electronic literature is complicated by the interdisciplinary nature of the field and perhaps most importantly by the fact that it is driven in equal measure by cultural and technological contexts. While the authors and artists working in the field are informed by the historical influence of other arts disciplines and practices, their work is equally shaped and delimited by technological innovation. The software and platforms used to develop works of electronic literature constrain and afford properties of these emergent genres in significant ways.

While electronic literature must be read from a standpoint of media and platform-specificity, these new literary genres did not emerge from a cultural vacuum, but in response to and in conversation with literary and artistic traditions. The various genres of electronic literature such as hypertext fiction, kinetic poetry, combinatory poetics, interactive fiction, networked-based collective narrative, locative narrative, interactive textual installations, and interactive cinema in fact owe significant debts to specific twentieth-century literary and avant-garde movements such as Dada, Surrealism, modernism and postmodernism, Situationism, Fluxus, and others. This book tries to frame the emerging genres of electronic literature within these historical contexts, enabling better understanding of the continuity of literary and artistic practice as well as the innovation enabled by new technologies.

Defining electronic literature

The term "electronic literature" is controversial within the field itself. Detractors of the term claim that it is not specific enough – after all "electronic" refers essentially to any device powered by electricity, and the boundaries of "literature" are equally murky. Others prefer that "digital literature" should refer to roughly the same body of work. John Cayley (2002) offers "writing in networked and programmable media" as a more specific term. "E-Poetry" and "hypertext" also have their specific adherents, and Aarseth's "cybertext" is a narrower term for texts with specific interactive properties. A key advantage of the term "electronic literature" is its generality, and thus its ability to include those emerging genres that did not exist in the 1990s, when the term was first widely circulated. This may have contributed to the term's longevity.

The establishment of the Electronic Literature Organization (ELO) in 1999 produced a need for a single term to be agreed upon, and the widespread adoption of "electronic literature" to refer to the types of work we consider and survey in this book likely has as much to do with the Electronic Literature Organization as with any innate quality of the term itself (Rettberg, 2014a). Even in the late 1990s, it was clear that the type of work writers were creating in digital media, using the specific computational properties of the computer and produced within cultural contexts of the global network, could not easily be pigeonholed into one specific category. At the time there was some distance between "hypertext fiction" and "E-Poetry" writing communities. I was one of the founders of the ELO and took part in the conversations that lead to the adoption of "electronic literature" as a term to establish our frame of reference. The ELO board wanted to use a term that could encompass work produced in both of those contexts and others, independent of literary tradition or form. Virtually any definition or specific typology for electronic literature would likely become obsolete within a decade. New forms were already emerging then that challenged established generic boundaries, and there was need for a term that would be open enough to encourage diverse approaches to writing in digital media. During this early period in the popular adoption of the Web, the ELO board was also trying to choose a term that might appeal to a general audience, one that would not sound so technical or jargon-heavy that it would scare away potential readers or writers who were coming from print traditions. During our discussion of the term at one of the first ELO board meetings, Robert Coover characterized the term as "charmingly old-fashioned." The term was purposefully anachronistic from the beginning – intended to mark both a break and continuity between contemporary literary practices in digital media and hundreds of years of literary tradition.

In 2004, the ELO put together a committee, led by Noah Wardrip-Fruin, to try to establish once and for all a definition that would be applicable to the forms of literary practice that the organization centrally focused on. The result was this statement and list of exemplary forms:

> Electronic literature, or e-lit, refers to works with important literary aspects that take advantage of the capabilities and contexts provided by the stand-alone or networked computer. Within the broad category of electronic literature are several forms and threads of practice, some of which are:

- Hypertext fiction and poetry, on and off the Web
- Kinetic poetry presented in Flash and using other platforms
- Computer art installations, which ask viewers to read them or otherwise have literary aspects
- Conversational characters, also known as chatterbots
- Interactive fiction
- Literary apps
- Novels that take the form of emails, SMS messages, or blogs
- Poems and stories that are generated by computers, either interactively or based on parameters given at the beginning
- Collaborative writing projects that allow readers to contribute to the text of a work
- Literary performances online that develop new ways of writing

The list was not intended to be exhaustive, but instead to identify existing threads of practice and to encourage new ones to develop. A distinction that has clearly remained important over time is that between "e-books" and "e-lit." What we talk about when we talk about electronic literature is not primarily the digital environment as a new means of distribution for literature that could just as easily be printed in a book. There is no doubt that e-books have in the past two decades had significant effects on the way that literature is published, distributed, and consumed. E-books have brought some new innovations in their own right – such as social bookmarking of texts and "whispersync" features that merge the experience of text and audio-book across different reading and listening devices – but they are not essentially, to use N. Katherine Hayles' term, "born digital" (Hayles, 2008).

Works of electronic literature are native to the digital environment – for the most part they could not easily be produced or consumed in print literary contexts. Stephanie Strickland argues that electronic literature "relies on code for its creation, preservation, and display: there is no way to experience a work of e-literature unless a computer is running it – reading it and perhaps also generating it" (Strickland, 2009). These works depend in some essential way on the computer. Electronic literature is fundamentally experimental literature: the writers and artists producing these works are centrally concerned with new narrative forms and poetic approaches that could not exist in the absence of this computational context.

Considering the ELO's definition of electronic literature, Hayles (2008b) took particular notice of the phrase "important literary aspects," pointing out that in some cases works of electronic literature operate in a literary context beyond the boundaries of what is typically considered literature. Some works refer to literature or inscription, without themselves operating in the same signifying apparatus as literature in print contexts. Some examples of works in the *Electronic Literature Collection, Volume One* such as Giselle Beiguelman's *Code Movie 1* (2006) or Jim Andrews' *Nio* (2001) use language not as a direct semantic signifier, but instead as conceptual or visual material. The process of inscription and recoding, in Beiguelman's work, or the relationship between letters as visual form and representation of sound, in Andrews' work, take the place of representational semantics. The corpus of electronic literature is a literature of new literary forms, genres that have varying degrees of correspondence with those from previous traditions and contexts.

Novelty is undoubtedly central to electronic literature – its authors are trying out new tools and approaches and in some sense conducting experiments in the same way as scientists do in a lab, testing how materials work together, what sorts of reactions occur when new mixes of computational method and literary practice are cast into the same cauldron. But it is also the case that the new forms and thematic concerns of electronic literature do not merely emerge from the technology itself: instead they emerge from the interaction of new technologies with aesthetic concerns that have much longer histories. While the works this book addresses are born digital, they are not exclusively of digital lineage. They have particularly deep connections to experimental writing and avant-garde art movements of the twentieth century.

This book considers what is new and essentially digital about electronic literature, but also and perhaps even more importantly how these genres connect with and expand upon prior movements. Kinetic digital poetry could not exist in its current form without traditions in concrete poetry. Lettrism, visual poetry, and sound poetry emerged well before there was a computer in every home, much less a smartphone in most pockets. The aesthetics of combinatory poetry may not have been explored so extensively were it not for the Dadaist desire to overcome language, or the surrealist yearning to uncover the logic of dreams, or the Oulipian fascination with writing under constraint. Electronic literature not only takes us forward to explore new horizons but also on a retrospective journey that can lead to better understanding of how the past of literature propels us toward its future.

Reconsidering genre in electronic literature

Tzvetan Todorov begins his essay "The Origin of Genres" by observing that to "persist in discussing genres today might seem like an idle if not obviously anachronistic pastime" (Todorov, 1976, p. 159). Like the term "electronic literature" the concept of genre is one that might seem "charmingly old-fashioned" when we are discussing literary forms native to the digital media. Digital media are after all not only multimedia but also variable media, malleable and transcoded (Manovich, 2002). The general-purpose computer is defined by the fact that it can perform the tasks of any other machine if that machine's processes can be understood as computable. Thus we no longer encounter computers as single-purpose devices. No contemporary computer would only be capable of calculating missile trajectories – with different software the same machine could be used to regulate traffic patterns, or emulate human speech, or to play *Angry Birds*, or to watch cat videos on YouTube.

The material aspects of electronic literature do not themselves determine genre – while we could speak of a sculptor working with marble, or bronze, or wood, or ice to be working within a particular medium, computational artists work with a medium that can function as many different media simultaneously. While we can speak of modalities of computational media – text, sound, voice, image, moving image, interactive image, etc. – those modalities can themselves be made to transform from one to the other. A text can be morphed into an image, which can again be transformed into sound. Because we can transcode from text strings, lines of code, into images, audio recordings, telephony, and video, computational media cannot be understood as fixed.

Perhaps it is folly even to consider "the work" of electronic literature. Many of the examples we will look at in this book are in fact better understood as "projects" than as works in the conventional literary sense. We usually consider a "work" of literature to have reached a state of fixity and of completion. The technology of the printed book exemplifies the quality of fixity. Writing in digital media on the contrary can and will change over time. A "publication" of electronic literature has at least one of the same effects as a publication in print, in that it involves something being brought forth to a public, but its publication does not imply fixity in the same way. The publication of electronic literature is not finished just because it has reached its public – it could change right before the reader's eyes. Many electronic literature projects have multiple iterations that involve not only revisions in the text or the underlying code, but also the form and nature of the artwork itself. Judd Morrissey's *The Last Performance [dot org]* (2007) offers one example – it is a collectively written database narrative project that has been variously presented as an online project, as a museum installation, and as a dance performance work (see Rettberg, 2010). The variety of venues for electronic literature also complicates the situation of genre. If the same work is presented first online for readers sitting at their computers, and then as a performance for a live audience, and then as an installation in an art gallery, can we even break its genre down into categories as basic as literary text, performance, or visual art?

Genre from a literary studies perspective

In this book I identify threads of practice and argue that these can be understood as genre, that it is useful to understand them as genre, but I do so with a keen awareness of the fact that most works of electronic literature are what N. Katherine Hayles has dubbed "hopeful monsters" (Hayles, 2008, p. 4). These new creations emerge not in a smooth and linear progression from existing genres but in a more chimerical fashion. I write separately of combinatory poetics and kinetic poetry, but many kinetic poems are also combinatory. Likewise, many works that could be described as locative narratives or literary installations are also hypertext fictions. So while literary genre in the sense that I will use it serves to concentrate our attention as readers on specific aspects that individual projects share within a group, none of these genres can be said to have fixed or immutable boundaries.

Literary studies has taught us to approach the idea of genre with caution and awareness that genres are better understood as situational framings rather than immutable categories that correspond to deep structures inherent in the literary work itself. Of course, that has never stopped thinkers from trying to devise systems that account as comprehensively as possible for categories of literary production dominant during their day – and ideas of genre dating back to the ancient Greeks still have substantial influence on the way that we experience and process literary experience today. In his *Poetics* Aristotle offered tragedy, epic poetry, and comedy as core genres and provided a detailed analysis of the dramatic structure of tragedies as they were written in his time (Aristotle, 1997). Neoclassical approaches continued to seek universally valid systems for classifying and describing texts (Barwarshi and Reiff, 2010). Northrop Frye discusses the archetypal mythos and the triad of comedy, romance, and tragedy within principal genres of rhetoric including drama, epos, fiction and lyric (Frye, 2000). While some works of electronic literature can be described in broad strokes as comic or tragic, dramatic, fictional, or poetic, the classic archetypal genres typically do not apply to electronic literature.

More contemporary discussions have treated literary genre as situated action rather than universally applicable typology. Todorov sees genre primarily as the result of institutional discourses that constitute norms. Individual texts are produced and understood in relation to those norms:

"A genre, literary or otherwise, is nothing but this codification of discursive properties" (Todorov, 1976, p. 162). Todorov understands the origin of genres to be prior genres, and genre to be a process of continuous transformation: "by inversion, by displacement, by combination" (p. 161).

Jacques Derrida discusses "the law of genre" – the idea that genre has the function of imposing norms on literary and cultural practices: "As soon as the word 'genre' is sounded, as soon as it is heard, as soon as one attempts to conceive it, a limit is drawn. And when a limit is established, norms and interdictions are not far behind: 'Do,' 'Do not' says 'genre,' the word 'genre,' the figure, the voice, or the law of genre" (Derrida, 1980, p. 56). In Derrida's view, genre functions more to exclude forms of literary practice than to elucidate them: "… as soon as a genre announces itself, one must respect a norm, one must cross a line of demarcation, one must not risk impurity, anomaly, or monstrosity" (p. 57). Electronic literature is considerably resistant to clear lines of demarcation. Hybridity and perhaps monstrosity (see Leclair, 2000) are par for the course in a multimedial field whose cycles of creation move at the speed of technological change.

After reader response theory and the rise of cultural studies, we can assert that genres are actions, as is any other kind of typology. Genres do not uncover a code or deep structure, but are the product of an active and interested process. These frameworks do not simply emerge from the culture; they are imposed. John Frow (2006) writes: "genre is not a property of a text but is a function of reading. Genre is a category we impute to texts, and under different circumstances this imputation may change" (p. 102). The "function of reading" that genre performs is particularly important to consider as we encounter electronic literature.

Frow describes "reading regimes" – institutions that comprise a cultural apparatus for reading: for example, schools, organizations, publishing companies, and marketing agencies that reify and regulate practice of reading. The reading regime of electronic literature has a complex composition. There are now institutions of electronic literature. There are organizations like the Electronic Literature Organization and the E-Poetry Festivals. In universities electronic literature is taught within various disciplines: English, comparative literature, creative writing, communications, art, and design. There are a number of publishers and online journals – such as the *electronic book review, Dichtung Digital, Hyperrhiz: New Media Cultures*, and *The New River* – that have made sustained efforts to publish electronic literature and criticism of it, and there are a few annual awards on offer, such as the Electronic Literature Organization's Robert Coover Award for a Work of Electronic Literature and the New Media Writing Prize. At the same time the cultural apparatus of electronic literature is unstable in comparison to longer-established fields of literary culture: individual authors might forget to renew their web hosting or abandon web projects, functionally un-publishing them from the Internet; some of the most important journals in the field during the 1990s and 2000s are no longer online; technological platforms used to develop works might become obsolete as software companies go out of business or are acquired; and mechanisms of evaluation for digital work in both academia and in the culture at large are still insufficiently developed. The varying norms and standards of different electronic literature venues and audiences further complicate the reading regime of electronic literature.

Thomas O. Beebee (2004) proposes that generic difference is "grounded in the 'use-value' of a discourse rather than in its content, formal features, or its rules of production" (p. 7). We claim genres for particular purposes. The body of work we survey here has been described as "electronic literature" at least in part in order to make a claim that the work *is* literature and should be read as such. In distinguishing genres within electronic literature, we also make assertions about the use-value of those genres for writers and readers. Rather than understanding electronic literature as an undifferentiated mass of experimental literary practices in digital media, by naming these genres and linking them to historical contexts, we also make certain claims to legitimacy. These practices are not ahistorical and did not materialize from thin air with the dawn of the digital age, but are grounded in literary and artistic traditions. Jessica Pressman considers for example the work of Young-Hae Chang Heavy Industries and finds explicit connections to modernist poetry being used to serve a claim to cultural legitimacy, to "highlight their literariness, authorize their experiments, and situate electronic literature at the center of a contemporary digital culture that privileges images, navigation, and interactivity over narrative, reading, and textuality" (Pressman, 2008, p. 300). I argue that the connections between genres of electronic literature with modernist and postmodernist literature go deeper than that, as in certain cases both the thematic concerns and structural models of the works can be read as clear extensions of the same cultural projects.

Ultimately, the reason for reading electronic literature from the perspective of genre is pragmatic. Genre provides a map to a certain territory, even as the process of mapping also defines the territory. By considering electronic literature in terms of genre we develop a shared vocabulary and set of referents. When we identify, if not themes, then at least formal and stylistic qualities that a group of cultural artifacts and practices share in common, we establish a frame of reference. We establish an understanding of the conventions writers are working with and against. Genre provides students and researchers with a background that makes it easier to discern the particular qualities of whatever work is set into view. An understanding of genre begins to give us a sense of "how to read" and perhaps in the case of electronic literature, where and what to read, enabling movement past the interface to the content of the work that lies beyond its form and apparatus. Genre further provides writers with models that they might adopt or subvert. In some of the cases discussed in this book, even the source code of the work itself is publicly available to read and perhaps to modify and tinker with. Writers can study works of electronic literature in a very specific way, not only in terms of content or style, but also rules of operation, as represented in the code.

The technological apparatus plays a special role in the formation of electronic literature genres distinct from print literary genres. Joseph Tabbi (2009) notes that both genre and media are "being transformed concurrently – and those transformations (as much as the work itself) are what need to be tagged and traced." Technology is not entirely determinative of genres of electronic literature, but the capabilities and limitations of systems, platforms, and software used to create and distribute electronic literature afford and constrain digital works in ways that are essential to understanding them.

Genre from a media and technology perspective

Our understanding of electronic literature must be informed by our understanding of the technological context in which it is produced. A central project for readers of electronic literature is more to deeply engage with questions of how technology is changing cultural practices in a more general sense. In *Gramophone, Film, Typewriter* Friedrich Kittler quotes Friedrich Nietzsche's reflections, after he started writing with a typewriter, on how the writing technology he was using to produce his work was reflexively informing the very structure of his thought and its expression on the page: "Our machines are also shaping our thoughts" (Kittler, 1999, p. 249). During this period, Nietzsche's writing style changed from the discursive style of *The Birth of Tragedy* and *The Genealogy of Morals* to the more epigrammatic and staccato style of his later work.

One of the long-standing debates in the theoretical discourse of technology has been the varying degree to which humans alternately shape technology through its social construction and in turn how humans may themselves become shaped by the technologies that structure their environment. Technological determinists argue that we are more shaped by our technology than vice versa. "Media," Kittler writes, "determine our situation" (Kittler, 1999, p. xxxv). N. Katherine Hayles alternately proposes that we consider a process of technogenesis, in which humans and technology are coevolving in a process of mutual symbiosis (Hayles, 2012). That is to say that technologies determine our situation even as we determine our technological apparatus. The two processes are in a feedback loop and cannot be simply separated from one another. I concur with Hayles – while it would be inaccurate to characterize our situation as entirely determined by our technology, it would similarly be wrong to claim that we have complete control of our tools. We rather co-evolve with our technologies.

Bernard Stiegler describes the potential of digital media to be reciprocal media – anamnetic mnemotechnology. Our abilities to both decode and recode digital media are essential but threatened aspects of the creative potentiality of digital media (Stiegler, 2010). Many of the current genres of electronic literature are good representatives of anamnetic technology. At the same time, approaches to computing have increasingly moved to a market-driven model, in which the computer user is more driven to consume media, or to produce it within the templated confines of social networks, than to actually create independently in the medium. The iPad is a consumer device focused on catering to the needs of an information consumer rather than the engagement of creative users of the technology. It marks a move toward computational devices that we can easily read from but only write to with more difficulty. Lori Emerson notes that some works of electronic literature can be read as a kind of resistance toward the power relations implicit in the vanishing interface "by hacking, breaking, or simply making access difficult, they work against the way in which digital media and their interfaces are becoming increasingly invisible – even while these interfaces also increasingly define what and how we read/write" (Emerson, 2012). Authors of electronic literature work within the bounds of interfaces, and the interface must be understood as mediating both the writer's creative process of production and the reader's experience of the work. As Christian Ulrik Andersen and Søren Pold (2014) note, interfaces are not neutral: "Whether the interface mediates between man and computer, between computers or between humans it will always reflect a balance of submission and control. This balance is often conditioned by ideology."

The technological environment constrains the genres of electronic literature not only through the form and capacities of software and hardware but also through codes in Lawrence Lessig's sense – legal strictures, copyright regimes, and labyrinthine software terms of use that often involve deep surrender of personal rights (Lessig, 1999). For creators and users of electronic literature these codes constrain and limit the types of materials that can be used and in some cases the life span of the work itself. An important concern in the field is the effect that using proprietary technology and software can have on projects developed in those platforms. Once its corporate owner does not support a platform, works developed in that platform may become obsolete. Some of the classics of 1990s hypertext fiction made in Storyspace and interactive poetry made in Shockwave are now functionally inaccessible. In some cases, publishers of works of electronic literature have even held onto copyright and refused to let even the authors republish their own work, long after they have discontinued support of the work.

Gunther Kress (2010) and others have written on the semiotics of digital objects in their essentially multimodal nature. The general-purpose computer offers authors a full panoply of options to affect, change, and operate simultaneously mixes of modalities that could not be executed in analog media. This results in particular consequences as we consider genres of electronic literature: depending on the technology used to create and distribute a particular work, and on the context of its manifestation, we may for instance be called upon to read images, sounds, music, interface, interaction, design, layout, spatial situation, temporality, and perhaps even code as well as the surface text.

We read the poetics and language of works of electronic literature, but we may also read to understand their structures, rules of operation, platform, and algorithms. Nick Montfort and Ian Bogost have led a drive toward "platform studies": scholarship that investigates the relationships between the hardware and software design of computing systems and the creative works produced on those systems (Bogost and Montfort, 2009). The MIT Press Platform Studies series provides examples of how platforms such as the Atari 2600, the Commodore Amiga, and Flash are developed in particular historical, economic, and cultural contexts and both those contexts and the technical capabilities and limitations of the platform itself play important roles in forming the creative works produced within them. Thus, while we can still think of poetry, fiction, and drama as genres involved in electronic literature, we can also think of Flash (platform) animated poetry, Processing (platform) interactive poetry, and HTML (platform) hypertext fiction. The platforms involved in the production of these works also must be considered formative of their genre. Mark Marino, Matthew Fuller, and others have pushed for "software studies" and "critical code studies" – these can be understood in relation to platform studies – if a platform is the system or operational layer which can be programmed, software studies focuses on the level of writing and creative practice of the programming itself. For analysis of computational literary works this would mean critical reading of the code underlying the surface text as it is experienced by the reader – to use the terms set out by Espen

Aarseth in *Cybertext*, such reading entails the analysis of the *textons* of code underlying and operating the text-machine in addition to the *scriptons* manifested for the readers' consumption (p. 63). While there is by no means a widespread consensus that a deep understanding of code is necessary for critical analysis of works of electronic literature – there may in fact sometimes be benefits to focused surface-only readings of works – critical code studies offers the opportunity to engage with works under the hood, not only as literary works, but as computer programs.

Overview of key theoretical, critical, and analytical work in the field

A substantial body of work in the theory and criticism of electronic literature has been published from the 1990s to the present. Early studies of electronic literature such as George Landow's monograph *Hypertext: The Convergence of Contemporary Theory and Technology* (1992), the collection he edited *Hyper /Text /Theory* (1994), and the second edition of Jay David Bolter's *Writing Space: Computers, Hypertext, and the Remediation of Print* (2001) introduced general concepts related to hypertext and related them to topics such as interface studies and post-structuralist theory. These texts made important theoretical contributions, if referencing only a few early works from a slowly emerging corpus of electronic literature. Some studies such as Jane Yellowlees Douglas' *The End of Books or Books Without End* (2000) and her earlier work from the 1990s focused specifically on close readings of that relatively small body of early hypertext fiction. Michael Joyce's essay collection *Of Two Minds: Hypertext Pedagogy and Poetics* (1996) offered the perspective of an author and writing teacher on the practice and poetics of the emerging form. A second wave of scholarly monographs such as Espen Aarseth's *Cybertext: Perspectives on Ergodic Literature* (1997) and Marie-Laure Ryan's *Narrative as Virtual Reality: Immersion and Interactivity in Literature and Electronic Media* (2001) recast the generic boundaries and conceptual dimensions of digital literature by moving the discourse of the field to more explicitly narratological territory, and by pushing the field toward broader categorical dimensions than hypertext alone, for instance encouraging the serious theoretical consideration of interactive fiction and computer games. Markku Eskelinen's *Cybertext Poetics: The Critical Landscape of New Media Literary Theory* (2012) builds further upon typologies of cybertext and narratology. Loss Pequeño Glazier's *Digital Poetics: The Making of E-Poetries* (2001) also attempted to expand the scope of critical inquiry to include emerging poetic practices specific to the Web, while situating them within experimental print poetry tradition. Brian Kim Stefans has written two critical books, *Fashionable Noise on Digital Poetics* (2003) and *Word Toys* (2017), that consider digital poetics as an element of broader movements in contemporary poetry.

A number of monographs about specialized subtopics and individual genres of electronic literature or focused theoretical approaches have been published in recent years. Nick Montfort's *Twisty Little Passages: An Approach to Interactive Fiction* (2003) provides a thorough introduction to the history of that specific genre. Noah Wardrip-Fruin's *Expressive Processing* (2009) considers the evolution of procedural narrative. Matthew Kirschenbaum's *Mechanisms: New Media and Forensic Textuality* (2012) considers works of electronic literature from a forensic perspective, considering how even such contingencies as the physical storage media on which works are distributed and preserved can affect both our experience of a work and the material conditions of its survival. Lori Emerson's *Reading Writing Interfaces* (2014) considers how writing technologies mediate the production of writing including electronic literature, and to some extent set poetic parameters for writers to work with and against. David Ciccoricco's *Reading Network Fiction* (2007) examines hypertext fiction on and off the Web through network tropes. Belinda Barnet's *Memory Machines* (2013) narrates a history of the development of hypertext and early hypertext fiction based on interviews with key actors with innovators responsible for its creation. Jessica Pressman's *Digital Modernism: Making it New in New Media* (2014) explores a collection of digital works through the lens of historical modernism. Manuel Portela's *Scripting Reading Motions* (2013) considers how combinatory and kinetic poetry self-consciously play with the processes and dynamics of reading and writing. Somewhat broader and more historiographical in approach are Chris Funkhouser's two monographs, *Prehistoric Digital Poetry: An Archaeology of Forms, 1959–1995* (2007) and *New Directions in Digital Poetry* (2012), that together establish a comprehensive record of landmark developments in the history of digital poetry. Sandy Baldwin's *The Internet Unconscious: On the Subject of Electronic Literature* (2015) reframed "electronic literature" as the collective and alienating act of writing the Internet and becoming subject to it. David Jhave Johnston's *Aesthetic Animism* (2016) makes an important contribution focused on the poetics of kinetic and interactive typography. Rita Raley's *Tactical Media* (2009) situates electronic literature and activism in a digital art context. Roberto Simanowski's *Digital Art and Meaning* (2011) wrestles with the balance between meaning and spectacle in a number of works of electronic literature and digital art. Jeremy Douglass, Mark C. Marino, and Jessica Pressman's *Reading Project: A Collaborative Analysis of William Poundstone's*

Project for Tachistoscope [Bottomless Pit] provides an analysis of a single work by three different authors using three distinct analytical methods. Dene Grigar and Stuart Moulthrop's *Traversals: The Use of Preservation for Early Electronic Writing* (2017) documents the process of archiving and documenting several early hypertext works and develops deep readings of the works concerned. A number of N. Katherine Hayles' books, such as *How We Became Posthuman* (1999), *Writing Machines* (2002), *My Mother Was a Computer* (2005) and *How We Think: Digital Media and Contemporary Technogenesis* (2012) laid out theories of posthumanism and materiality important to the discourse of electronic literature and used works of electronic literature as tutor texts to support broader theoretical claims. N. Katherine Hayles' *Electronic Literature: New Horizons for the Literary* (2008) is perhaps the book that has had the most impact in establishing an initial set of referents and laying out some forms that characterize the field. The first chapter of Hayles' book provided a swift and solid introduction to genres of electronic literature, even as other chapters used electronic literature to weave together threads of Hayles' theoretical project. I take the liberty of using *Electronic Literature* as the title for this volume in part because this book, written a decade later, carries on the first part of Hayles' project to more extensively describe contemporary genres of digital writing and the discourses surrounding them to a non-specialist audience.

Edited collections have also been important to establish in the field of electronic literature. Collections such as *New Media Poetics: Contexts, Technotexts, and Theories* edited by Adelaide Morris and Thomas Swiss (2009); the *First Person, Second Person, Third Person* series edited by Noah Wardrip-Fruin and Pat Harrigan (Wardrip-Fruin and Harrigan 2004; Harrigan and Wardrip-Fruin 2007, 2009); *The Aesthetics of Net Literature: Writing, Reading and Playing in Programmable Media* edited by Peter Gendolla et al. (2007); *Reading Moving Letters: Digital Literature in Research and Teaching* edited by Simanowski et al. (2010); *Beyond the Screen: Transformations of Literary Structures, Interfaces and Genres* (2010) edited by Jörgen Schäfer et al.; *Analyzing Digital Fiction* edited by Alice Bell et al. (2014); *Interactive Digital Narrative* edited by Hartmut Koenitz et al. (2015); and *Electronic Literature Communities* edited by Scott Rettberg et al. (2015) gather together voices of critics, authors, and artists working in the field, and establish critical perspectives on niche aspects of the field. *Electronic Literature as Model of Creativity and Innovation in Practice: A Report from the HERA Joint Research Project* (Rettberg, 2014b) provides an extensive account of the most substantial Digital Humanities research project to date in the field. *The Bloomsbury Handbook of Electronic Literature* edited by Joseph Tabbi (2018) is the most recent edited collection of this kind, providing an excellent representation of approaches and debates that have defined the field in the 2010s. Research and teaching in the field also rely heavily on historical readers and reference works such as *The New Media Reader* edited by Noah Wardrip-Fruin and Nick Montfort (2003) and *The Johns Hopkins Guide to Digital Media* edited by Marie-Laure Ryan, Lori Emerson, and Benjamin J. Robertson (2014), which place electronic literature in broader digital culture contexts.

Joseph Tabbi (2010) argues that literature *becoming a network* is fundamental to its "renewal and emergence in the networked environment of computers, interfaces, and tagged content" (p. 40). I have gone in some length here at the outset to identify critical and theoretical works that have played important roles in developing the discourse of the field, both because I hope that readers of this book will want to dig deeper in specific genres and topics discussed here as well as to acknowledge that the present work owes a great deal to this network of prior research. More than establishing a new theory of electronic literature or bringing a single aspect of the field into sharp focus, this book is an aggregation of views, a portrait of genres of electronic literature that brings in a chorus of many voices from the field and serves as an invitation to an ongoing and multifaceted conversation centered on literature and digital media.

Why read electronic literature?

Electronic literature helps us to understand how digital technologies and digital culture impact writing in the broadest sense. The genres of electronic literature represented in this book are digitally native forms that involve the computational and multimedial properties of the computer both in the production of the text and in its traversal. In studying electronic literature we ask what it means to "read" computer programs as literary artifacts – and in so doing perhaps expand our notion of what the act of reading entails.

Electronic literature is experimental literature in the sense it functions much like basic scientific research: there is as much to learn from failure in this field as success. Studying electronic literature is less about tackling a canon than it is about building a collective understanding of the creative potentialities of digital media. Electronic literature drives us to consider how computation affords new modes of literature, at the same time as it constrains them in contextually specific ways. While some experiments in electronic literature are simply tests of the poetic potential of a particular platform, other works pioneer techniques later used in mainstream cultural production.

Electronic literature teaches us approaches to reading and writing digital media. In this sense it has applications not only for literary scholars and for creative writers, but for anyone interested in understanding or creating in digital media. The majority of the students who have moved through my electronic literature courses over the years have not gone on to become literary scholars or creative writers, but have instead found careers as web designers, as teachers, as journalists, as librarians, as marketers, as media consultants, and in information technology. As objects of study and as processes of creative production, works of electronic literature may be used to teach digital media skills, interactive media strategies, and new ways of understanding digital culture.

Perhaps the most important reason to read electronic literature is that the study of these works provides us with opportunities to consider what is happening to our situation within a world increasingly mediated by digital technology. As self-reflexive literary artifacts, works of electronic literature present us with crafted experiences that reflect changes wrought by the digital turn taking place in the nature of communication, textuality, society, and perhaps even the structure of human thought.

The structure and method of this book

Works of electronic literature referenced in the chapters of this book will include a balance of historical examples from the 1950s to the early 2000s and contemporary work produced in the last decade. The book focuses primarily on work written in English, but it is important to note that there are significant works and active communities writing in French, Spanish, German, Portuguese, Catalan, Polish, and many other languages. The selection of works will include some works that are now out of circulation but will emphasize those that remain accessible and available for study – particularly work from the three volumes of the *Electronic Literature Collection*. The majority of the chapters in this book have a roughly parallel structure, each approaching a different genre or set of related practices. Each core chapter of the book includes:

- Consideration of how the genre is informed by and emerges from preceding cultural and artistic practices and movements;
- Discussion of how each genre is shaped by a technological apparatus, by particular software and hardware platforms and the cultural contexts surrounding them;
- Description of the particular medial and artistic properties that

distinguish the focused group of digital literary works as a specific genre;

• Presentation of the history of each genre, including an overview of key works, core theoretical concepts informing practice, analysis of how each genre has evolved and its potentialities for future practice; and

• Suggestions of how the genre informs and opens up new ways of understanding contemporary media and culture.

The five chapters that follow engage substantively with core genres of practice in electronic literature: combinatory poetics, hypertext fiction, interactive fiction and other gamelike forms, kinetic and interactive poetry, and network writing. The majority of creative works presently shown and studied as electronic literature exhibit elements of one or more of these genres. The concluding chapter "Divergent Forms" briefly considers practices that have built upon these genres in ways that extend them to other environments and other disciplines, such locative narrative, augmented and virtual reality work, interactive installations, and expanded cinema.

2 Combinatory Poetics

When scholars of electronic literature discuss its history, they often start with hypertext fiction, because hypertext was the first form of digital writing to receive sustained critical attention in the English-speaking literary studies context. We will instead begin with combinatory poetics, the oldest genre of electronic literature. Christopher Strachey's *Love Letters* generator (1952) is most likely the first computer program made to generate literary text, and combinatory poetics have remained an essential genre of electronic literature through to the present day. Like many of the other genres considered in this book, combinatory writing has deep connections to experimental writing traditions and art movements of the twentieth century.

One way of understanding computers is through a paradigm of database and algorithm. Computer programs access and present data, whether internal to the program or provided by external sources and user input, and then through algorithmic processes, modify or substitute the data presented by the system. It is in this procedural substitution of data, and of language, that computation is most concretely connected to combinatory poetics in experimental writing traditions such as Dada, Surrealism, and Oulipo. In this chapter we will consider how elements of chance and procedurality served as the foundation for combinatory and generative art and literature. Combinatory poetics emerged in twentieth-century avant-garde movements, further developed in poetry generators in the early history of computing and remains today an essential mode of practice in electronic literature.

Artistic and literary contexts for combinatory poetics

Dada was a multimedia avant-garde art movement that began in Zurich during World War I and flourished in Berlin, Paris, and New York from 1916 until, roughly, 1920. Beginning as a disgusted response to the war and the blithely nationalistic bourgeois attitudes the Dadaists felt were at the root of the conflict, the Dadaists developed and refined the notion of "anti-art" as an expression of dissatisfaction with the dominant contemporary ideology. Although the period in which Dada was an active organized cultural movement was quite short, its legacy is widespread and profound. Individual Dada artists including Hugo Ball, Tristan Tzara, Max Ernst, Francis Picabia, Man Ray, Marcel Duchamp, and others went on to influence many of the twentieth century's most important art movements, such as Surrealism, modernism, and conceptual art. Some important elements of Dada art include the rejection of the dominant modes of distribution and valorization of cultural artifacts, the elevation of the importance of audience response to and interaction with the art object or event, interdisciplinarity and anti-disciplinarity, the abstract use of language and sound as material, the use of diverse "at-hand" media and found objects, the representation of the human body as man/machine hybrid or grotesque deformity rather than as idealized beauty, and most importantly for the purposes of this chapter, an embrace of randomness as an aspect of artistic practice.

Dada ostensibly advocated the destruction of art practices and cultures that preceded it. At the same time, the Dadaists were consummate ironists, who both recognized and declaimed with great vigor their own hypocrisy. To be Dadaist was to negate, to endorse an extreme vision of duality. In his first "Dada Manifesto," published in 1918, Tristan Tzara writes:

> In documenting art on the basis of the supreme simplicity: novelty, we are human and true for the sake of amusement, impulsive, vibrant to crucify boredom … I write a manifesto and I want nothing, yet I say certain things, and in principle I am against manifestos, as I am also against principles … I write this manifesto to show that people can perform contrary actions together while taking one gulp of fresh air; I am against action, for continuous contradiction, and for affirmation too, I am neither for or against because I hate common sense. (Tzara, 2006, p. 36)

Out of context, it may be difficult to "make sense" of Tzara's hatred of "common sense," but it is important to remember what common sense implied at the time Tzara was writing. Europe was just emerging from the fog of the World War I and the horrors of trench warfare. Much of a generation was lost and as the war wound down, the streets of Europe's capitals were littered with the amputated and deformed victims of those atrocities. The casual embrace of nationalism and bourgeois "common sense" were precisely what had led Europe to the abyss. Rationality, it seemed, had resulted in a world gone mad. Emerging from Zurich, one of the few neutral centers during World War I, Dada was intended to be as non-aligned as possible. In contrast to the various flavors of national romanticism that had characterized much of the art world in the years preceding the war, the Dada were self-consciously anti-nationalist and individualistic.

Tzara's manifesto clearly argues that the one thing binding Dadaists together is a rejection of the values of European civilization of the day. The artistic production of the Dadaist demands to be understood as an act of destruction as much as an act of creation, "there is a great negative work of destruction to be accomplished. We must sweep and clean. Affirm the cleanliness of the individual after the state of madness, aggressive complete madness of a world abandoned to the hands of bandits, who rend one another and destroy the centuries" (Tzara, 2006, p. 41). Given the general tenor of negativity in Tzara's manifesto toward groups generally and toward art specifically, it may be surprising that the Dadaists produced anything at all. Wouldn't the ultimate act of negativity have been to simply stop producing art, or perhaps even to set about destroying the art popular among the bourgeois by setting upon the galleries and museums with scissors and torches? Yet ultimately the Dadaists were not terrorists, they were artists, and if they were going to set about an act of destruction, they would do so through their art, which was conceived as anti-art. And while their impulse was toward radical individuality, by virtue of working within a shared community of practice, in which their works were produced and presented in the same context, and in conversation with one another, certain similarities and trends in the artifacts they produced nonetheless emerged. The Zurich Dada were among the first movements to embrace abstract art, for instance, and their works present abstraction in forms ranging from Hans Arp's constructions, drawings and wood reliefs, to Marcel Janco's cardboard masks, to Tristan Tzara's simultaneous poetry and Hugo Ball's sound poetry.

Tristan Tzara described the recipe for a Dadaist poem in the July/August 1920 issue of *Littérature* as follows:

TO MAKE A DADAIST POEM:
Take a newspaper.
Take a pair of scissors.
Choose an article in the newspaper of the length you wish to give your poem.
Cut out the article.
Then cut out carefully all the words that make up the article and put them in a bag.
Shake gently.
Then remove each cutting one after the other in the order in which they emerge from the bag.
Copy conscientiously.
The poem will be like you.
You will now become 'an infinitely original writer with a charming sensitivity, although still misunderstood by the common people'. (Tzara 2006, p. 34)

The cut-up technique is clearly posited as an antidote to the romantic (bourgeois) notion of the author as inspired, "infinitely original" genius (see Rettberg, 2008).

In his *Dada: Art and Anti-Art*, Hans Richter describes chance as one of the essential elements of the Dada movement, "a magical procedure by which one could transcend the barriers of causality and conscious volition, and by which the inner eye and ear become more acute, so that new sequences of thoughts and experiences made their appearances" (Richter, 1995, p. 57). Richter attributes to this attitude of embracing chance, as in Tzara's cut-up poems, the wide variety of innovative forms created by the Dadaists.

One of the distinguishing aspects of digital art objects is that they are often what Lev Manovich describes as variable media. Manovich writes, "a new media object is not something fixed once and for all, but something that can exist in different, potentially infinite versions" (Manovich, 2001, p. 36). One powerful way to take advantage of the variable nature of new media objects is to introduce an element of indeterminability, of chance, into the operations of a given work. Aarseth (1997) uses the term textons to describe static bits of content, and scriptons to describe various arrangements of textons encountered by a reader, and distinguishes between determinate and indeterminate texts: "A text is determinate if the adjacent textons of every scripton are always the same; if not, the text is indeterminate" (p. 63). Because computers provide a variety of ways to easily select at random and quickly arrange material within a random or preconceived structure, and because the global network offers artists such a wide variety of data sources to choose from, authors of electronic literature have embraced and refined the cut-up technique and used randomization and chance in an array of ways.

In their extension and reaction to Dada, the surrealists also embraced aleatory writing methods, often as an aspect of collaborative writing practices. To some extent Surrealism sprang from the Dada, but surrealists were less interested in the concept of "anti-art" and more in the relation between art, nonconformity, and the subconscious. While the Dada were embracing chance and the random in writing primarily as a rejection of the corruption of language they perceived in bourgeois society, to the surrealists, Tzara's cut-up method represented a mystical method of accessing the subconscious or "unconscious" mind, in order to produce work that would speak in the language of dreams.

In his 1924 "Manifesto of Surrealism", André Breton defined it as:

> SURREALISM, *n.* Psychic automatism in its pure state, by which one proposes to express – verbally, by means of the written word, or in any other

manner – the actual functioning of thought. Dictated by the thought, in the absence of any control exercised by reason, exempt from any aesthetic or moral concern. (Breton, 1972, p. 26)

The method that Breton proposed to express the actual functioning of thought was automatism: essentially the abandonment of forethought and conscious structure. For Breton, random access to the unconscious is the best fuel for creative practice. Breton proposes automatism that entails a loss of authorial control:

It is true of Surrealist images as it is of opium images that man does not evoke them; rather they "come to him spontaneously, despotically. He cannot chase them away; for the will is powerless now and no longer controls the faculties." (p. 36)

Breton understood automatic writing as offering random access to one's own dream logic and memory.

Surrealist automatic writing practices extended to social writing practices – writing games. In this social extension, the aleatory practices are less about the operation of any individual imagination but instead reach toward an expression of a kind of collective unconscious. The random here is not access to one's own interiority but a social process of feedback loops. Among the many different kinds of writing games that involved collaboration, chance, and attempts to access the unconscious, the exquisite corpse is best known. The first and most basic exquisite corpse game called for a minimum of three players seated at a table. Each player would write a definite or an indefinite article and an adjective, then fold the paper over to cover the word and pass it to the player next to them. Each would then write a noun, repeat the folding procedure and pass it again, and continue to repeat the procedure with a following verb, article, adjective, and another noun. The first sentence resulting from this game, which the surrealists named the game after, was "Le Cadavre exquis boira le vin nouveau" ("The exquisite corpse shall drink the new wine") (Aspley, 2010, p. 267). The game of the exquisite corpse subsequently inspired many variants: one player might write a question, and the next write an answer without knowing the question; one player might write a conditional statement and the next a result; it might extend into a sequence of events, one sentence at a time, and so on. The exquisite corpse technique was applied in the production of images as well as texts. In the variation known as "picture consequences" portions of a person were drawn before the paper was folded, with only bits of lines from the previous drawing showing, often resulting in comic or monstrous depictions of a person that none of the artists saw until the drawing was complete. Collage is another visual technique that both the Dada and the surrealists used to produce work. Although elements in collage are not always selected at random, they are "found" insofar as they are composed of elements of other printed images or texts recombined, rather than "originally" produced.

Several elements of surrealist practice have influenced computational combinatory writing and other forms of electronic literature. Among these is the essentially *procedural* nature of surrealist writing games – the creative act begins not with inspiration but with a set of agreed-upon practices. The *collaborative* and *multimedia* elements of many of their practices have also inspired subsequent work in digital media – surrealist writers and artists were just as likely to write together, and to freely mix image and text, as they were to write alone or in one medium. The use of *found texts* and images also coheres with the practices of many writers working with combinatory practices in digital media. This is a sort of practice that tends to value the idea that collective narratives (see chapter 6) may be as worthy material for creative practice as texts that are consciously written by any individual. For instance, texts sampled from contemporary news sources, or websites, or mailing lists are often used as material for generative poetry. Contemporary Flarf and conceptual writing or "uncreative writing" values found texts recombined or even simply reframed over individual creativity (see chapter 6). Automatic writing, unconscious writing, and collectively produced writing all challenged contemporary ideas of what writing should be, demonstrating that new kinds of texts could be produced and generated from little but the creative application of rules and sampling – both from individual imaginations, and from any other texts that happened to be at-hand.

Artist and poet Brion Gysin – expelled from the surrealists during his late teens by Breton (Kern, 2009, p. 90) – is an important figure in the history of combinatory writing both for his extension of Tzara's cut-up technique and for his "permutation poems." Gysin's work with these techniques began with a Stanley blade but eventually also involved the use of a computer. Living in Tangier in the 1950s, Gysin was a close friend of William S. Burroughs. Gysin is alleged to have discovered his cut-up technique accidentally while cutting through some photographs. He noticed that some newspapers under the photos had also been cut. He pulled out these fragments, and began assembling them into a new text, which he titled "Minutes to Go," subsequently expanded into a co-authored book of the same title (Belles et al., 1960). Gysin proposed to Burroughs that writers should use the techniques of collage that painters had been using for decades, by cutting apart and splicing together words and phrases. William S. Burroughs was deeply influenced by this method, which he used extensively in the composition of his novel *Naked Lunch* and other subsequent works. Burroughs understood the cut-up method to be a way of producing unpredictable spontaneity that could lead to fruitful discoveries, and wrote:

> The cut-up method brings to writers the collage, which has been used by painters for fifty years. And used by the moving and still camera. In fact all street shots from movie or still cameras are by the unpredictable factors of passers by and juxtaposition cut-ups. And photographers will tell you that often their best shots are accidents … writers will tell you the same. The best writing seems to be done almost by accident but writers until the cut-up method was made explicit – all writing is in fact cut ups. I will return to this point – had no way to produce the accident of spontaneity. You can not will spontaneity. But you can introduce the unpredictable spontaneous factor with a pair of scissors. (Burroughs, 2003, p. 91)

In addition to cut-ups, Gysin produced "permutation poems" – poems derived from permutations of a series of words or a sentence. He performed a series of these as sound poems on BBC radio in 1960, such as "I Am That I Am," "a cyclical, randomized representation of the three words contained in that phrase" (Funkhouser, 2007, p. 39). Reviewing recordings of Gysin reading these poems, one notices that the permutations themselves differ on the basis of their mediality. When Gysin performs "I Am That I Am" for the radio, his inflections and stresses on different phrases add a layer of variation to the phrases and suggest different interpretations than would be evident if reading the text from the printed page alone. Gysin and Ian Sommerville applied the permutation technique in producing one of the earlier examples of poetry generation in the 1960s, *Permutation Poems*, which recombines the words of an input phrase in all possible permutations.

One aspect of the cut-up method used by Gysin and Burroughs worth foregrounding as we consider electronic literature is that, although we typically think of cut-ups as resulting in written recombined language or text, both artists thought of the techniques more intermedially. Burroughs frequently cut up and recombined audio recordings, and sometimes produced written texts by transcribing these cut-up audio recordings. The technique, first inspired by the technique of visual collage, is remediated into textual practices, audio production, and video. In this sense the cut-up method anticipates and is in conversation with the transcoded and remediated nature of many works of electronic literature. Procedural technique is not tethered to any single media but can result in many different types of outputs that can be fed back and through each other again.

A third group of literary experimentalists that influenced electronic literature and combinatory poetics in particular is the Ouvroir de Littérature Potentielle (Oulipo), a group of writers and mathematicians who gather for dinner once a month in France to exchanges ideas, creative works, and challenges involving writing under constraint. Founded by mathematician François de Lionnais and writer Raymond Queneau in 1960, and continuing into the present, the group has focused primarily on structural systems guided by rules; constraints that can themselves be generative. These constraints can range from some that are conceptually quite simple to others that are quite complex. Oulipian work has been produced as print poetry, fiction, and in many other forms. Oulipian constraints typically do not concern the content of a literary work but instead its form. Two of the most frequently referenced works include *La Disparition* (in English *A Void*) by Georges Perec (1969), a lipogram novel that was written without using any words that contain the letter E; and *Cent mille milliards de poemes* (in English *Hundred Thousand Billion Poems*) by Raymond Queneau (1961), a set of ten sonnets that were identical in structure and rhyme scheme, so that when the pages were cut line by line, individual lines could be substituted individually and still produce a valid sonnet with 10^{10} possible variations.

Many Oulipian constraints can be understood as procedural writing games or as algorithms – Jean Lescure's N+7 constraint simply involves substituting every noun in any given text with a noun seven nouns after the given word in the dictionary. Oulipian author Harry Mathews' "snowball" technique provides another example of a relatively simple constraint: write a poem where each line contains one letter more than the last.

Mathews describes the function of Oulipian games in the writing process:

> The Oulipo supplies writers with hard games to play. They are adult games insofar as children cannot play most of them; otherwise they bring us back to a familiar home ground of our childhood. Like Capture the Flag, the games have demanding rules that we must never forget (well, hardly ever), and these rules are moreover active ones: satisfying them keeps us too busy to worry about being reasonable. Of course our object of desire, like the flag to be captured, remains present to us. Thanks to the impossible rules, we find ourselves doing and saying things we would never have imagined otherwise, things that often turn out to be exactly what we need to reach our goal. (Mathews, 1997)

While it would be easy to dismiss Oulipian techniques as "fun and games," as much of the activity of writing with constraints is in fact playful in nature, these games have resulted in a remarkable corpus of work. Constraints are core to the Oulipian practice but their engagement with language does not stop at the constraint. Many of the Oulipian writers describe the constraints as liberating: by focusing on the constraints, they can allow the writing they produce to surprise them. They can write about subjects that might otherwise be difficult. When Perec was writing *La Disparition*, he was not only writing a novel without using the letter E, he was also writing a novel about the disappearance of his parents during the Holocaust.

Like the Dada and the surrealists, the Oulipo use *procedures* to *generate* writing that they would not have imagined in the absence of those procedures. In contrast to the Dada and the surrealists, who respectively embraced the random and the unconscious, Oulipian writing is generative as a result of its strict adherence to the formal rules that guide its creation. In this sense the writing process is determinative – not left to chance.

Several ideas at the core of Oulipian practice are enormously influential on combinatory writing made with the computer. The first can be found in the name of the group itself, which translates in English as the "Workshop for Potential Literature." The idea of *potential literature* is essential for understanding combinatory and generative poetics: text generation programs themselves can be considered *potential literature machines* – all of the elements of a poem or story are in place before the given program runs, but the actual poem or story is not produced until that operation takes place. Secondly, as Mathews elucidates above, is the idea that limitations, constraints on the writing process, somewhat paradoxically can become the mechanisms for "doing and saying things we would have never imagined otherwise." While there is a difference between wrestling with these constraints as an aspect of one's own creative engagement with writing and hard-coding them as algorithms in a computer program, both can result in writing that the writers themselves may never have imagined. Oulipian procedurality led some Oulipo members toward an interest in making use of the computer in the production of literature. The offshoot group ALAMO – Atelier de Littérature Assistée par la Mathématique et les Ordinateurs (in English "Workshop of Computer- and Mathematics-Assisted Literature") led by Paul Braffort and Jacques Roubaud, was founded in 1981 specifically to explore the coupling of literature and computer (Braffort, 2002).

The Oulipo were neither the only nor the last artistic movement to engage with procedural poetics before the widespread popular adoption of the personal computer. The Fluxus artists and writers active mainly during the 1960s and 1970s, for example, focused on procedures and their variation in performance. Fluxus artworks, performances, and happenings are perhaps best distinguished by Dick Higgins' term of "intermedia" and centered on the interplay between and boundary meshings of different art forms and non-traditional contexts and venues, but the idea of the Fluxus script was important for the movement. As opposed to traditional theatrical performance scripts, Fluxus scripts typically do not dictate dialog or even setting, but describe a context-free procedure, often an absurd one.

Consider two of George Maciunas' "12 Piano Compositions for Nam June Paik" (1962):

> Composition No. 5: Place a dog or a cat (or both) inside the piano and play Chopin.
> Composition No. 6: Stretch the 3 highest strings with a tuning key until they break.

While some of the Fluxus scores may have been intended as conceptual rather than actualized (subjecting a dog or a cat to Chopin in this manner seems a bit cruel) in fact many such scripts have been performed repeatedly. The nature of Fluxus directives vary widely – they might just as likely involve the preparation of a meal or a time-based performance as a piano – but they have a procedural element in common. There is a given procedure or set of procedures, but the event or output will invariably change on the basis of numerous factors: the performer's interpretation of the instructions, the environment and materials used to implement the instructions, and the audience's reception of the event. In this sense the Fluxus scores operate much like algorithms in poetry generators. Depending on the variables and in some cases the user's input, the output of the same algorithm (the performance or the poem) can change radically. Not surprisingly, some of the Fluxus artists, most notably Alison Knowles, integrated computational practice in their work.

Combinatory writing practices are not simply the domain of obscure art movements but in fact have extended more generally into popular culture. I have fond childhood memories of playing with Mad-Libs in the back seat of the car on many a road-trip family vacation. Although these simple interactive stories are rudimentary in comparison to most poetry and fiction generation programs, the general principle on which they operate is quite similar. A general story frame is established by the text, but certain words in the text are left blank and the reader is instructed to fill in a type of item or a part of speech – a noun here, an action verb there, an adjective, a type of fruit – and the story changes on the basis of the reader's input. One of the basic principles of many poetry generators is indeed that of substitution, if most often from the arrays of a database rather than on the basis of the whims of a young reader. But the principle of substitution, and the resulting pleasure of surprise, are consistent across the two forms.

Combinatory principles have also played a role in contemporary music culture. The principle of indeterminacy was core to the works of John Cage who frequently introduced aleatory elements into his compositions, for example by rolling dice to select particular elements of a composition. Brian Eno coined the term "generative music" as he was interacting with and developing musical compositions in the 1990s. In early 1996 during a talk Eno asked:

> With this generative music that I played you, am I the composer? Are you if you buy the system the composer? Is Jim Coles (?) and his brother who wrote the software the composer? – Who actually composes music like this? Can you describe it as composition exactly when you don't know what it's going to be? (Eno, 1996)

Eno points to one of the complications of authorship involved in generative poetics and indeed in most genres of electronic literature. The output of any given program is not derived only from the work of the specific writer/programmer who develops the given generator, but also the work of those who developed the platform, as well as the procedural operations of the computer itself. Creativity is best understood here as the result of a distributed process, rather than a product of individual inspiration.

Composers Cage and Eno are not alone in their engagement with generative techniques in composition. The use of computation in music is a field in itself and has been a key aspect of modern music. But generative poetics in music are not the exclusive domain of experimental composers and musicians. No less a pop icon than David Bowie made use of computational generative techniques in the production of his lyrics. In a 1997 documentary, Bowie is seen demonstrating the "Verbasizer" on his Mac PowerBook – a program he developed with collaborators which spliced together input sentences provided by the songwriter, producing new phrases and verses (Apted, 1997). Bowie is said to have used this program while writing his album *1. Outside*.

The early history of digital combinatory writing

Until this point we have considered cultural contexts for generative poetics, and artistic and literary movements that we can understand as influences on and antecedents to current computational generative poetics. But, like most forms of electronic literature, generative poetics emerge not only from cultural but also from technological contexts. From the time of the first Turing machines, one of the primary concerns of computer science has been to work out how computers can be made to engage with language in ways similar to the human use of language, and how to model or perform many of the same functions as human intelligence. Two related fields within computer science, artificial intelligence and natural language processing, have had particularly important influences on generative and combinatory poetics.

Alan Turing's 1950 essay "Computing Machinery and Intelligence" put forth the example of the imitation game, which Turing proposed might replace the question of 'Can machines think?' The imitation game he proposed includes three parties: a man, a woman, and an interrogator. Interacting with the two only through textual questions and answers, the role of the interrogator is to determine only through their textual responses the gender of the respondents. Turing asks us to consider what might happen when a machine takes the place of one of the respondents. Could a machine fool the interrogator as often as a human interlocutor? In other words, Turing is asking us to consider not whether or not machines can think but whether or not machines can manipulate language to a sufficient extent that it could convince humans that they are communicating with another human being. If this sets a considerably lower (and more measurable) bar than asking whether machines can think, it also serves to define one of the central concerns of computer science: how can computers use human language? In the last section of his article, Turing put forth the possibility of learning machines and suggested that if we were to hope that computers might one day "compete with men in all purely intellectual fields" the best one to start with might be to "teach it to understand and speak English" (Turing, 1950, p. 460). It has followed from this that an ongoing concern of AI researchers that one of the ultimate end goals of developing an artificially intelligent learning machine should be to develop a machine that could not only beat a grandmaster at chess, but also compose poetry and write novels. If we have yet to see a computer program that can compete with Shakespeare, the practices of generative writing and combinatory poetics are nevertheless a poetic response to Turing's challenge.

One of Turing's contemporaries was Christopher Strachey, who came into contact with Turing while studying at King's College, Cambridge. Strachey was interested in various ways to use the computer creatively. Through Turing, he was allowed access to the Mark I computer at the University of Manchester and developed a number of programs for it, including a program to use the computer to play Draughts (Checkers) and several computer music programs that enabled the Mark I to play songs such as "Baa Baa Black Sheep" and "In the Mood." He was also the author of one of the first literary computing text generators, and most likely the first work of electronic literature, with his 1952 program *Love Letters*. Strachey wrote the program while working for the National Research and Development Corporation. Strachey apparently developed the program for a lark and not as an aspect of his official duties. Strachey's colleagues at the University of Manchester became aware of the program's existence when they noticed that someone was pinning printouts of quixotic love letters up on the office bulletin board. Nick Montfort's translation of Strachey's program provides us with some examples of how these letters read:

DARLING LOVE
MY ADORABLE DEVOTION WISHES YOUR LONGING. YOU ARE MY LOVEABLE EAGERNESS. MY ADORATION BEAUTIFULLY CLINGS TO YOUR CRAVING APPETITE. MY CRAVING ENCHANTMENT WANTS YOUR UNSATISFIED EAGERNESS. YOU ARE MY EAGER ENCHANTMENT.
     YOURS WISTFULLY
     M.U.C.
HONEY MOPPET
MY PASSIONATE AMBITION LOVINGLY PINES FOR YOUR EAGERNESS. YOU ARE MY DARLING WISH: MY LOVEABLE DESIRE. YOU ARE MY LITTLE ENTHUSIASM: MY LOVEABLE LOVE.
     YOURS SEDUCTIVELY
     M.U.C. (Strachey, 1952)

If these letters are clearly not *great literature*, they are literary writing produced by the procedural operations of the computer. In an article in the journal *Encounter*, Strachey described the scheme of the program as "almost childishly simple." Pulling words from a list categorized by parts of speech, the program produces an address of two words pulled from lists, followed by one of two types of sentences: either "My – (adj.) – (noun) – (adv.) – (verb) your (adj.) – (noun)." or "You are my – (adj.) – (noun)." The program loops five times, randomly choosing one of these two types of sentences each time, and inserting a colon if the second option repeats, and then produces a salutation of "Yours – (adv.)" M.U.C. The M.U.C. of course stands for "Manchester University Computer."

Strachey himself presented the love-letter generator very lightly, writing that "very little thought went into its devising." Instead Strachey asserted, "The chief point of interest, however, is not the obvious crudity of the scheme, nor even in the ways in which it might be improved, but in the remarkable simplicity of the plan when compared to the letters it produces." It is neither the program nor the individual texts that Strachey finds compelling but the fact that something so computationally simple and requiring so little authorial effort can produce so many varied results. If the computer might appear to think, Strachey reminds us that the "computer is not really 'thinking' at all." Instead computer programs that make the computer appear to think are merely performing "nothing more than complicated tricks." Nevertheless "these tricks can lead to quite unexpected and interesting results" (Strachey, 1954, p. 27).

Noah Wardrip-Fruin (2011) examined Strachey's generator and its contexts extensively in "Digital Media Archeology: Interpreting Computational Processes." He considers the "inhuman" tone of the outputs of Love Letters and argues that the program must be understood as parody, not "a process for producing parodies," but rather "a parody of process" (p. 316). That is to say that in crudely replicating the human/heterosexual process of writing love letters in a way that produces uncanny outputs more likely to produce a chuckle than to read as a window into anyone's soul, Strachey's generator may be parodying this courtship ritual itself: highlighting the fact that love letters are rarely actually as intimate or thoughtful as they seem, but are instead a phatic genre that could be reduced to a formula. There is some evidence that like his friend Alan Turing, Christopher Strachey was homosexual. Wardrip-Fruin notes that in 1952 at the same time as Strachey was sharing his first generator with his friend Turing and laughing at its absurd outputs, Turing was undergoing forced hormone treatments as punishment for his illegal sexual orientation. The treatment was designed to render Turing impotent and it had severe side effects, causing Turing to grow breasts, and contributed ultimately to his decision to take his own life. Wardrip-Fruin argues that through this simple program that parodied heterosexual courtship conventions, Strachey and Turing may have been "laughing at a society all too willing to reject, incarcerate, and hormonally alter them for the simple fact of their homosexuality" (Wardrip-Fruin, 2011, p. 318). If Wardrip-Fruin's reading of the first work of electronic literature may be testing the boundaries of intentional fallacy, it also provides us with a model for reading electronic literature procedurally and contextually: while poetry and story generators produce surface texts which can and should be read as texts in their own right, rich readings of them often entail reading and understanding them as formal procedures, as systems that generate complexity from simplicity, and entail reading them within broader social contexts.

In 1959 German mathematician and computer scientist Theodore Lutz developed *Stochastic Texts* (*Stochastische Texte* in the original German) on a Zuse Z22 computer – a program that produces random short sentences based on a corpus of chapter titles and subjects from Franz Kafka's *The Castle*. Lutz's goal in producing the program was not to produce high-quality writing but instead to demonstrate how a random number function, producing a probability distribution that when combined with a structured linguistic logic could produce meaningful text. Lutz (1959) explained: "The results so far let us hope that program-controlled electronic data processors can be used with great success in language research and analytical language areas. It is to be hoped that the distrust of some more traditionally minded philologists toward the achievements of modern technology will soon make way for widespread and fruitful co-operation." In other words this generator, which produces rudimentary literary texts, was primarily intended to demonstrate that computational linguistics could be an area worthy of further exploration. Lutz suggests that beyond the basic combinatory operations of his program, it may be "possible to change the underlying word quantity into a 'word field' using an assigned probability matrix, and to require the machine to print only those sentences where a probability exists between the subject and the predicate which exceeds a certain value" (Lutz, 1959). David Jhave Johnston notes that Lutz's observation here anticipates an important idea for further work in both computational linguistics and poetry generation, as it "implies the matrice of language is analogous to a network and that proximal sets may evoke meaningful relations" (Johnston, 2008).

Funkhouser argues that Lutz's experiment constitutes the first exploration of computer-operation-based composition of poetry (Funkhouser, 2007, p. 37). While the texts produced by *Stochastic Texts* are somewhat elementary, they nevertheless produce results that can be read as poetry:

NOT EVERY LOOK IS NEAR. NO VILLAGE IS LATE.
A CASTLE IS FREE AND EVERY FARMER IS FAR.
EVERY STRANGER IS FAR. A DAY IS LATE.
EVERY HOUSE IS DARK. AN EYE IS DEEP.
NOT EVERY CASTLE IS OLD. EVERY DAY IS OLD.
NOT EVERY GUEST IS ANGRY: A CHURCH IS NARROW.
NO HOUSE IS OPEN AND NOT EVERY CHURCH IS SILENT.
NOT EVERY EYE IS ANGRY. NO LOOK IS NEW. (Lutz, 1959)

It is worth considering how these phrases, aggregated together, suggest poetic meaning. Certainly, Kafka deserves some credit: the words are his. Lutz, in his fifty-instruction program, provides syntax, a grammar, and rules of operation. The computer implements those instructions and outputs the text. I would however suggest – and I think this is the case for much generative poetry – that the reader plays the most significant role in perceiving these texts as poetry rather than simply as aggregated data. In these texts we might recognize poetic conventions such as personification or synecdoche. We might hear echoes of Beckettian reduction of experience to the "bare bones" of minimalist representation. We are drawn to "fill in the blanks" and interpret what lies between the lines of the poem, to take these minimalist expressions and from them imagine a mood and a scene. Repetition with variation has its own poetic power. As Funkhouser observes, the program results in a "nonrational ordering of subjects and thoughts" (Funkhouser,

2007, p. 38). Perhaps this nonrational ordering is one of the qualities that drive us to interpret a text as poetry rather than as ordinary language. The nonrational, slightly off, uncanny presentation of subjects produced by the generator kindles a desire for re-ordering, interpretation, and closure from the perspective of the human subject. The reader who is presented with a text that is described as a poem feels compelled to make meaning of it, whether that text is written by a human poet or composed by a machine. *Stochastic Texts* also demonstrates how constraints can have poetic effects in a computational context. The difference between the constraints here and those of the Oulipo is that in the case of a poetry generator they are encoded in the text machine.

Lutz's research was explicitly scientific in nature. We find electronic literature not only in the present but retrospectively: Strachey and Lutz were likely not thinking of themselves as digital writers at the time of their experiments. We will see throughout this volume that authors of electronic literature tend to defy simple disciplinary differentiations between poet, programmer, scientist, engineer, researcher, artist, critic, performer, or designer. A mathematician might produce a poetry generator, a fiction writer might function as a visualization researcher, or a performance artist might function as a digital archivist.

In 1962, the software "Auto-Beatnik" by R. M. Worthy was announced in *Horizon* magazine (1962). Writing at in the *Antioch Review* Robert Oliphant (1961–1962) described the program as follows:

> Using an LGP-30 computer, an input was programmed consisting of 32 grammatical patterns, a vocabulary of 850 common English words classified into 40 grammatical and syntactical groups, and a random selection procedure for selecting sequences of patterns and words to fit those patterns. The output of the machine was arbitrarily segmented into groups of six patterns, or "lines." Each group of six lines is called a "poem." (p. 408)

The program reportedly produced poetry close enough to read as if were human-written. An example outputted poem of the *Auto-Beatnik* demonstrates this:

> Adieu, most moons are floating or neurotic.
> Act me,
> Or on the insect, she fell gayly,
> You tiptoe openly around an earth,
> And singing softly is like spinning drunkenly,
> That insect was very torrid. (p. 408)

These lines are almost convincing: compelling poetry often relies on strange juxtapositions and ambiguities. The phrase "singing softly while spinning drunkenly" suggests a recognizable state. Moon and earth create a correspondent pairing of images. We are willing to accept the insect as some kind of symbol. While it is difficult to process how one would "tiptoe openly around an earth," the language is suggestive enough to make the reader want to process and understand it as poetry.

Some of the most important works of digital art and literature have resulted from conscious attempts to bring collaborators from literature and the arts together with computer scientists and designers. One such example is Alison Knowles' and James Tenney's *House of Dust* (1967), which is often cited as the first computer poem. James Tenney was a composer who made important contributions to the development of digital music. From 1961 to 1964 Tenney was a composer-in-residence at Bell Labs, where he worked with Max Mathews and others in developing software that allowed the computer to determine certain aspects of musical composition. Tenney was interested in stochastics and chance operations and applied those interests in his work with digital music. Tenney and Alison Knowles participated in an informal Fluxus workshop together in 1967, during which Tenney demonstrated how the FORTRAN-IV computer language could be used to introduce chance elements in the creation of artworks. Knowles contributed a poem with the following structure:

> a house of (list material)
>   in a (list location)
>   using (list light source)
>   inhabited by (list inhabitants)

The program simply pulled one of each element from arrays of 4–25 items. The program was typically iterated many times, creating long poems with quatrains such as:

A HOUSE OF TIN
  IN A DESERT
    USING NATURAL LIGHT
      INHABITED BY VARIOUS BIRDS AND FISHES

A HOUSE OF STRAW
  IN AN OVERPOPULATED AREA
    USING ELECTRICITY
      INHABITED BY PEOPLE WHO SLEEP ALMOST ALL THE
      TIME
(Knowles and Tenney, 1967)

Funkhouser refers to this type of combinatory poetry as a "slotted work" (Funkhouser, 2011, p. 60) as each line of the poem includes a blank slot that pulls one element at random from the array. While the quatrains do not result in much stylistic diversity, the project is important for the fact that it was consciously conceived as a literary artwork composed using the computer. It also took on other dimensions as the project proceeded. Knowles for instance published different versions of *House of Dust* poems in several different journals, so this is likely the first work of electronic literature to circulate in conventional publishing channels. As a Fluxus artist, Knowles was also intimate with the idea of the "intermedia" artwork, and so, rather than stopping at a poem, she took the project one step further by actually attempting to use one randomized output of the poem as the basis for a work of sculptural architecture and interactive sound installation – a physical house of dust inspired by the quatrain "A HOUSE OF DUST/ ON OPEN GROUND/ USING NATURAL LIGHT/ INHABITED BY FRIENDS AND ENEMIES" – which was first built in New York and then in 1970 moved to the campus of Cal Arts (Taylor, 2009). The structure became the basis for a number of performance events, including a "Poem Drop Event" organized by her student Norman Klein, which featured 1,000 feet of the poem printed on dot-matrix computer paper dropped over the house of dust structure at Cal Arts from a helicopter (Woods, 2012). It has also inspired contemporary authors of electronic literature, such as Stephanie Strickland and Ian Hatcher, whose *House of Trust* (2015) uses a similar structure in a generative paean to libraries.

In retrospect, *House of Dust* is important for several reasons: it was the first work of electronic literature circulated on a widespread basis; it was born of interdisciplinary collaboration; it was *iterative* in nature, and best understood as a *project* rather than as a single instantiation. It was iterative not only in the sense that the generator produced diverse variable outcomes, but also that the project was iterated as a computer generator, as print publications, as physical sculpture, and as performances. It is increasingly the case that contemporary works of electronic literature have multiple instantiations and take place in multiple culture venues. When a project can be presented and understood as a computer program, as a print publication, as an installation, and as a performance, it changes in a context-specific way with each iteration.

Procedural, syntactic poetry generation systems

Poetry and story generators and other combinatory writing systems are characterized by structured complexity and procedurality. Of the genres of electronic literature, these programs have the most direct correlation with elementary principles of computation, driven as they are by algorithmic procedures applied to textual datasets. From a literary standpoint they challenge classical notions of authorship and close reading. From an aesthetic standpoint they typically involve elements of chance and surprise, constraint, and variability, and explore the poetic and narrative potentialities of text machines. Combinatory and generative writing, procedural and computationally enhanced writing, constitute the oldest and most continuous set of practices in electronic literature. Some earlier texts have already been discussed in the first section of the chapter. If the majority of the generators we have considered so far were essentially computational experiments, in the field of electronic literature there is less of a concern with artificial intelligence milestones and instead a focus on the creation of more consciously aesthetic poetic works that explore different models of procedural and aleatory structure.

We will focus here primarily on generative literature produced in the English language, but it is important to note that generative literature is an international phenomenon, and many of its most important works have been produced in other languages, particularly in Portuguese and French. During the 1970s and 1980s, a number of authors began to explore the potentialities of computer-generated literature. Portuguese author Pedro Barbosa published *A Literatura Cibernética 1: Autopoemas Gerados por Computador* (1977) and *A Literatura Cibernética 2: Um Sintetizador de Narrativas* (1980), books which included outputs of poetry and narrative generative systems, as well as a critical framework for approaching cybernetic literature (see Seiça, 2018a). The French author Jean-Pierre Balpe is another important innovator in generative literature during a long career exploring its potentialities. From the mid-1980s to the present, Balpe has produced work in forms ranging from generated novels such as *La Mort dans l'âme* (1993) and poetry generators such as *Babel poésie* (2003), generative work produced in collaborations with composers and theatrical producers, to texts published by fictional characters on contemporary social networks. Both Barbosa and Balpe have continued to produce generative work to the present day.

Hugh Kenner and Joseph O'Rourke's *Travesty* (1984) is a text generator in the form of a procedural operation by the program on any given text. The texts *Travesty* produces are not written by the authors of the program but are instead fed into the system by the user. The program then searches through vocabulary of the source text, substituting elements of the text from one position to another based on a measure of linguistic probability, n-grams. Kenner and O'Rouke explain n-grams well in a 1994 *BYTE* magazine article:

Write "th", and the probability is very high that what follows will be "e". If it is, then the character after "e" is most likely to be either a space or an "r". Pairs like "th" are called digrams; triplets like "the" are trigrams. They have frequencies, like letters. The most common English digram is "he": you will find it three times in the sentence you are reading now, 15 times in this paragraph. And you will guess correctly that as we move up from single letters to diagrams and trigrams, the probabilities that govern the next character grow ever more rigorous. (p. 131)

Travesty's user sets the bounds of the n-gram by a number of letters. The program then scans the text and returns a result based on the most statistically similar letter sequence within another word in the text. Depending on the length of the n-gram chain, the resulting language might be similar to Lewis Carroll's nonsense poetry, such as "Jabberwocky," or it might be closer to comprehensible verse. Kenner and O'Rouke provided an example based on feeding the entirety of T. S. Eliot's of "The Hollow Men" through *Travesty*. A resulting travesty of the text reads:

We are not appear/ Sight kingdom/ These do not appear/ This very long/ Between the wind behaving alone/ And the Kingdom/ Remember us, if at all, not/ appear/ Sightless, unless/ In a fading as lost kingdom

Compare this to the first verse of Eliot's poem:

We are the hollow men/ We are the stuffed men/ Leaning together/ Headpiece filled with straw. Alas!/ Our dried voices, when/ We whisper together/ Are quiet and meaningless/ As wind in dry grass/ Or rats' feet over broken glass/ In our dry cellar.

The style of the original text is largely preserved in the travesty, if not the semantic intent or the ordering of elements.

A number of other computer programs that could apply procedures to any input text in order to mangle and restructure the text into poetic form were developed during the 1980s. William Chamberlain and Thomas Etter's *Racter* is one such notable system, as it resulted in what may have been "The First Book Ever Written by a Computer" as claimed on the cover of *The Policeman's Beard Is Half-Constructed* (1984). In his introduction to the book, Chamberlain described the abilities of *Racter*. It "conjugates both regular and irregular verbs, prints the singular and the plural of both regular and irregular nouns, remembers the gender of nouns, and can assign variable status to randomly chosen 'things.' These things can be individual words, clause or sentence forms, paragraph structures, indeed whole story forms." The texts published in *The Policeman's Beard Is Half-Constructed* tend toward the absurd, but they are largely coherent and more polished than many examples of generated text. Some commentators believed that the texts for the book were heavily edited. Regardless of the level of human input into the process or extent of editorial post-processing, the resulting texts often read as competent prose poetry, as in this example:

> A crow is a bird, an eagle is a bird, a dove is a bird. They all fly in the night and in the day. They fly when the sky is red and when the heaven is blue. They fly through the atmosphere. We cannot fly. We are not like a crow or an eagle or a dove. We are not birds. But we can dream about them. You can.

The book is also notable for its beautiful surrealist-style collage illustrations by Joan Hall, and it was also printed with a number of the poems angled diagonally or scattered across the page, reinforcing connections to historical literary avant-garde traditions.

Charles O. Hartman describes many of his poetry generation experiments in *Virtual Muse: Experiments in Computer Poetry* (1996). Hartman had a sustained engagement with what he called "computer poetry" and developed his work modularly. Hartman explored combinatory poetry first with *Poetry Composer*, a simple program that stores twenty lines and displays them in a random order. While the program was simple, the challenge of composition was that the lines needed to work in any order. He followed up with a kind of utility, the *Scansion Machine*, which could determine the meter of a line fed to it. He produced poetry using a modified version of *Travesty* as a basis before developing *AutoPoet*, a more complex system. Hartman first developed a dictionary of a few thousand of the most frequently used words in the English language, in addition to five hundred handpicked "specials" – words that Hartman picked out of his own interest. The dictionary included the number of syllables in each word, the stressed syllable if there was one, and the part of speech. Finally, he developed a syntax-building system. The program would:

1. Create a syntactical skeleton or template – a list of parts of speech in sentence order (e.g. determiner, adjective, noun, verb).
2. Pick words at random from lists of determiners, adjectives, nouns, verbs, and so on, to build a sentence on this template.
3. When the words have accumulated to about the length of a pentameter, test it for metricality.
4. If it passes the test in step 3, print it. If it doesn't, go back to step 2. (Hartman, 1996, p. 70)

This represents a sophisticated level of generation, which can produce poems that are both syntactically plausible and metrical. Yet Hartman felt that it did not ultimately work very well. He realized that what was wrong with *AutoPoet* was that it produced "*imitation poetry*. All our habits of reading are called upon, all the old expectations, and then let down" (p. 72). His follow-up to *AutoPoet*, *Prose*, built sentences that were syntactically correct. But only one in five or ten lines held the slightest appeal to Hartman as poetry. He then changed his perspective on the project. Rather than treating the output of his program as poetry, delivered whole to the screen as finished verse, he began to treat the system as a first draft writer. Hartman would read the lines the program produced, select those he felt interesting or evocative, and using those lines as a basis, would edit the poem. In this sense, the program didn't write the poem, but instead provided the poet with language to use as source and inspiration.

Contemporary combinatory digital poetics

Combinatory text and text generation are important components of contemporary electronic literature authors' toolkits. As with the other genres discussed in this book, text generation is not an exclusive genre – generative text is often combined with other multimedia and network-writing techniques. The combinatory poetry generation systems themselves have in recent years tended toward simplicity in comparison to systems such as Hartman's. The poetic effect of a relatively simple process can in many cases work more effectively than generators that build language at a more granular level.

Many of the most often cited works of combinatory electronic literature make use of quite simple techniques. Nanette Wylde's *Storyland* (2002), published in the *Electronic Literature Collection, Volume One* (2006), produces short stories, six-paragraph fictions that feature minimal interactions between three characters that read as minimalist contemporary parables. Consider one output:

> In the not-too-distant past, a misogynist cried for your sins. The misogynist was guilty.
> Species dwindled.
> The misogynist wrote a letter to a talk-show host. The talk-show host was also guilty when no one was looking.
> While their inner storms were brewing, a bank teller lit a candle. The bank teller had a broken heart.
> Money changed hands.
> The bank teller was angered by the misogynist. The misogynist longed for the talk-show host.

While this story does not offer a lot of context, it does not come across as nonsense. This might well be kind of vignette or parable of contemporary sociopolitical life. It is not difficult to imagine that the misogynist is some kind of politician embroiled in a scandal, who goes on a talk show in order to perform a public *mea culpa*. The talk-show host meanwhile is just as corrupt as the politician. The bank teller, watching from afar, is disillusioned and heartbroken by the state of affairs, but nevertheless implicated in the same system that has produced the misogynist and the talk-show host, if powerless to change anything.

This sort of story, like the output of many text generators, invites the reader's involvement not by providing an excess of detail but, instead, by providing the reader with a minimal sketch, with a great deal of interpretative space left for the reader to fill in. As readers we tend to have a desire to *make sense* of texts presented to us, minimal outlines such as this can serve as provocations, engaging our imaginations with prompts to flesh out a richer storyworld than actually denoted by the text that appears on the screen.

Running the program multiple times and analyzing output from the same generator allows us to consider and decipher the program's structure. In this case, we can determine that the combinatory schema is quite simple in form. This program was written in Flash, so we cannot read the underlying source code, but by reading through multiple iterations of the program's output we can intuit its structure. It likely has about a dozen or so variables in arrays. Each time it is reiterated, the program pulls randomly from those arrays and sets the elements into place. For example, in the first sentence:

[Time setting], a [stereotype character A] [past tense action verb] for [object]. The [stereotype character A] [past tense of a condition].

Storyland is a simple program and yet I would argue that it is a *good* work of electronic literature because of the fact that its output almost always provides for a brief but engaging reading experience. One of the most frequent criticisms of poetry and story generators is that they produce nonsensical or even unreadable output, and this may well be the case for many text-generation systems. This does not necessarily mean that they are lesser works of art – the author may be striving for some other effect than producing compelling poetry or prose, such as exercising a particular constraint or mode of conceptual writing. Personally, however, I favor generative and combinatory systems that produce output that is not only readable but engaging in a literary sense. The texts produced by *Storyland*, for example, are more engaging than those produced by earlier systems such as *Tale-Spin*, which are much more complex under the hood, but which do not produce stories that are very interesting at the surface level of language.

It is important to read poetry and prose generators with an understanding that the author function is fundamentally different from that of writing a single poem or story. While the author of a poem intended for print publication is striving for a singularity – the one perfect expression of what they are trying to communicate – the author of a poetry generator is striving for multiplicity. A combinatory poetry generator uses variables to produce a factorial number of outputs. When this is the case, not all the outputs will be equally interesting as literature. But the best systems will produce outputs that are compelling literary experiences more often than not. The goal for the author of a combinatory work is not to produce the *best* literary expression of an idea, but the most interesting *range of possibilities* the literary system can produce. If a generative system only operates to demonstrate a concept while producing texts that can only be appreciated as output of a computer program but not as compelling language, in my view it fails as a work of electronic literature.

Could a poetry generator produce poems of adequate quality to be published in literary magazines? This, roughly, is the challenge that Jim Carpenter set for himself in developing the *Erica T. Carter Project*, an ambitious poetry generator. The project used corpuses and styles (analyzed by Carpenter as "tree adjoining grammars") from famous poets such as Emily Dickinson, Frank O'Hara, Sylvia Plath, Gary Snyder, and Rachel Blau DuPlessis, and mixed their words and styles together algorithmically to produce new poems. In addition to developing a complex program, Carpenter pushed things a bit further, creating a virtual persona for the generator, and had her submit poems to literary magazines, a number of which were published. In 2004 Carpenter exhibited the generator and a collection of its output at the Slought Foundation in Philadelphia as "Erica T. Carter, The Collected Works" (Carpenter, 2004). In 2008, along with Stephen McLaughlin, Jim Carpenter released *Issue 1: Fall 2008*, a 3,785-page work that was allegedly a compilation of poems by more than 3,000 contemporary American poets. In reality, Carpenter's generator produced all of the poems. Carpenter's project was both a complex and accomplished poetry generator and a Dadaistic performance, which thumbed its nose at the poetry establishment. Many of the poets listed as authors were in fact not pleased to find their names attributed to published poems that they had not written (Goldsmith, 2008). In a final gesture of the program/performance (or perhaps to mollify the angry poets), Carpenter removed most traces of the program from the Web – in a Sylvia Plath-style act of robotic self-annihilation – a loss for researchers and digital poets, who would still like to work with it.

Nick Montfort's *ppg256* poetry generators (2012) are a series of works that operate within an extreme constraint: the name of the project stands for "perl poetry generator 256 characters in length." Each of the poetry generators in the series is a single line of code of exactly 256 characters. In this sense, *ppg256* is a form of conceptual writing. The author's goal is not so much to write a generator that produces rich imaginative writing or even poetry that would be published in a literary magazine but, instead, that can produce readable language in poetic forms: no small feat in itself, when the number of characters the programmer allows himself are fewer than those in this sentence. Montfort's project here is a *tour de force* in the computer science conception of "elegance": the idea that the best code is that which produces the most substantial desired effect, while utilizing the minimal computer memory and processing power necessary to do so.

The majority of the *ppg256* programs write progressively and continue to scroll on, delivering new stanzas, until the user quits the program. Consider the code of *pp256–1* in its entirety:

```
perl -le 'sub b{@_=unpack"(A2)*",pop;$_[rand@_]}sub w{" ".b(cococa-
camamadebapabohamolaburatamihopodito).b(estsnslldsckregspsstedbsnele
ngkemsattewsntarshnknd)}{$_="\n\nthe".w."\n";$_=w." ".b(attoonnoof).w
if$l;s/[au][ae]/a/;print;$l=0if$l++>rand 9;sleep 1;redo} #Rev2'
```

When run, it produces output such as this stanza:

```
the coat
bans no hack
moat no poat
mash of coed
moes at hams
```

Words and phrases are being produced here in an arranged format that resembles poetry. There is some rhyme, and some alliteration, recognizable pattern, but the result is just shy of language that suggests intended meaning.

The output of the program *ppg256–3* likewise flirts with the edge of narrative, producing stanzas such as:

```
the_boyape
and
the_godman
ran_her

the_big_apebot
and
one_wan_botgod
jam_her
```

There are named characters, there are actions or events, but there is no causal connection or coherent thread between events as the program continues its endless production of language. Montfort's minimalist generators indeed challenge us to reconsider our definitions of poetry or narrative, through the use of extremely bare-bones code that delivers almost-meaningful poetry, almost-coherent feints at narrative. The *ppg256* set redirects our attention to the code-as-operable-language, and to the operations of computer itself.

As a whole, the *ppg256* project can be considered a work of conceptual writing. If the output produced is often such that it would not be accepted for publication in a literary magazine for traditional poetic values of heightened language or meaning, they often function well as performance works, both in the sense that they produce visual and sound poetry, and in the sense that they perform the potentialities of language within the constrained system. Montfort has in fact published a book, *#!* (2014a), which includes output from these minimal generators and others, along with the source code of the programs. As a set, the *ppg256* generators also demonstrate how extensively variable generators produced within a single minimal constraint can be, producing everything from wordplay poetry to minimalist narrative to concrete poetry.

Some combinatory texts work through interactive substitution or "overwriting," such as Jim Andrews' and collaborators' *Stir Fry Texts* (1999). Andrews describes the stir fry texts as consisting "of n distinct texts. Each of the n texts is partitioned into t pieces. When you mouse over any of the t parts of a text, that part is replaced with the corresponding part of the next of the n texts" (Andrews, 1999). The result is a kind of nervous text, a story or poem with elements that change and recombine as you navigate through them. In this sense the text is combinatory but not generative. The program cycles through a fixed number of elements, not in a completely random fashion but within a range of possibilities predetermined by the author. As the reader moves over certain phrases, they stir and change from within the range of possibilities, overwriting and providing a new version of the original text.

Judd Morrissey's *The Jew's Daughter* (2000) works with a similar navigation mechanic. The story is comprised of a text that appears to be a single screen or page of text with one word highlighted in blue, as in a hypertext fiction. But as the reader moves over each "link," rather than moving to a different page, some elements of the page change while other phrases remain intact. The work is linear in the sense that there is only one possible path through it, but combinatory in the sense that every new page overwrites the preceding page.

Randomization functions can lead to the production of absurdist texts, and a number of authors have effectively embraced and harnessed this quality of generative and combinatory work to literary ends. Talan Memmott's

Self Portrait(s) [as Other(s)] (2003) for example recombines elements from a corpus of text and imagery. The images the program produces are elements cut from self-portraits by famous artists. When recombined, we might end up with the eye of one artist, the nose of another, the chin of a third. The pseudo-biographical text accompanying the images is composed of slotted elements from biographies and curatorial texts about artists and their works. In one example Edouard Delacroix is described as a Futurist artist (who lived 153 years!) and influenced Mark Rothko. If none of the fake biographies produced are plausible, the remarkable thing about this piece is how easy it is at first glance to glaze over their historical inaccuracies. Through its absurdist construction, the work reveals how formulaic the genre of artist biographies actually is. The details of the artists' lives and works vary, but in a sense the construction of the artist's identity-as-artist is always the same.

Jason Nelson's *this is how you will die* (2005) engages expressly with absurdity and fatalism. In this case, the reader/user/player (as we will see a later chapter these roles are often combined in Nelson's works) is presented with a slot machine apparatus, including "demise credits" and "death spins." There are five slots that spin each time the user hits the death spin button. Every spin produces a new variant narrative of "your" death. Lucky players will get bonus demise credits along with the story of their deaths (and sometimes in the place of cherries, bonus videos and short poems about the nature of death). Though you can earn more credits as you spin your wheels, there is no jackpot in this slot machine. Just as in any real-world gambling concern, the system is rigged. No matter how lucky you are, you will run out of credits and stories of your demise. The combinatory element is effective here because the arbitrary nature of the random element is, in fact, no less arbitrary, and no less absurd, than mortality itself.

Nelson represents the combinatory procedure through the easily understandable metaphor of a slot machine. Other authors have similarly demonstrated the generative nature of their work topologically, for example by producing output that manifests as a three-dimensional cube. Daniel Howe and Aya Karpinska's *open.ended* (2004) is a 3D poem with texts that appear on the faces of cubes nested within each other. Each face of the cube includes a phrase or line of a poem. An additional multimedia layer is provided by the spoken voices of the authors reading other lines of the poem. The user can pull particular faces of the cube forward by selecting them, and when this occurs the other lines of the poem change dynamically. The work thus provides some element of choice and user control, but every iteration of the work is largely aleatory.

Nick Montfort's *Taroko Gorge* (2009) is a poetry generator Montfort authored in Python during a trip to Taiwan, after he had visited the national park of the same name. It is a relatively simple script that produces an endlessly scrolling poem, cascading ceaselessly in the web browser until the reader closes the window in which it manifests. It is neither the most ambitious work Montfort has produced nor the most complex – though as in much of Montfort's work, complexity and simplicity are closely joined. It does not produce a dense reading experience, and its combinatory potential can be exhausted in a matter of perhaps ten or fifteen minutes. Yet *Taroko Gorge* resulted in nothing short of an electronic literature phenomenon, as it has now been hacked and remixed dozens of times by other writers.

Montfort ported the project to HTML/CSS/JavaScript and published it online. When I read Taroko Gorge, I was impressed with its elegance and its structure. Like much of Montfort's work, it is a compact and efficient computer program. It produces output that is authentically poetic and what you might call "ambient." I also really loved the inversion embedded in the fact that *Taroko Gorge* is a poetry generator, a machine-driven system, that produces calm, almost Zen nature poetry. As with most of Montfort's work, the code is open and accessible. When I opened up the source and studied the structure, it occurred to me that it might be fun to hack Montfort's work and see if I could use the same code base to produce a generator that resulted in different poetic output. Doing so was a relatively simple matter. Since Montfort's script pulls words from arrays and places them within a structured grammar, the main way I changed the generator was by replacing all the words in its vocabulary. *Taroko Gorge* yields the first stanzas:

> Mists exercise the basin.
> Mists dream.
> Stones pace the veins.
>   run the arched cool –
> Shapes pace the vein.
> Coves relax.
> The crag roams the basins.
>   shade the encompassing –

A sample run of *Tokyo Garage* delivers in contrast the first stanzas:

> Translator endures the strangers.
> Authors fail.
> Atomic bombs adore the politicians.
>   remember the digital blinking scantily clad –
> Massively multiplayer games proselytize the altruists.
> Detectives destroy.
> Addict adores the vintage Cadillac.
>   apologize for the robust electric –

I transformed Montfort's meditative poetry generator, with its minimalist vocabulary, into a maximalist work about ideas of cities, populating a frenetic, cosmopolitan, and comic landscape of absurdity.

I titled the new work *Tokyo Garage* (2009), put a strikethrough through Montfort's name on the author credit, and placed my own name beneath it. Then I published it on the Web and sent Montfort the link, informing him I had "made a few improvements" to his piece. At the time, I was thinking that the main audience for *Tokyo Garage* would in fact be Montfort, as my remix/hacking/overwriting of the poem was essentially a lark for our mutual amusement. What happened next was a surprise I don't think anyone expected. First J. R. Carpenter took the same code-base and developed *Gorge* (2010), a work that produces poems about eating and digestion, and then two more variations. Talan Memmott's *Toy Garbage* (2011b), focused on kitsch and plastic toys, came soon after. Eric Snodgrass delivered up *Yoko Engorged* (2011), an erotic generator that produced poetry about Yoko Ono and John Lennon. Mark Sample paid tribute to *Star Trek* cast member and net luminary *Takei, George* (2011) and so on. Montfort added each of the rewrites to his site. More than two dozen variations of the *Taroko Gorge* codebase have been published, and it has become a kind of mini-genre of its own. The gesture of hacking, remixing, and subverting the original work has been repeated many times, with each iteration resulting in a new work.

Aden Evens points out that much of the appeal of *Taroko Gorge* rests in the invitation it represents: both to become a digital author and a co-author with the machine, promising to produce simultaneously "an authorial role and its cession to the machine, a poem at once one's own and entrusted to the algorithm" (Evens, 2018). Perhaps the most important aspect of the *Taroko Gorge* phenomena is that literally anyone can produce a new version of the work. This has proven useful for bringing people into writing electronic literature. When writer friends tell me they'd like to make work in digital media but don't know how to write code, I simply open up the source code and show them where to rewrite the vocabulary in the arrays. If you can write nouns and verbs and adjectives and have an idea of what theme you would like to work with, you can build a new poetry machine on top of the architecture of another one. It is an aspect of the ethos of the electronic literature community that many of its authors embrace this remix and reuse mentality and embrace digital writing as a form of productive play, just as the Oulipo do in their writing games.

Regenerating and mutating existing texts

A number of poetry generators begin with a source corpus of poetic language that is modified by procedural recombination and driven by the user's interactions with the interface. Nick Montfort and Stephanie Strickland's *Sea and Spar Between* is one such example, and it is innovative in several ways. It is a generator "which defines a space of language populated by a number of stanzas comparable to the number of fish in the sea, around 225 trillion" (Montfort and Strickland, 2012). The authors defined an information lattice of 14992383 x 14992383 possible permutations. The number of recombinations of the poems permitted by system poem is therefore finite but staggeringly extensive. The corpus of language the authors used to develop the work is exclusively composed of words and phrases from the poems of Emily Dickinson and the complete text of Herman Melville's *Moby Dick*. When launching the work in the browser, the user is placed at an arbitrary but defined address within the virtual space (e.g. 13885482,11069694). The reader can then navigate from there either by entering another address or by scrolling horizontally or vertically in the browser window. The stanzas are each composed of two couplets. The page presents a virtual sea of these four-line stanzas, dark blue stanza of text on a light blue background. If the reader zooms out in their browser window it is possible to see the scale of the information space, and as the stanzas become too small to remain legible they can indeed be read abstractly as fish in the sea. The stanzas can be read individually or in connection with one another. Any connections found by the reader between them will be entirely subjective. While some of the stanzas produced are better than others, they all "work" at the level of syntax. When readers open up the JavaScript source code of *Sea and Spar Between* they find that the source code (in the 2012 "cut to fit the toolspun course" version of the work) includes a full-length essay about the work with glosses both on the code that drives the work and on the poetic sources and decisions the authors made about the literary system as they developed it. It also includes language indicating that the work is free software and can be re-used by others.

Frequency (Rettberg, 2009) is a poetry generator based on a constrained writing project. Working with a list of the 200 most-used words in the English language, I wrote 2,000 lines of poetry. I wrote ten lines beginning with each of the words on the list, using only the words on the frequency list. The program, developed in Ruby, assembles subsets of these lines in rhyming and syllabic poetry forms such a sonnets and haiku, in addition to constrained forms, such as the Oulipian snowball, and concrete forms such as "two towers" or "four square." Because of the fact that the system's vocabulary is constrained, there are always semantic connections across the lines and the lines tend to work fairly well together thematically. Working with this large but finite set of already written lines, the program is not so much a generator as it is an arranger. *Frequency* demonstrates how we can think of traditional poetic form and computational processing as intrinsically related, how we can use one to model the other, and how poetic lines can be made to flow into variant contexts and forms algorithmically.

Evolution (2013) by Johannes Heldén and Håkon Jonson is a poetry generator developed with a complex relation to authorship in mind. Heldén, a visual artist, poet and musician who lives and works in Stockholm, set out with Jonson to create a poetry generator that would make his own function as a poet redundant, by passing a form of Alan Turing's "imitation game." *Evolution*'s authors asked themselves some challenging questions, as they explain in the project's abstract:

> With *Evolution* we aim to examine and dissect the role of the author; when new poetry that resembles the work of the original author is created or presented through an algorithm, is it possible to make the distinction between "author" and "programmer"? And is it even relevant? When the work of the algorithm is extrapolated to the point where the original author becomes redundant, how does this affect copyright, legacy, future writings, etc.?

The program is generative on a number of levels. The authors modeled elements in Heldén's print poetry, such as vocabulary, use of spacing, and syntax, modeling the generator on Heldén's own style. The program uses particular templates for "ambience" and then uses a series of arbitrary data sources, such as weather data from various locations or the "RADIUS OF UNCONFIRMED EXOPLANETARY SYSTEMS" to determine the sequence of modifications made to the text. The text moves rapidly through generations of change based on these variables, modifying the text in a continuous cycle of revision that resembles the author's own writing style and process. A generative soundtrack mixing samples of Heldén's music plays in the background as the process unfolds. *Evolution* was also published as a book (2014) that included the source code of the generator as well as several critical responses to the work and the conceptual issues it raises. The book was the winner of the 2014 N. Katherine Hayles Award for Criticism of Electronic Literature.

Abra: A Living Text (2017) by Amaranth Borsuk, Kate Durbin, and Ian Hatcher treats poetry generation as an act of interactive play. If *Evolution* was a poetry generator designed to replace its author, the iPad app *Abra* presents a poetry generation system that is itself the artwork, a system designed for users to write and play with language. It merges aspects of algorithmic generativity with interactivity. Its authors describe the work as functioning "much like the magic word of its origin – abracadabra – as an unpredictable living text. Not only does the text grow and change on its own, readers also take part in the process, touching to mutate, graft, and prune the text, watching words shift under their fingers." Using various "spells" the user can launch processes of addition, reduction, erasure, and substitution, mutating the work in an ongoing process, pausing to capture screenshots of satisfying states of the poem as the process unfolds. The tactility of the tablet interface adds another dimension to the reader's interaction with the text. Words are produced and processes launched as a result of the reader's physical engagement with the text.

Bots

After the 2016 American elections, the social media platform Twitter may forever be associated with bots of a malevolent kind – those that are used to spread propaganda and create the impression that fake news items have credibility on the basis of their popularity on the network. But these are not the bots we're looking for. Many people have taken to making bots that produce poetry, prose, or concrete visual forms in ASCII text and deliver them on a scheduled basis to a Twitter stream. The bots produce a wide variety of types of poetry. According to Leonardo Flores (2013) they work with "poetry in many forms (haiku, couplets, sonnets, and more), techniques (n-grams, Markov chains, templates, variables, etc.), and datasets (self-contained, data mining, streaming APIs, user-generated, dictionaries, and more)."

Pentametron is a classic example of a poetry Twitter bot. The avatar icon for the bot is Shakespeare's face silhouetted by the Twitter egg icon. *Pentametron* scans the public tweets on Twitter and picks out those that happen to be in iambic pentameter. When it has collected some of those it scans for rhyme and then posts a couplet in two tweets. Some recent sample output includes "A double blessing is a double grace,/ The Center is a crooked place" and "A lie in on Friday seems unreal./ WILL SOMEONE GET THE KID A HAPPY MEAL?!"

The New York Times offers a bot, *Times Haiku*, which like *Pentametron* scans for a specific syllabic arrangement. In this case, the *Times* bot searches for haiku in the articles published in the paper, sentences that can break down into a 5/7/5 syllable arrangement. Some *Times* editors are delivered the haiku every time they appear, and occasionally post those that appeal to them, along with a link to the article that provides the bot's source. An apropos haiku "All of the papers/ continue to operate/ autonomously" was for example found in a November 17, 2017 story titled "The Media Mogul of Maine."

Bots can pull from static as well as dynamic sources for different generative effects. Some of these are conceptual, for example the *@everyword* bot by Allison Parrish (2007). The bot posted every word in a dictionary of the English language, in order, one word at a time, every half hour. The performance was durational, and unfolded over a seven-year period from 2007 to 2014. Kati Rose Pipkin's *tiny star fields* is a bot that periodically produces a short visual representation of stars in the sky in the confined space of a Twitter post using stars, asterisks, and other ASCII symbols. There are far too many variants of bots to describe extensively in this book, but the *Electronic Literature Collection, Volume 3* includes a good introduction to the breadth of approaches that authors are taking to working in this uniquely form of generative networked writing.

There are a number of tools available to help authors develop Twitter bots. Kate Compton's *Tracery* project streamlines the process of setting up a text or graphics generation for bots. A site called *Cheap Bots, Done Quick* can be used to host them. Another set of tools of interest to writers interested in any sort of text generation is Daniel Howe's RiTa software toolkit for computational literature. The RiTa library provides capabilities including from grammar and Markov-based generation to text mining, and can make use of a user-customizable lexicon or the WordNet database (a large language corpus). The tool can be used in a number of different programming environments including Android, Processing, Node, and p5.js (Howe, 2015).

Big data poetics

Neural nets are a contemporary approach to artificial intelligence and machine learning using data models that are inspired by the way biological neural networks in the human brain process information. David Jhave Johnston's *BDP (Big Data Poetry)* (2016) is a project that investigates the use of neural nets for literary creation. Using tools such as Tensorflow, Keras, and PyTorch, Johnston is "training" these neural net systems on a corpus of 600,000 lines of poetry in English harvested from online archives, and then asks the resulting models to produce poems on an infinite loop. In comparison to the other sorts of poetry generation discussed in this article, the process of using neural nets is considerably "black boxed." After training the model with a corpus and configuring it, the developer plays little role in the process or understanding of how it works. The underlying source code is largely the property of research wings of major corporations, such as Facebook and Amazon, who have made the facility available to researchers to use. Once started, the models learn and develop of their own accord. During 2017, Johnston set out to publish a series of books of poetry, publishing a book every month for a six-month period. His role in the process is largely editorial. Every morning he scans through thousands of lines of poetry produced by the machine. He then culls and groups lines from the system, forming them into readable poems. This is perhaps a new role for the human poet: as editor for poetry entirely generated by machine intelligence based on a process that remains both invisible and largely incomprehensible for the human poet.

What can we learn from combinatory poetics?

Combinatory and generative approaches result in forms of electronic literature that flow natively from principles of computation. While aleatory and variable writing practices have a long history in print literature, we can say that they were comparatively minor tributaries of print literary tradition. The computer however allows for automation of complex generative procedures and enables authors and writers to exploit these techniques in the production of text machines that materialize the idea of potential literature. If the notion of a computer program that could competently write an engaging novel has yet to be fully realized, complex procedural poetry and fiction generation systems have been produced. Related techniques and procedures underlie many aspects of contemporary networked culture from spambots to massively multiplayer online games. Combinatory poetics can result in strange, uncanny, and beautiful texts resulting from an amalgamation of human and machine intelligence and serve as heuristic devices to help us better understand computation.

3   Hypertext Fiction

Hypertext fiction was the first form of electronic literature to garner sustained critical interest during the late 1980s and early 1990s. A small but dedicated group of writers began to work seriously in the genre at the same time as the personal computer and then the Internet were becoming widely adopted, writing stories designed as interlinked fragments of text, with multiple possible reading sequences to be navigated through the reader's selection of links between them. At the same time, postmodernism was reaching the peak of its literary and theoretical interest. Hypertext fiction represented a bridge between the literary experimentation of the late twentieth century and the cultural shifts accompanying the move to networked computing. Although other practices of digital writing preceded literary hypertext, without the small critical industry that developed around hypertext fiction during this period, electronic literature would likely not have been established as a field of academic research and practice in the way that it is today. While we cannot understate the importance of hypertext for the development and growth of the electronic literature community, there is less recent activity in this genre than in some of the others discussed in this book, though in some ways the core ideas and basic techniques of hypertext have migrated into genres such as installations, interactive 3D works in CAVEs, and apps for mobile devices. In this chapter we will consider how hypertext emerged within a particular literary, historical, and technological context, and how it served to facilitate the foundation of a critical and creative community of practice.

Literary antecedents to hypertext

Thus far I have not commented extensively on the critical theorists active in the 1990s and 2000s, whose attention to connections between theory and hypertext did much to spark academic interest in hypertext, most notably George Landow. This influence should not be overlooked. Landow's *Hypertext: The Convergence of Contemporary Critical Theory and Technology* (1992) made explicit connections between literary hypertext and poststructuralist theory. In the second edition of the book, *Hypertext 2.0* (1997), for instance, Landow claims "hypertext has much in common with some major points of contemporary literary and semiological theory, particularly with Derrida's emphasis on decentering and with Barthes' conception of the readerly versus the writerly text. In fact, hypertext creates an almost embarrassingly literal embodiment of both concepts" (p. 32). If later critics have contested the idea that hypertext can literally *embody* these concepts, there is still general agreement that, at least, hypertext makes for a decentered reading experience. Another frequently debated claim from Landow's work is the degree to which hypertext entails a "transference of authorial power" (Landow, 2006, p. 125) from the author to the reader. Landow describes the configurative choices made by the hypertext reader as embodying the death of the author – or the reconfiguration of the author function described by Foucault (1988). Aarseth (1997) questioned whether links are themselves not actually further constraints put on the text and on the reader by the author, restricting a reader's choices rather than enabling free configuration of the text. Rather than revisiting the finer points of the relationship between postmodern theory and hypertext, however, we will focus here on the ways that the thematic concerns and formal characteristics of postmodern American print fiction informed (and may continue to inform) the practice of hypertext, and how some of the early hypertext authors emerged from immersion in postmodern fiction in ways that have effects on their aesthetic sensibilities and their practices in digital media.

Modernist influences

Just as computational poetry and narrative generators were informed by aleatory and combinatory poetic practices of earlier avant-garde movements, hypertext fiction and poetry has a lineage in twentieth-century cultures of experimental writing, most clearly in relation to modernism and postmodernism. There are many different ways to characterize modernism and postmodernism (and the terms are used to describe varied practices in different fields such as critical theory, art, architecture, and literature). In this context, we will primarily consider the relation between literary modernism and postmodernism to hypertext. The distinction between modernism and postmodernism can likewise be understood from a variety of perspectives but for the most part postmodernism is best understood as "late modernism" rather than as completely separate from it.

Most understandings of modernism are not solely based on periodization – modernism is not simply literature produced during the modern era – but instead as techniques and practices that made a significant formal break with the traditions that preceded them. Particular concerns of literary modernism included a heightened interest in the materiality of language, an increased use of referentiality and intertextuality, and ways of using language to represent interiority and the flow of human consciousness. Generally modernist writers followed Ezra Pound's injunction to *renovate* literature, to "Make it new" (Pound, 1934). In Pound's work and that of other contemporaries such as T. S. Eliot and James Joyce, the idea of making it new presumes not necessarily that literature will be made of new ideas cut from whole cloth, but that ideas, themes and motifs from earlier traditions should be remixed, recycled, represented, shaped into new forms.

In the work of Eliot, Joyce, and other high modernists we see substantial use of intertextuality and referentiality. A given text, whether *The Waste Land* (1922) or *Finnegan's Wake* (1939) is through its structural dependence on and extensive links to other texts woven into a larger web of literature. In the work of writers such as Gertrude Stein and Virginia Woolf, we also see a turn toward representing events not primarily through their manifestation in the exterior world, but as an interior process that can itself be represented not only through shifts of narrative voice and point of view, but also through the material form of the text itself – its pacing, its use of grammar, and its patterns of association. In *To the Lighthouse* (1927) for example Woolf describes words as making a "pattern on the floor of the child's mind" (Woolf, 2014, p. 67). The most influential concept here in relation to hypertext is the notion that literary devices can be used to represent language differently in portraying associative thought than in communicating conversational discourse. Another modernist narrative structure present for example in Woolf's *Mrs Dalloway* (1925) or in the "Wandering Rocks" chapter of Joyce's *Ulysses* (1922) is that of rapid shifts in point of view, focalization, and narrative style through words, locations, or associations. The connections which drive the movement of the narrative are derived not from following the perspective of any of the individual characters but instead by a panoramic approach through which we experience moments, fragments, partial experiences, before linking over to the next perspective. This technique helps the narrative achieve a sense of simultaneity, and reinforces the idea that the main character of that novel may not be Stephen Daedalus or Leopold Bloom, but the city of Dublin itself.

Postmodern multilinearity

The formal, structural, and linguistic experimentation of the modernists was extended in the work of the writers collectively referred to as "postmodernists." The American brand of literary postmodernism was deeply influential on the authors of hypertext fiction writing in the 1990s and early 2000s. If the formal innovations of the postmodernists do not represent a huge break from those of the modernists, we can identify certain formal approaches and tendencies that had greater emphasis in the work of these writers, who were most active from the 1960s until roughly the end of the twentieth century. Some of the qualities of literary postmodernism most influential on the development of hypertext fiction include a shift away from linear storytelling toward a multi-threaded approach or a "fiction of possibilities," a general distrust of the idea of representational mimesis, a turn toward interrogating the narrative structure and materiality of the text, an embrace of reflexivity, and a movement toward collage, pastiche, and remix in works of fiction and poetry.

Many of the possibilities of narrative structure that so interested hypertext writers and theorists during the 1990s were explored by experimental writers of earlier periods, stretching back to the authorial intrusions and formal innovations of Laurence Sterne's *The Life and Opinions of Tristram Shandy, Gentleman* (1761). Among the works most often cited as antecedents to hypertext are Jorge Luis Borges' short story "El jardín de senderos que se bifurcan" (1941), published in English as "The Garden of Forking Paths" (1962). A central element of that story was a novel by the character Ts'ui Pên that was itself a labyrinth in that it described a world where all possible outcomes of a given event would occur simultaneously, thus forking out to other chains of event, which would themselves fork in an infinite tree of possibilities. Very early in his career Stuart Moulthrop made a hypertext version of Borges' story, titled *forking paths* (1987), though the work was never published as Borges' story was under copyright. The story also had a clear influence on Moulthrop's *Victory Garden* (1991).

Julio Cortazar's *Hopscotch* (Spanish: *Rayuela*) (1963) plays with the arbitrary nature of chronology in story in a number of ways. The novel has 155 chapters, but the last 99 of them are described as "expendable" (Cortazar, 1987). Cortazar further offers the reader three different ways to read the book: either by reading the chapters in the printed order of 1–56, or by reading according to an alternate order provided in a "table of instructions," or simply hopping about the novel in whatever order the reader likes.

Following on Cortazar, a number of authors took the abandonment of linearity even further. Mark Saporta's *Composition No. 1*, originally published in French in 1961, and translated into English by Richard Howard in 1963, is a novel printed on 150 loose-leaf pages, each with a separate section of the novel.

Saporta gives the reader instructions to shuffle the pages like a deck of cards, as if at a fortuneteller's. The operations of chance play an oracular role in structuring the narrative. The novel follows the lives of several different women during the WWII German occupation of France. Ben Carey (2015) notes that the author uses both certain ambiguities, particularly in framing the beginning and ending of each segment of narrative, as well as certain constants, through focus on three central characters, and a recurring focus on an assault suffered by Helga, one of the novel's central characters. Because there is a focal event in the novel, reflections on that event can be presented before, during, and after the central episode without much of a break in narrative continuity. Visual Editions released an iPad edition of *Composition No. 1* in 2011, which performs the shuffling on demand.

B. S. Johnson's *The Unfortunates* (1969) was similarly published not in a bound codex but instead in twenty-seven unbound sections in a laminated box. Only the first and last chapters are specified, the other sections are to be ordered at random by the reader. The play with arrangement and chronology we see in Cortazar and Johnson perhaps hearken back to the modernist interest in the associative properties of the mind and of memory. If fiction often lays life out as one long linear or carefully ordered progression in which time's arrow only moves forward, the subjective experience of human consciousness is messier than that, as memories of past and projections of the future interpellate our experience of everyday life.

Robert Coover was and remains one of the postmodern authors most influential on the electronic literature scene. His short story "The Babysitter," published in *Pricksongs and Descants* (1969), is a classic of postmodern fiction. The story consists of over one hundred fragments – paragraphs set off from each other by space breaks, that take us through multiple and divergent sequences of what might have or what could have occurred during the course of one evening between a babysitter, a baby, her boyfriend, and the mother and father of the house. Although chronological progression takes place in the story, as we move from 7:40 p.m. into the late hours of the night, the distinction between objective reality and fantasy falls away as we read the fragments, and every possibility has equal opportunity to be visited. As Brian Evenson notes:

> The third-person narrator presents every event, many mutually exclusive, as if it were a reality. There is no clear line drawn in the story between fantasy and reality. The relation between the external world and the interior world of the imagination has been abolished on the page. Television shows which characters watch seem to take over the larger story, rape and playing pinball get confused, people peep in windows, events at the party seem to trickle back into the Tucker's home, and nearly all of the character's fantasies

spring to life. Coover refuses to choose one possibility over all of the others. (Evenson, 2003, 91)

"The Babysitter" is one of the best examples in print of the idea of *multilinearity* that digital hypertext seemed poised to exploit, a story that is not one progression of events, but many possible progressions of events branching from the same tree. Few hypertext fiction authors in the first couple of waves of work in the genre actually pursued a branching path narrative structure in terms of possible outcomes, although it is a more popular strategy in more recent Twine games (see chapter 4). More prevalent uses of multilinearity in hypertext include the representation of cognitive associations between nodes and shifts in point of view on the same events.

Metafiction and reflexivity

One of the clearest threads running through much of postmodernist fiction is a tendency toward *metafiction*, fiction that is reflexive and as much about narrative structure and the apparatus of storytelling as it is about the characters, plot or themes of its ostensible subject. Reflexive texts all in some sense "turn back toward themselves." Reflexivity can however come in a number of different forms: within the corpus of postmodern American fiction I would describe these forms as authorial, intertextual, generic, and medial reflexivity.

Authorial reflexivity entails the appearance of the author, or a character named after the author, within what might have appeared to be an enclosed diegetic system. Kurt Vonnegut, Richard Powers, John Barth, Paul Auster, and David Foster Wallace, for instance all at some point in their careers included characters that are either named after themselves, clearly represent the author as character, or in some way consider the tenuous ontological condition of the author. At the same time as poststructuralist theory had declared the death of the author (see Barthes, 1977), many postmodern authors wrestled with the nature and the function of the author as they wrote their texts. Inserting their fictional doppelgangers into their stories served not only as a form of resistance, a *cri de coeur* against the barrier between the author's living consciousness and the static text, but also as a way to break down the structure of relations between author, book, and reader, and to highlight the fundamental artifice on which those relations are based.

Intertextual reflexivity, developing from the modernist intertextual tendency, was also a common trait of postmodern fiction. Intertextually reflexive fictions invite consideration of their relation both to other texts and to themselves as texts. Jeanette Winterson's *Sexing the Cherry* (1989) reconstructs elements of Jonathan Swift's *Gulliver's Travels* (1726) and subverts classic fairy tales and stories from the Bible. Kurt Vonnegut's *Breakfast of Champions* (1973) features characters from his previous novels who appear and interact with each other. In postmodern fiction, inter-textuality is often used in some sort of disruptive way – not only to bring into play the cultural frame of narrative structures of prior texts but also to break the diegetic frame. When Kathy Acker plagiarizes or "overwrites" William Gibson's *Neuromancer* (1984) in *Empire of the Senseless* (1988), she is not simply referencing the source text, but occupying it in a subversive way. Both the idea of overwriting and the actual remix of source texts were important in many of the early hypertext fictions such as *afternoon, a story* (Joyce, 1987), *Patchwork Girl* (Jackson, 1995), *The Unknown* (Gillespie et al., 1998), and *The Jew's Daughter* (Morrissey, 2000).

Postmodern fictions are often formally or generically reflexive, concerned with the processes and apparatus of reading and writing fiction. When Donald Barthelme wrote the story "Sentence" (1969), he was questioning both the form of the sentence and the minimal condition under which a text can be considered to constitute story. Similarly, John Barth's "Frame Tale" (1968) consists, in its entirety, of the phrase "once upon a time there was a story that began" along with directions to cut out the text and fold it into a Möbius strip, resulting in an infinite loop of a frame tale. When David Foster Wallace buried important plot points of *Infinite Jest* (1996) in footnotes, or when Mark Z. Danielewski did the same in *House of Leaves* (2000) in footnotes to other footnotes, they were reflecting on the inherent limitations of fiction to depict the complexity of reality and exploring the potentiality of the note itself as a sort of technological apparatus to enable a less-bound maximalism, a type of perspectival exteriority not available in the same way in conventional narrative form.

Postmodern fiction also engaged with medial reflexivity, which follows from this same awareness of the artifice, the machinery of storytelling, and other kinds of semiosis. One aspect of the postmodern turn was not only to reconsider the form and genres of narrative, but also the relations of written narrative to other media forms. This reflexivity could take a number of different forms: one is the impulse to use techniques from other art forms in the creation of novel forms: Donald Barthelme's collage technique, for example, which consisted not only of sampling from other texts, but literally cutting out illustrations from nineteenth-century books, and gluing them into his own stories, or Tom Philips' *A Humament* (1966), a novel made by painting over every page in another novel, obscuring and enhancing the meaning of particular passages through both verbal and visual registers (see chapter 5). Conversely, there are the examples of Robert Coover's collection *A Night at the Movies, or, You Must Remember This* (1992), which adapts and interrogates the language of film through fiction, or Curtis White's *Memories of My Father Watching TV* (1998), a chained sequence of stories that uses the language, plots, and formal characteristics of 1950s television shows to work through a boy's painful relationship with his father. Many works of electronic literature are in a similar way thematically concerned with the materiality of the digital as writing environment.

Both formal and medial reflexivity are in keeping with an impulse toward testing the boundaries of what N. Katherine Hayles describes as media specificity (Hayles, 2004). That is, in using footnotes in an unconventional way, Wallace isn't necessarily critiquing the fact that footnotes are not usually used this way, but instead, pointing out that this affordance of the apparatus of the book or the magazine article is available to us, and when Coover and White adapt the language and conventions of film and television to the short story or memoir form, they aren't so much demonstrating the capabilities of film or television as they are exploring which sorts or expression are uniquely available via language on the page.

Many of the works of postmodern fiction referenced here share a level of consciousness of a media apparatus that, in Jay David Bolter and Richard Grusin's terms, remediates (Bolter and Grusin, 1999). Media reflexivity is an important concern for hypertext and for other genres of electronic literature. Indeed, as the first forms of literary expression native to digital media, this reflexivity may be one of their most important functions, providing us with a literary record of – to paraphrase Hayles (1999) – "how we became posthuman."

Another quality of postmodern fiction also characteristic of hypertext fiction is a tendency toward increased fragmentation. In some cases, this takes on the form of a very extreme extension of modernist referentiality. Two of the later works of David Markson, *Wittgenstein's Mistress* (1988) and *This Is Not a Novel* (2001) consist almost entirely of references, anecdotes, quotes, and aphorisms, but arranged in a such a way that the reader can feel immersed in a sense of consciousness. Carole Maso's novel *Ava* (1993) takes us into the consciousness of a dying woman but does so through fragmented memories both of her past lovers and the literary and cultural referents that shaped her experience. In *Dictionary of the Khazars* (published in Serbian in 1984 and published in an English translation in 1989), Milorad Pavić offers us a novel in the form of a lexicon (printed in two slightly variant "male" and "female" editions). In her short stories, Lydia Davis (2010) offers us fiction as an extreme form of compression of experience, with stories that may be as short as a paragraph but that nevertheless feel fully formed, acute, and rich. These shifts toward fragmentary, nodal structures, narratives presented in shards and glimpses, disconnected moments, and transclusions to other cultural artifacts, are moves that authors of electronic literature have further embraced.

The relationship between American literary postmodernism and early hypertext was not only one of casual formal similarities but also personal connections. Although too much can be made of interconnected social networks insofar as there are social networks at work in literary culture, Robert Coover has been a key figure in both literary postmodernism and the emergent culture of electronic literature. Shelley Jackson, Robert Arellano, Judd Morrissey, and a number of other active electronic literature authors passed through the Brown University literary arts program where Coover taught the first digital writing workshops. Before he was one of the best-known hypertext authors, Stuart Moulthrop was a Thomas Pynchon scholar. Talan Memmott was a friend and art-school student of Kathy Acker. Before he wrote *Grammatron*, Mark Amerika was a protégé of Ronald Sukenick. Before William Gillespie, Frank Marquardt, and I worked on *The Unknown* (1998) we studied fiction writing with David Foster Wallace and Curtis White. Many writers in the early hypertext fiction writing community and postmodernism were in conversation and connected with each other both socially and aesthetically.

We will revisit the formal qualities and reflexive concerns of literary postmodernism later in the chapter as we consider individual works of hypertext fiction, but before we turn to the works, we should also consider the technological milieu from which hypertext emerged.

Hypertext in technological context

Hypertext is not only or even primarily a kind of writing. It is more fundamentally a text technology, and an approach to organizing, structuring, and sharing information. Anyone who has ever used a web browser has encountered hypertext: the H in HTML stands for hypertext (HyperText Markup Language), as does H in the "http://" that precedes every web address. Everyone who uses the network uses hypertext every time they turn on their computer or smartphone. Linking and browsing the Web, following connections between documents, has by now become so second nature to most of us that we no longer think about it – the technology of hypertext has become as transparent to us as the technology of the book. It is useful to remember that this was not always the case: as recently as the late

1990s the idea of "following a link" while reading a text was still novel. But if the ubiquity of hypertext and the everyday use of associative reading are comparatively new, the idea of hypertext originated much earlier.

In his 1945 essay "As We May Think," Vannevar Bush (1945) made a number of proposals for the future of research and technology. Bush was the director of Office of Scientific Research and Development, the forerunner to DARPA, the agency responsible for the Manhattan Project and other advanced scientific projects organized by the US government during World War II. During this period there was an unprecedented push to gather the leading scientific minds of the era in order to develop and implement technologies to better prosecute the war effort – Bush had coordinated the efforts of six thousand scientists. After the development of the atom bomb, and after Hiroshima, Bush's essay could be read as part of an effort to "turn the swords into plowshares" and to redirect the energies of this collective scientific effort toward peacetime goals and toward the advancement of civilization. Bush proposed a number of new technologies and approaches in his essay: most significant among them for our purposes is the "memex": "a future device for individual use, a sort of mechanized private file and library … a device in which an individual stores all his books, records, and communications, and which is mechanized so that it may be consulted with exceeding speed and flexibility … an enlarged intimate supplement to his memory." When we read this description through the lens of our present culture, the memex sounds very much like a personal computer, though projecting from the advanced technologies of his time, Bush imagined a desk-sized object that would be used to control and manipulate a library of microfilm. Users would both acquire published material and would be able to add materials of their own (using a microfilm camera about the size of a walnut worn on their foreheads). In a way, Bush was anticipating both personal and wearable computing, but the aspect of his essay that would have the most impact on the future of digital culture was the idea of associative indexing on which his memex would be based. The key feature of the memex is a creation of "trails" that users could build between articles. Bush provided an example of a researcher exploring the origins and properties of the bow and arrow:

> Specifically he is studying why the short Turkish bow was apparently superior to the English long bow in the skirmishes of the Crusades. He has dozens of possibly pertinent books and articles in his memex. First he runs through an encyclopedia, finds an interesting but sketchy article, leaves it projected. Next, in a history, he finds another pertinent item, and ties the two together. Thus he goes, building a trail of many items. Occasionally he inserts a comment of his own, either linking it into the main trail or joining it by a side

trail to a particular item. When it becomes evident that the elastic properties of available materials had a great deal to do with the bow, he branches off on a side trail which takes him through textbooks on elasticity and tables of physical constants. He inserts a page of longhand analysis of his own. Thus he builds a trail of his interest through the maze of materials available to him.

Bush also imagined that these trails "would not fade" – that the researcher would forge connections between the materials and save those trails in a way that the trail itself could be passed onto others, who could then build new connections. This idea of writing as a process of not only producing language but also developing links between materials is core to the idea of hypertext. In some ways, Bush's idea of how trails work is more flexible than hypertext as implemented on the Web. While hypertext authors build trails through links, once those trails of links are shared in simple hypertext, users cannot add paths or insert additional materials of their own.

Theodor Holm Nelson first introduced the term "hypertext" in his 1965 paper "A File Structure for the Complex, the Changing, and the Indeterminate." Nelson described hypertext "to mean a body of written or pictorial material interconnected in such a complex way that it could not conveniently be presented or represented on paper" (Nelson 2003, p. 96). In *Computer Lib/Dream Machines* (1974), Nelson provided a more expansive definition of "hyper-media" as "branching or performing presentations which respond to user actions, systems of prearranged words and pictures (for example) which may be explored freely or queried in stylized ways" (Nelson, 2003, p. 313). Among the types of hypertexts he discusses in that essay, which focused on the potential uses of hypermedia in new systems that could potentially revolutionize education, are "discrete hypertexts" which "consist of separate pieces of text connected by links" (p. 314) The majority of hypertext fictions published during the 1980s and 1990s would fit within this rubric though, as Noah Wardrip-Fruin (2004b) argued, this conception of hypertext as "chunk-style" linked nodes is somewhat narrower than hypermedia as Nelson originally envisioned it. Nelson for example imagined "stretchtexts" that would expand or contract to provide the reader with more detail about a given part of the text, and interactive diagrams that would perform as the reader interacted with particular parts of them or zoomed in for detail.

The "hyper" in hypertext suggests extensibility. Picking up from Bush, Nelson conceived of hypertext by considering any given text as existing within "a literature" – a web of interconnected documents. The connections between texts might be direct and visible – as in citations and footnotes – or they might be indirect – as when the author of one text is influenced by or reacting to another. But embedded within and surrounding any book or article in a particular field is this web of connections. This network of relations is in fact what composes the field itself. In Nelson's view, one of the grand promises of hypertext would be to make those connections accessible. Nelson conceived of a hypertext system called "Xanadu" that would represent these connections through transclusions – any part of any document within the system could be embedded within any other document in the system. Nelson even conceived of a system of micropayments that would be built in the system both to address the problems of copyright and to provide content creators with an income stream from the use of their work. Nelson did not think of links as being one-way connections from one document to another, but as two-way streets – when part of one document was linked to another, the transclusion would also be visible on the source document, and this would allow for another kind of trail to form. You would not only see the quote from *Hamlet* in the research article about madness in Shakespeare, you would also be able to get to the research article from the text it cited in the Xanadu version of *Hamlet*. Nelson's Xanadu system was never fully developed, though he has continued to work on the system. Nelson is a vociferous critic of hypertext as it has been implemented in HTML on the World Wide Web, as he considers it to be a dumbed-down version of his original conception.

Nelson's idea of hypertext inspired many researchers in computer science, information science, human computer interaction, and other fields, and "hypertext" became a component of the discourse of these fields. The Association for Computing Machinery (ACM) Hypertext conference series began in 1987 and continues to this day. Hypertext systems developers were essentially interested in the ways that computation could be used to develop systems of writing: organizing, associating, navigating, and sharing documents that would be interconnected with other documents.

The Hypertext Editing System (HES) produced at Brown University in 1967 by Andries van Dam, Ted Nelson, and Brown students was one of the first hypertext systems to organize text into links and branching texts (Barnet, 2010). The use of the prototype system was limited, although it was notably used for documentation of the Apollo space mission. Elements of HES were integrated into a follow up project, File Retrieval and Editing SyStem, or FRESS. It was also the beginning of Brown University's long engagement with hypertext, which would eventually result in some of the most important works of hypertext fiction. From 1987 to 1992, researchers at Brown developed and used the IRIS Intermedia system, a UNIX-based networked hypertext system, for projects including the first hypertext fiction writing workshops. During the early 1990s, a number of writers based at Brown University used Storyspace software to author hypertext fiction, establishing a writing community that would be essential to the development of contemporary electronic literature.

A number of different hypertext systems were produced during the 1980s and 1990s, before the development of the World Wide Web, including systems designed specifically for writing. When Apple released the first Mac, one of its selling features was HyperCard – a simple program but one that was oriented in a very different direction: toward using hypertext and simple programming to enable users to create applications of their own with their own content and for their own specific purposes. HyperCard was a hypertext program, built around the metaphor of index cards. Users could create stacks of hypercards that included programmable behaviors and links, and could embed simple imagery and multimedia. Writers used HyperCard to create some of the earliest examples of hypertext fiction and poetry, such as the first version of Deena Larsen's *Marble Springs* (1993) and unpublished electronic poetry by William Dickey (see Dickey and Landow, 1991; Kirschenbaum, 2016). Like much early electronic literature, the majority of the work produced in this platform has been lost to technological obsolescence, though Larsen's *Marble Springs*, a hypertext fiction centering on the interwoven lives of characters living in a Colorado mining town from the mid 1800s until the early 1900s, was transitioned by its author through several platforms and is now accessible on the Web.

Although authors produced hypertext fiction in a number of different systems during the 1980s and 1990s, the Storyspace platform developed by Jay David Bolter, John B. Brown, and Michael Joyce, first released in 1987, was particularly important for the genre of hypertext fiction, as it was developed specifically for writing. It was developed in tandem with both new media theory and creative practice. Bolter, at the time a classicist, would go on to be one of the most significant theorists of digital textuality. Joyce, a fiction writer, used Storyspace to author his pioneering hypertext *afternoon, a story* and subsequent works. Storyspace provided a visual environment focused on the process of structuring and writing hypertext, with textual nodes presented as individual writing spaces, and links as lines between them. It offered writers a number of different ways of clustering and organizing their material and included other scripted options such as Boolean search and guard fields that could prevent readers from encountering a textual node until certain conditions had been met. It also allowed for limited use of graphics and multimedia. Another factor that made Storyspace important in the early history of hypertext fiction is that when Mark Bernstein and Eastgate Systems took over its development and distribution, the platform became part of a publishing enterprise. Eastgate was modeled in most ways on a traditional small press, but published its literary products on digital storage media (first floppy discs, then CD-ROMs, and currently USB sticks). This provided authors and audiences with a recognizable publishing platform and a way of distributing hypertext fiction to a wider audience before most people had access to the Internet. Eastgate published a small but influential corpus of works upon which most of the early critical attention to electronic literature was focused.

The most important contemporary hypertext system, the World Wide Web, began in a relatively modest way. While he was working at CERN during the late 1980s, Tim Berners-Lee grew increasingly frustrated with what was at that time a very common problem for anyone sharing files over the network – a lack of interoperability among competing file formats, and no way to access one related document from a citation within another. Further, it was often difficult to rely on the accessibility of journal publications of the latest cited research. Why should researchers working in a physics laboratory, in a fast-moving cutting-edge discipline, have to spend excessive time and resources tracking down cited articles when they had in place the Internet – an ever-expanding global network? In an ideal world, getting to those references would not involve subscribing to a multitude of scientific journals or having the resources of a major research library at hand. Ideally, citations would not only provide paratext. They would be links to the actual cited research, ready-to-hand on the global network, instantly accessible with the click of a mouse.

The key to solving this simple problem of finding information would be a shared, open standard for marking up text and linking between documents, HTML. In 1989 Berners-Lee wrote the white paper "Information Management: A Proposal" (1989), proposing the development of a hypertext markup language standard, and in 1991 set up the first World Wide Web server. Initially the community of hypertext researchers was lukewarm to Berners-Lee's proposal – after all the system he proposed was remarkably simple in comparison to many hypertext systems that had already been developed. It had a minimal feature set. Links were "dumb" and one-directional, and the platform itself entailed very little programmability. This simplicity would however turn out to be advantageous. Very little background knowledge or training were required to produce an HTML document: anybody who learned a set of tags could do it, which made it simple for many people to begin using the standard very quickly. The standard had another key advantage that the majority of the existing hypertext platforms did not: it was completely non-proprietary. Berners-Lee didn't develop HTML so that any one software company would profit from it, but so that publicly funded researchers (and by extension, everyone else) could easily share documents on a global network and link between them.

Finally, and crucially, HTML was designed to be extensible. If the initial version of markup language itself was focused on simple text formatting and embedding images in documents, it allowed for the use of other scripting languages and extensions.

The National Supercomputing Agency based at the University of Illinois launched the first web browser, NCSA Mosaic, in 1994. It was adapted and popularized as a commercial product, Netscape Navigator, and soon after that web browsers would be installed on virtually every new personal computer on the planet. And then we were off to the races on the World Wide Web, which has brought much of the world's population online. For the first time hypertext, if not hypertext fiction, found a mass audience. While other hypertext systems, including platforms that are specifically intended for creative writing, such as Twine, have emerged in the years since the widespread adoption of the Web, HTML on the World Wide Web remains the dominant hypertext platform today.

Early hypertext fiction

Having considered the cultural context of literary postmodernism, the literary antecedents to hypertext fiction, and the technological context in which hypertext developed, we move now to the genre itself. Although there are a number of examples of poetry and nonfiction work produced in hypertext, the majority of the works most discussed and addressed in critical contexts are works of fiction. Authors are still producing hypertext fiction today, but its short heyday was during the 1990s and early 2000s. Common characteristics of hypertext fiction include link and node structures, fragmented text, the use of associative logic, alternative narrative structures, complications of character development and chronology, spatialized texts, intertextuality, pastiche and collage, new forms of navigational apparatus, and a focus on interactivity and user choice.

We can describe three different stages of hypertext fiction: works published before the emergence of the World Wide Web during the 1980s and early 1990s, those published on the Web during the late 1990s to 2000s, and contemporary "post-hypertext" works produced in the years since, which use techniques, ideas, and narrative frameworks similar to those of hypertext fiction, but within a different media environment and cultural frame.

The majority of the earliest hypertext fictions were developed in hypertext platforms that were oriented toward the individual personal computer, such as HyperCard and Storyspace. Eastgate Systems, mentioned earlier, published hypertext fiction written in Storyspace using a distribution model that was very similar to that of a conventional small press. This presented both advantages – in modeling a hypertext publisher after traditional literary publishing, Eastgate in some sense contributed to the development of a literary culture focused on work produced in digital media – and disadvantages – for when the open-access free-for-all culture of the World Wide Web emerged, that publishing model did not hold up particularly well.

Unlike many of the most studied early hypertext works, what most consider to be the first work of hypertext fiction, Judy Malloy's *Uncle Roger* (1986) was in fact initially published on the Internet, not on the World Wide Web, but on the WELL (the Whole Earth 'Lectric Link) (J. W. Rettberg, 2012; Berens, 2014; Grigar and Moulthrop, 2016). During the 1970s, Malloy had experimented with "card catalog" artist books using "molecular units of narrative to create nonsequential narrative." In 1986, when the Art Com Electronic Network was launched, Malloy was invited along with artists including John Cage and Jim Rosenberg to create work for an interactive arts magazine. The first instantiation of *Uncle Roger* included two files of interactive hypertext, and a third file of randomly presented narrative. The story is set in 1980s Silicon Valley culture, during a period when computer companies were competing with each other to see who could develop the fastest chip. The story is told from the narrative point of view of a babysitter named Jenny who has recently moved to California from the East Coast to work for the family of Tom Broadthrow, a tech company CEO. The first of the three scenes, "A Party at Woodside," was a narrative of seventy-five lexia (narrative fragments) contained within a database structure. The setting of a big party offered Malloy a framework that she felt worked well for the fragmented style of hypertextual storytelling, as she writes in the documentation for the piece: "As at any party, the reader may see some occurrences but not others; may meet some of the people but not others. As at any big party, neither the narrator, nor the reader understands every observed action" (Malloy, 2015). The second section, "The Blue Notebook" also used a similar keyword structure, while the third, "Terminals" delivered fragments at random. The story mixes elements of corporate espionage and intrigue with elements of a love story, coming-of-age story, and observations on the culture of the tech industry. Over the course of the three files, Jenny is gradually and reluctantly pulled into her uncle Roger's shady dealings in Silicon Valley. Malloy started the first version of the work in Applesoft BASIC before switching to a UNIX shell development environment. The reader navigated the work not through the types of links familiar to us now, but instead by keywords that the reader could use to search through the text (for example retrieving nodes with the character keywords "Jenny" or "Uncle Roger" or by the element "food and drink"). The first publication of *Uncle Roger* on the WELL was actually in serial form on a discussion board. While most readers most likely simply read the text fragments as they were posted, it was possible for users to download and re-implement the work as intended in its earlier BASIC version.

Malloy transitioned *Uncle Roger* through several platforms, ultimately releasing a web version which approximated the database navigation structure of the previous versions in HTML by making the row of keywords visible in "Party at Woodside," by using image icons to represent threads and themes in "The Blue Notebook," and by presenting the reader with an unmarked keyboard to be struck at random to deliver one of the unordered segments of "Terminals." *Uncle Roger* represents a significant contribution to the development of hypertext narrative, in particular in its exploration of several different methods of navigating through fiction in the absence of linear storytelling. At the same time, *Uncle Roger* has a rough and unfinished quality common in many hypertext fictions. While it explores many potential narrative directions and is skillfully written, it never really arrives at its own denouement, leaving a sense that there is more to the story than was actually revealed. This sense of narrative incompletion may be endemic to hypertextual storytelling, which often drives the reader (and the writer) to explore so many different threads that it ultimately becomes difficult to tie them all together in a satisfying way.

Michael Joyce's *afternoon, a story* was the first hypertext fiction developed and published using the Storyspace platform. *afternoon, a story* is one of the first hypertext fictions and also one of the most critically examined. *afternoon* is told in paragraph-length screens of text connected by hyperlinks, but these links are more complicated than most web links are: they are unmarked, and some links are conditional, so that clicking a particular word may lead to a different place if you have already read another part of the work than if you have not yet read that node. Peter, the narrator of *afternoon*, drove past an accident on his way to work, and worries that his ex-wife and son were involved in the accident. He tries to determine whether this is the case by calling his son's school and the hospital, but also diverts himself from thinking about the accident by calling other people and drinking coffee with a colleague. As we read on and return to certain scenes, we begin to wonder whether Peter himself may have been more involved in the accident than first seemed the case. The most common interpretation of *afternoon* is that the digressive structure of the nodes, by forcing the reader through detours without coming to a clear end, mirrors the way that Peter himself attempts to avoid looking the truth in the face

(Douglas, 2000, p. 105). In this way the form, structure, and indeterminacy of the work become objective correlatives for the psychic state of its protagonist.

Building on work by reader-response theorists that emphasizes how texts in general are experienced differently when they are reread, a number of scholars (Joyce, 1996; Walker, 1999) have focused on ways in which rereading shapes interpreters' understanding of hypertext fiction. For its part, *afternoon* not only invites rereading but also thematizes recursivity, suggesting the need to view events from multiple perspectives, even if no final authoritative synthesis of those perspectives is possible (see Joyce, 1987b). Perhaps the greatest strength of *afternoon* is that Joyce was very conscious of relating the material of the story and the ambiguous situation of the central character to the affordances and constraints of hypertext and the particular platform that he was working in. The nonlinear structure of the story is intrinsically related to gaps of memory and trauma as experienced by the protagonist. As an author deeply steeped in modernism, Joyce also produced a deeply intertextual work, which is densely packed with references to Greek mythology and the *Odyssey*, to James Joyce's *Ulysses*, Goethe, the Grimm Brothers, Tolstoy, and others. Many of the nodes also feature a stream-of-consciousness writing style familiar to readers of Virginia Woolf. Moving through the text entails rapid shifts in point-of-view and style, and in the type of material one encounters: we might move from an interior monologue to a quotation from a poem. Joyce's writerly relation to literary modernism drives his use of hypertext.

Uncle Buddy's Phantom Funhouse by John McDaid (1993) offers an example of a hypermedia work that straddled different media on both conceptual and theoretical levels. The work was originally published in a box that included four 3.5" floppy disks, printed materials including letters and annotated draft manuscript, and two cassette tapes. The HyperCard stacks contained on the disks included diverse forms of textual material and images, for example a contract, a deck of oracle cards with images that offered a sort of tarot reading, maps, song lyrics, letters, a screenplay, and other fragments found in the house of the main character, the late Arthur "Buddy" Newkirk. These fragments do not ultimately comprise a story in a traditional sense, as Anju Rau (2001) notes: "The Funhouse offers the reader (not necessarily coherent) glimpses into the different parts of Buddy Newkirk's life – bits and pieces from which the reader can sample an idea of this life. But the parts of the mosaic do not come together to form a unified image." The process of navigating the funhouse is a kind of scavenger hunt and a sort of media archeology project. McDaid presages questions that have become mainstream as culture has increasingly moved online, as personal computers and social networks function not only as tools and communication platforms for the living, but memorials for the dead. What becomes of our messages, our photographs and memories, our digital detritus, after we are gone, and what does this mean for the archivists and biographers of the future? The time machine referred to in *Uncle Buddy's Phantom Funhouse* may very well be this collection of artifacts and digital traces left across a diverse media ecology, which can be uncovered and investigated and searched, but can never comprise a complete and coherent understanding of the person who left them behind.

After Joyce's *afternoon*, Shelley Jackson's *Patchwork Girl* (1995) is likely the most-referenced work of first-generation hypertext fiction. Jackson wrote *Patchwork Girl*, a feminist retelling of the Frankenstein story, when she was a student in George Landow's class at Brown. Perhaps because of the fact that Jackson was so thoroughly steeped in postmodern fiction and theory, *Patchwork Girl* and Jackson's subsequent works present some of the clearest examples of reflexivity in hypertext.

Patchwork Girl is an acutely self-conscious text, which includes five sub-sections: the journal, story, graveyard, crazy quilt, and the body of the text. The story section includes a somewhat nonlinear narrative of the monster's creation, escape to America on a ship, relationship with another woman, and eventual dissolution. Jackson's hypertext took great advantage of the visual layout capabilities of Storyspace. The graveyard section of the work includes image maps of different parts of the body. When the reader selects each individual body part, she learns the story of the woman from whom the part came. Each donor has a strong defining character trait. Jackson uses this patchworked body as a metaphor for the idea that identities are always multiple, and personalities are always pastiches of multiple and sometimes conflicting drives. The crazy quilt section of the hypertext takes this notion of pastiche further still, stitching together quotations from Jacques Derrida's *Dissemination* (1983), Donna Haraway's "A Cyborg Manifesto" (1991), Mary Shelley's *Frankenstein* (1818), L. Frank Baum's The *Patchwork Girl of Oz* (1913), Barbara Maria Stafford's *Body Criticism* (1991), and the *Storyspace* user's manual (Bolter et al., 1999), creating mashed-up quotations that comment on the text itself. The journal section of the hypertext focuses on the monster's relationship with her author, Mary Shelley, by stringing together appropriated bits of *Frankenstein* with responses from the monster herself.

The body of text section is the most explicitly metafictional part of the novel, including a variety of authorial asides on the writing process and the nature of authorship. We leap between the female monster, Mary Shelley, the author of *Frankenstein*, and Shelley (Jackson), the author both of the fictional Shelley, the monster, and in textual form, herself. Jackson's authorial intrusion here is based on her experience as an author encountering a new medium. Jackson's writing is characterized by a sharp wit and sense of linguistic play, by ongoing interest in mediality, in the relation between image and text, and in the body itself as a medium. Jackson is a visual artist as well as a writer and images in her work often function as texts in their own right.

Jackson's web hypertext *My Body & A Wunderkammer* (1997) picks up on the theme of body/image with a playful autobiography that the reader navigates by selecting different parts of her body, represented through woodcut drawings. Jackson investigates the way that the body becomes a kind of inscription surface for personal history and memory, and how its surfaces, limbs, and organs function both as individual entities and as indivisible aspects of a human subject's identity. The links between nodes function as connective tissues that tie both individual anecdotes and parts of the body together. The body functions as a cabinet of curiosities and as a repository of stories. Many of the vignettes focus on the body as a surface that is written, marked, and scarred by experience, and how its parts in turn frame, enable, and limit identity in a recursive process. *My Body* is presented as a personal memoir, if one by an author playfully engaged in processes of self-fabrication. Jackson plays with the indistinct boundaries between fiction and nonfiction and the unreliability of narrative memory. The body is also a canvas of the imagination, onto which aspirations and anxieties are cast: though the majority of the work reads as plausible autobiography, at one point Jackson describes being born with a short tail that takes on improbable and metaphoric dimensions as over time as "It thickened and grew lithe. At night in bed it explored, violating me shamelessly."

Similar themes are explored further in *The Doll Games* (2001), a work that Jackson coauthored with her sister Pamela Jackson. In this case the work builds upon a series of narrative games that the two sisters used to play with their dolls as prepubescent girls, but these games are framed by faux-academic discourse. In "sitting uneasily between" different styles of discourse, the work teases the reader to differentiate between authoritative knowledge and play, serious knowledge and farce, identity and make-believe.

The Doll Games is a metafiction. At its center are the actual games that Shelley and Pamela Jackson played when they were in their youth. The section of the work titled "definition" and subtitled "a funhouse mirror" is ostensibly written by J. F. Bellwether, PhD, a scholar who has made the study of "ground-breaking series of theatrical performances by Shelley and Pamela Jackson that took place in a private home in Berkeley, California in the first half of the 1970s" a focus of his scholarly work. In some ways the project picks up on "the cabinet of curiosities" approach of *My Body*, and uses hypertext more indexically than associatively. The project, which is presented as a set of interlinked web pages, includes sections focused on the dolls, artifacts, documents, commentary, and tapes of transcripts of the two women discussing the games, as well as interviews with others who played similar games. The dolls themselves become characters with their own identities, writing stories and letters to each other.

The Doll Games explores hypertext as an extensible form, and one that can fluidly integrate many different types of materials and medialities. The project is alternatively an academic study, a psychological analysis, a documentary, a "making of" special, an archaeological investigation, a photo study, and a comic book. The work takes a layered metafictional approach, taking a phenomenon – playing with dolls – that is often dismissed as an ordinary idle pastime of young girls and wrapping layers of commentary around it from the imagined voices of the dolls themselves, to the reflections of the sisters on their games at different stages of their lives as writers and researchers, to the fictional voice of the scholar, to the relation of their stories to larger questions of how children use weird forms of play to wrestle with their emerging sense of identity and their place in the world.

In *The Doll Games*, we also see a heightened awareness of the network as a writing medium and play with its specific properties. The front page of the work includes a row of keywords including "… doll sex, doll mutilation, transgender dolls, prosthetic doll penises, doll death, doll dreams …" These keywords may be intended to cue readers as to the content of what will follow, but they also serve a function in how this particular HTML page will be read *by the network*. More likely than not, the Jackson sisters knew something of how search engines function and placed these keywords conspicuously on the front page in order to draw a particular readership for the work. Indeed, at the time of its publication, *The Doll Games* was the first site returned by a Google search for "doll mutilation." People searching the Internet for doll sex or doll mutilation might have been a bit puzzled to find themselves delivered to this strange work of postmodern fiction.

Hypertext fiction for transitional media: Stuart Moulthrop's explorations

We can consider hypertext fiction as a transitional genre between print literature and new forms enabled by digital media and perhaps even "post-digital" media (Cramer, 2014). Most authors of hypertext fiction started writing in the new media not only to explore the affordances of the digital, but also with an awareness of the position of literature within a broader and rapidly shifting media ecology. In part because of the novelty of the medium and the importance of the device to electronic literature, there is a heightened awareness not only of the specific capabilities of computational media, but also of media in transition and its unstable, ephemeral nature during the digital turn.

Of the hypertext fiction authors active in the first wave of experimentation with the form, Stuart Moulthrop has remained one of the most prolific, authoring some sixteen hypertext and cybertext works between 1987 and 2013. Moulthrop's work is particularly interesting as a case in hypertext, because he has explored so many of its technical and aesthetic possibilities even as some thematic concerns within his work have remained consistent. Moulthrop has a clearly postmodern sensibility – before he began writing hypertext he was a Thomas Pynchon scholar – and his works are consistently concerned with the struggle to make sense of the human position within postmodern culture. He is also one of the electronic literature authors most deeply invested in the interface between narrative and computation.

Moulthrop's *Victory Garden* is the most extensive of the hypertexts published by Eastgate Systems, including 933 lexia. *Victory Garden* experiments extensively with multilinear narrative structures enabled by hypertext: with multiple potential outcomes of given storylines, changes in perspective on given events, chronological jumps and flashbacks, and narrative loops that vary on recursion. Set during the beginning of the first Gulf War and centered on a group of characters living in a university town, *Victory Garden* is about how war is experienced on the home front, filtered through contemporary academic, popular, and media culture. The *Garden* of the title refers both to the "victory gardens" people were encouraged to grow during World War II in order to save resources for the war effort, and to Jorge Luis Borges' story "Garden of Forking Paths." In one lexia of the work, "All of the Above," Moulthrop references Borges' story, "In all fictional works, each time a man is confronted with several alternatives, he chooses one and eliminates the others; in the fiction of Ts'ui Pen, he chooses – simultaneously – all of them." *Victory Garden* is perhaps the single experiment in the hypertext canon that attempts to do just that. As Raine Koskimaa notes, "*Victory Garden* is clearly pointing toward the kind of hypertext fiction which, because of its size, is theoretically and practically, inexhaustible" (Koskimaa, 2000). Just as an event such as a blitzkrieg war unfolding both in the lived experiences of soldiers and civilians at home and abroad and on multitudes of cable television screens is in some sense fundamentally unknowable as a totality, Moulthrop provides a textual analogue in the structure of his fiction. Moulthrop's novel includes a great variety of different types of textual materials, and intertextual references to several works of print literature – Borges' fiction and Thomas Pynchon's novels serve as touchstones and make cameo appearances. Moulthrop also integrates images and maps as navigational tools to navigate the text.

Moulthrop's work has extended across multiple forms and modalities. He has produced work in many different platforms from early work in HyperCard and Storyspace through HTML, Flash, JavaScript and other scripting languages. He has often played at the boundaries between narrative, essay, poetry, and game. With the launch of the World Wide Web, Moulthrop moved swiftly toward creating works that explored the developing network media environment and the emerging vernaculars specific to it. As Moulthrop encountered new Web technologies, he explored their potential for literary ends and how they might challenge our expectations of narrative. In *Hegirascope* (originally produced in 1995, and published in a revised version in 1997) Moulthrop played with the idea of "push" content, the reader's agency of hypertextual choice, and the conflict between conventions of reading fiction and the fragmentary nature of attention online. As the reader encounters each fragment of *Hegirascope*, she is faced with a text and four hypertext links at each corner of a box around it. If the reader does not either complete reading the text or choose one of the links within a brief time frame, the page will reload and the reader will be delivered to another fragment. Some parts of the text can be described within the frame of conventional narrative fiction while others are more along the lines of what Shuen-shing Lee (2005) describes as non-narrative units – often ruminations that touch on media theory, narrative theory, and themes of apocalypse. Moulthrop invokes McLuhan's (1964) idea of hot and cold media and considers hypertext and the Web emerging as an "overheated" media. He engages with contemporary debates surrounding hypertext as "the end of books," poking fun at critics of the form such as Sven Birkerts. The challenges of contemporary political reality also make periodic intrusions, as events such as the 1995 Oklahoma City bombing and the attempted genocide in Bosnia surface in the texts.

In *Reagan Library* (1999) Moulthrop again explored the new-at-the-time technology of QuickTime VR panoramas, and this time integrated generative (and degenerative) text fragments. The reader/player navigated through VR panoramas with modeled 3D objects connected to texts. The title of the work references an American president who was approaching the late stages of Alzheimer's at the end of his term, and the work appropriately explored themes concerning the degeneration of memory within a virtual world that portrayed four different states of decay. QuickTime VR is unfortunately itself past the end of its term and no longer supported by Apple, so the work itself has also now decayed.

Moulthrop's works from the early 2000s onwards move to a significant degree away from the paradigms he embraced earlier in his career toward more explicitly computational forms. The subtitle of Moulthrop's *Pax: an Instrument* (2003) is indicative of this shift, as he decided not to describe the work as a fiction or a hypertext, but as a "textual instrument" (Wardrip-Fruin, 2005). *Pax* was produced in the wake of the September 11, 2001 terror attacks in the USA and subsequent shifts in the political and social environment. *Pax* readers interact with the work by selecting figures of nude bodies moving through space (floating up or falling down) and catching them. These characters are suspended in space when the reader mouses over the figure. They can be released by moving the cursor away or by clicking. As they are caught in space, a line of text materializes next to the body and takes shape as a word or simple phrase, for example "compliant," "act of god," "erasure," or "zero hour." If the reader clicks on a figure, a line of text will appear on the right side of the screen. The narrative unfolds on a temporal basis, arranged in six thematic movements: "Shaken Out of Time," "American Flyers," "Home Land," "Evil Ones," "Falling," and "Total Information." The text does not proceed linearly: the narrative will never be presented the same way twice. Some of the textual elements are part of a fiction while others are ruminations about terrorism, confusion, and moral ambiguity. The work centers on an incident in the airport in Dallas in which passengers were marooned in a security lockdown with little information about what precipitated the event. Many of the voices in the work – presumably those of people in the terminal – express anxieties related to both the specific incident and the general uncertainty of living in an age of terror, reduced privacy, and restricted liberty. The visual representations of the bodies, vulnerable, naked, falling through space, reinforce a sense of vulnerability. The texts that appear in gray are of a more aphoristic nature and include generated texts within the theme.

Like many of Moulthrop's works, *Pax* is difficult to pin down, sitting between forms. As the author describes in his introduction to the work, "this is not a work of literature in the ordinary sense; neither does it have the formal properties of a game, though it is meant to be *played* as well as read." As he worked on *Pax*, Moulthrop was in conversation with Noah Wardrip-Fruin about his idea of works of electronic literature as "textual instruments," as "playable media" that readers operate differently than they would conventional hypertexts that they simply point and click (Wardrip-Fruin, 2005). In this case, certain elements are unfolding a temporal flow, others are triggered by reader interactions, and others are randomized by the system. In his subsequent works, in the 2000s and 2010s, Moulthrop has moved increasingly into this boundary zone and, it could be argued, further away from narrative toward a more general engagement with language and code. In an interview with Judy Malloy, Moulthrop said that he has an "even-now-still-growing conviction that the idiom of code and the older idiom of human expression are both valid constituents of poetry" (Malloy and Moulthrop, 2011). Moulthrop's move from narrative hypertext fiction toward more formally complex kinds of textual instruments is representative of a migration that many of the early hypertext authors made from comparatively simple uses of hypertext to more expansive explorations of literary applications of computation.

During the late 1990s and early 2000s hypertext fiction authors largely moved away from producing works as individual applications for the personal computer toward hypertext as a sprawling network-based form. The rise of the World Wide Web signaled both new formal constraints and affordances for hypertext authors and a completely different model of distribution. While the hypertexts published by Eastgate modeled traditional publishing and bookstore sales, the majority of the hypertexts published on the Web are simply posted, announced on mailing lists and other websites, and spread virally through online sharing. In most cases they are freely distributed – readers do not pay to access the works and neither publishers nor authors are paid. While from an economic standpoint this presents certain obvious problems, it also provided opportunities for hypertext authors to reach new audiences, and to make their work available on a global basis virtually instantaneously. The Web also functions in a different way materially, as hypertexts on the Web are not fixed into a single version on distributed storage media but can be continuously changed and overwritten. The Web further changes the relationship between author and audience. Authors can interact with audiences not only through email but also sometimes even invite their readers to contribute to their work.

Olia Lialina's *My Boyfriend Came Back from the War* (1996) was one of the first hypertext fictions published on the Web. The work was designed around the early HTML convention of frames, which Lialina used for effects that she compared to cinematic techniques (Connor, 2016). The simple story of a conversation between a woman and her soldier boyfriend, just returned from an unnamed war, unfolds interactively as the user selects lines of dialog, all of which are either links or black and white GIF images. The links sometimes change the text or image in the frame they appear in and sometimes change material in a different frame or spawn a new frameset. The work begins with the single line "My boyfriend came back from the war. After dinner they left us alone." Clicking the link moves us to a page with a black and white image of a woman and a man, backs turned from each other, and another image of a window frame. When we click on the image of the couple, a close-up image of the woman appears in a new frame (a kind of elementary cinematic zoom). Clicking on that image in turn opens another frame in the center of the browser, with the line "Where are you? I can't see you?" Their conversation unfolds from there, with links often opening new frames, further dividing the space of the screen. The divisions of the screen into frames echo the emotional distance between the woman and her boyfriend. It emerges that she likely had an affair while he was away. He in turn has difficulty communicating with her and is blocked by inescapable memories of war. The piece communicates a bleak picture of their future. As the texts proliferate, the visual field grows cluttered and confusing, creating a visual representation of an argument that is going nowhere. Eventually clicking through every link brings us to black frames, effectively symbolizing a bad ending to the relationship.

At the time of its initial release in 1996, Robert Arellano's *Sunshine '69* was the first hypertext novel written specifically for the World Wide Web. *Sunshine '69* is a historical hypertext novel that attempts to encapsulate the zeitgeist of the 1960s by tracking events in the lives of nine characters from June through December 1969, concluding with the Altamont festival held on December 6, 1969. At different points in the novel, the reader can encounter a 'bird's-eye view' of the historical events in 1969, and the work includes a bibliography of the nonfiction sources that Arellano sampled. While the novel references historical fact, Arellano uses that context as a background for a metaphoric tale of corrupted visions. In the novel, Mick Jagger makes a deal with Lucifer that results in the tragedy at Altamont, and LSD is transformed from a substance for utopian mind-expansion into a sinister market commodity.

The characters of *Sunshine '69* are sketched as cartoonish types – in one section of the hypertext, a page including a cartoon drawing of a suit and a character sketch represents each individual character. The postmodern 'flatness' of the characters helps Arellano to avoid the problem of slowly developing characters in a novel that can be read in thousands of possible orders. The drawings don't include any faces – as if to underscore that these characters should be understood not as individual human beings, but as stereotypes, fictional personalities representative of the cultural forces at play in the novel.

The cast of characters of *Sunshine '69* includes Alan Passaro, a Hell's Angel, hired for security at Altamont; Lucifer; the Glimmer Twins, Mick Jagger and Keith Richards of the Rolling Stones; Ali a.k.a. Ronald Stark, a shady agent provocateur with connections to the CIA; Meredith Hunter, a young African-American hipster from South Berkeley; Orange Sunshine, alternatively a hippie girl-next-door and a brand of LSD; Norm Cavettesa, a discharged Vietnam veteran; and Timothy Leary, one of the leading advocates of experimentation with hallucinogenic drugs. Arellano freely mixed 'real' people with fictional characters. Leary, Jagger, and Richards are icons, and stand in for cultural movements. Hunter was an eighteen-year-old murdered at Altamont, and Passoro the Hell's Angel who stabbed him. The other characters are presumably fictional.

Real events, adapted from nonfiction texts, are juxtaposed with imagined events to create an alternative history, and underscore the idea that all histories are narrative constructs. In the context of the novel, characters who really lived through the events, or who died as a result of them, are no more or less real than those imagined by the author to represent flower children, government spies, or allegorical evil.

Sunshine '69 presents a range of navigational options to the reader, in addition to the in-text hypertext link. In the absence of the reading conventions of the book, authors of nonlinear fiction need to provide readers with other navigational tools to guide them. These tools can be as simple as the alternate reading order Cortazar provides for the reader of *Hopscotch* or can make more elaborate use of the multimedia capabilities of the computer. Once the readers get past the animated introduction to the work, each screen of the *Sunshine '69* has four buttons linking to "Calendar," "People," "8-Track" and "Map." Each button links to a different navigational apparatus, so that readers could navigate by character, chronologically, according to musical selections, or by a map.

Mark Amerika's *Grammatron* (1997) is another expansive web-based work of hypertext and hypermedia narrative. Emerging from the context of the Alt-X online publishing network and Mark Amerika's then-popular "Amerika Online" column, *Grammatron*, retells the Golem myth in digital form. The work centers on Abe Golam, a pioneering Net artist who creates the Grammatron, a writing machine. The creature becomes a kind of combinatory monster, wherein all texts recombine. Throughout the work, Golam searches for his 'second half' – a programmer, Cynthia Kitchen, who might provide the missing link to another dimension of digital existence.

Grammatron included more than 1,000 text elements (some of them scripted and some randomized), thousands of cross-links between nodes of the text, many still and animated images, a background soundtrack, and spoken word audio. *Grammatron* was pushing toward a *Gesamtkunstwerk* mode of hypertext and was as much a philosophical exploration of "network consciousness" as it was a novel. Amerika consciously positioned himself within an art world context in this and in later work. *Grammatron* was received as one of the first significant works of Net Art and was exhibited at the 2000 Whitney Biennial.

With *Grammatron*, we can see several strands that would become more marked in later years, including a move away from a specifically literary audience toward other cultural contexts, such as conceptual art and performance. *Grammatron* also marked a shift from hypertext *per se* toward hypermedia, in which text is one of many media elements. This multimodal shift became even more pronounced in subsequent years, particularly with the rise of Flash as an authoring platform in the late 1990s and early 2000s.

William Gillespie, Frank Marquardt, Scott Rettberg and Dirk Stratton's *The Unknown* (Gillespie et al., 1998) was co-winner of the 1999 trAce/ AltX competition. A comic novel, *The Unknown* begins with the premise that the hypertext novel is itself a promotional stunt for a printed book *The Unknown: An Anthology* (Gillespie et al., 2002), of experimental poetry and fiction. The hypertext is the story of the eponymous authors' book tour, which takes on the character and excesses of a rock tour. As *The Unknown* authors tour venues across the USA and abroad ranging from small used book stores to the Hollywood Bowl, they have encounters with literary and cultural celebrities ranging from Newt Gingrich to William Gaddis, from Marjorie Perloff to John Barth, from Terry Gilliam to Lou Reed. Complications arise as one of the protagonists becomes a cult leader before becoming a human sacrifice; another becomes a mean and withdrawn social outcast; and another a heroin addict enamored of celebrity and its excesses. As their fame reaches its apex and a Hollywood blockbuster is made of their hypertext fiction, things generally fall apart. A picaresque tale with classic elements of a road trip novel, *The Unknown* freely mixes writing styles and forms ranging from prose to poetry, credit card statements to freshman composition writing assignments, pastorals to corporate typing tests. Many scenes of *The Unknown* are parodies or tributes to other writers: scenes are written in the style of Jack Kerouac, Edgar Allan Poe, Cormac McCarthy, Nelson Algren, Kathy Acker, and many other notable American authors.

The Unknown tended toward exuberant expansiveness and embraced excess. As the project was written and distributed, the authors kept writing and adding material for several years after the novel was first published on the Web. While the main component of *The Unknown* is a fictional narrative, in its own words, a "sickeningly decadent hypertext novel," the work also included several other "lines" of content including documentary material, "metafictional bullshit," correspondence, art projects, documentation of live readings, and a press kit. *The Unknown* played a great deal with the conventions of postmodern fiction, such as the concept of the death of the author (one of the author characters, Dirk, is brutally murdered and then brought back to life), reflexivity (the authors are characters and in one scene, the authors and their characters meet), and the construction of alternate fictional realities nested within the same frame. David Ciccoricco (2007) describes *The Unknown* as evoking "*worlds* – worlds that never quite attain or even aspire to a coherent 'entirety' by any measure of verisimilitude or referentiality … The worlds of *The Unknown* leak, and the authors revel in the mess" (p. 129). Ciccoricco considers *The Unknown* in the context of Baudrillard's conception of the hyperreal, given the fact that the authors are on a fictional book tour for a book they did not publish until well after *The Unknown* itself was published, and that the fictional authors become increasingly divorced from their non-fictional and even prior fictional referents (p. 130).

As the project progressed and after it had won an award, the authors toured in person to a variety of venues and performed interactive readings of the work. During live performances, the authors would turn up wearing black jacket and tie – in an homage to the early Beatles – and would ring a call bell every time a link appeared on the page, encouraging readers to interrupt and shout out a link to follow whenever they encountered one they found particularly toothsome. The majority of these readings were recorded in audio and/or video, and audio recordings integrated into the given page of the hypertext, so that readers could listen to the authors reading the text of the page. These travels also provided further material and settings for writing. *The Unknown* is thus a novel; a work of performance writing; and in some respects, also a constraint-driven writing game.

The Unknown made extensive use of hypertext to cross-link scenes of the novel and provided other indices and apparatuses for navigation. Links are used in *The Unknown* in a variety of different ways: sometimes to guide the reader to the next section of a narrative sequence, sometimes to provide further referential information and other times according to a more whimsical logic: for example, every time the word "beer" appears, it is a link, taking the reader to another scene in which beer is mentioned. While we were writing *The Unknown*, I suggested that the links were used for functions including "referential, line break/double entendre, point of view shifting, comic subversion, and chronological" (Rettberg, 2002).

The Unknown represents an encyclopedic model of hypertext. It is a novel that attempts to fully integrate its own publishing and critical apparatus. As the authors' statement published in the *Electronic Literature Collection, Volume 2* (only half-jokingly) attests, *The Unknown* "attempts to destroy the contemporary literary culture by making institutions such as publishing houses, publicists, book reviews and literary critics completely obsolete" (Gillespie et al., 2011).

As was the case for the majority of the other hypertexts mentioned, *The Unknown* had a number of metafictional characteristics, including a number of asides on writing in the form itself, which are included in the "metafictional bullshit" nodes of the text. In the node "Hypertext is/ are Electronic Space" William Gillespie, for example, mused in Deleuzian fashion:

> Hypertext, to put it clearly, is a mapping of a text onto a four-dimensional 'space.' Normal grammars, then, do not apply, and become branching structures anew. Fragments, branches, links.

> The word is glowing and on a screen. It is electronic and cannot be touched. It has been copied over thousands of times and reverberates through virtual space.

Reflection on the form of hypertext seems an almost inevitable outcome of writing a hypertext novel. Hypertext fictions are often field notes as much as they are fiction.

Califia (2000) by M. D. Coverley (Marjorie Luesebrink) was one of the last hypertext fictions published as a standalone application by Eastgate Systems, developed in the ToolBook multimedia platform. The work was influential in its rich use of images and is notable for spreading the story across a diverse array of different types of textual artifacts and across a significant span of time. The story was focused on the search for a lost cache of gold buried in fragments of five generations of three California families. Fragments of the narrative were located not only in conventional fiction segments, but also in maps, newspaper clippings, diary entries, receipts, deeds, maps, and other visual texts and documents in this novel-length work. Coverley followed up with *Egypt: The Book of Going Forth by Day* (2006), a hypermedia novel set in ancient and contemporary Egypt, in which images, songs, and animations also played a prevalent role in communicating the story.

Increasingly sophisticated and inventive use of visual design was one of the hallmarks of hypertext fiction produced during the 2000s and after. *Lexia to Perplexia* by Talan Memmott (2000) is a complex work about the interface between the human and the machine. The work is notable for the fact that the author conceptualized the interface itself as developing and embodying the central metaphor of the piece. In his author's introduction to the work in the *Electronic Literature Collection, Volume One*, Memmott claims that the work "does what it says … certain theoretical attributes are not displayed as text but are incorporated into the functionality of the work." In exploring "network phenomenology" Memmott constructed a "a diagrammatic metaphor, emphasizing the local (user) and remote (server) poles of network attachment" (Memmott, 2006). Memmott's work blazed new trails both in terms of its articulate use of coding and design as material metaphor and its conception of hypertext literature as a form of critical media for considering the situation of the human in the network.

These Waves of Girls (2001) by Caitlin Fisher is a hypermedia novella, made in Flash, which explores memory, girlhood, identity, and sexuality. *These Waves of Girls* was the winner in 2001 of the Electronic Literature Organization's first award for a work of fiction. The work tracks these concerns through the perspective of a four-year-old, a ten-year-old, and a twenty-year-old girl in a series of interconnected stories and vignettes. Visual and audio design is an important aspect of *These Waves of Girls* – not necessarily for its sophistication, but because it has a loud, garish visual feel to it, suggestive in a way of the scrapbook of an adolescent. The visual design captures the exaggerated emotional states and heightened drama of the transition from childhood to adulthood.

In hypertext works such as *Entre Ville* (2006), *in absentia* (2008) and *The Gathering Cloud* (2016), J. R. Carpenter brings a deft hand at web design to experimental presentations of fiction and poetry within densely layered, collaged visual interfaces. In *Entre Ville*, drawings on notebook pages, cutout photograph elements, and short impressionistic pop-up videos are launched by clicking on the windows of an apartment building, which supplement the written narrative. Carpenter has an excellent sense of the uses of multimodality. In *in absentia* she explores the use of a Google map interface to situate a fragmented narrative in the space of a city. With *The Gathering Cloud* Carpenter layers visual elements that progressively launch on top of one another, supplementing and commenting prior elements in an elegant work of visual design that also functions as a critical essay on climate change and "the cloud" and the carbon footprint that all our networked activity leaves hovering over the planet.

A number of hypertext works produced in the 2000s were built in Flash or similar platforms to make particular use of hypermedia, extending the text to audiovisual elements and more sophisticated forms of interactivity. *88 Constellations for Wittgenstein* by David Clark (2009), a work that explores history through a kind of absurdist connectionism, is difficult to pin down into any one genre. As David Jhave Johnston observes, it is "a rapturous virtuosic sprawling labyrinth that confounds, nourishes and provokes" and "a consummate example of hybrid interactivity, future cinema, net-art and scholarship" (Johnston, 2011). Centering on the life and philosophy of Ludwig Wittgenstein, the work spins off from this central narrative into a web of connections that resembles a sophisticated conspiracy theory. Navigating from constellations in the night sky, the reader traverses the work through beautifully layered animations. The bulk of the text of the work is performed as voice-over narrative. Some elements of the work can also be played only with the left hand, as the keyboard launches visual shifts and audio elements. *88 Constellations for Wittgenstein* reconnects hypertext with a postmodern historiography, in which the reader can follow pathways and alternative histories based on chance connections. A web of historical figures and events, filled with improbabilities that are nevertheless plausible, sprawls out before us, if never quite assembling itself into a coherent objective reality.

Another notable hypermedia fiction produced in Flash is the *Inanimate Alice* series (2005), a collection of multimodal young adult stories about an itinerant digital native and her imaginary friend, first developed by Kate Pullinger and Chris Joseph, released over years in a series of online episodes and continuing through to a VR project, *Inanimate Alice: Perpetual Nomads* currently in development by Mez Breeze Design and Bradfield Narrative Designs. Christine Wilks' works such as *Fitting the Pattern* (2008) and *Underbelly* (2010) similarly use Flash to mix elements of memoir, documentary, and historical fiction with audio, video, and hypertextual navigation to create interactive narrative collages.

Queerskins (2012) by Illya Szilak is a hypermedia novel that is based in part on the author's experience as a physician working with HIV patients. The novel tells the story of a young man, Sebastian, who is dying at the beginning of the AIDS epidemic. The novel makes rich use of multimedia from a variety of sources. Pages from a diary provide a textual layer, while much of the rest of the story is delivered in spoken monologues. The work also makes use of images and videos from strangers culled from Creative Commons-licensed sources on YouTube and the Internet Archive and short ambient videos commissioned for the project. In each chapter the reader shuffles through multimedia collages of these materials while piecing together the narrative. Szilak is in the process of developing an adaptation of *Queerskins* for virtual reality.

Serge Bouchardon publishes the majority of his work in French and English simultaneously. Many of his works are driven by the reader's active ludic interaction with the work. Reading is not posited as a simple visual or cognitive act but as an embodied interaction with the digital artifact. His *Loss of Grasp* (*Déprise* in French) (Bouchardon, 2011) and other works explore the interface as both a source of inspiration and frustration. Although his work is typically more linear than many hypertext fictions, the works are "textual instruments" in the sense that the reader must play the interface in a variety of ways ranging from using the mouse to erase layers of text to activating the camera on their laptop to visually mirror a sense of deep ennui. The narrator of *Loss of Grasp* is a middle-aged man dealing with a variety of anxieties: over his work, his marital relationship, and his relationship with his son. Bouchardon describes his intent: "to get the reader to experience through gestures events which the narrator had already experienced" (Bouchardon and López-Varela, 2011). Through actions such as scrubbing away at the screen to "unveil" his wife, revealing questions and eventually the face of his spouse underneath the typography, or by moving the mouse to knock away portions of an essay by his son about "heroism" to reveal the narrator's doubts about that relationship, gestures serve both as comic effects and to increase the reader's sense of identification with the protagonist.

Hypertext's ends and means

Hypertext was emblematic of a historical moment, the period of the shift from personal computing to network computing during the 1990s and early 2000s. Of the genres considered in this book, hypertext is in the strange situation of being the genre that has been most written about in the field, while simultaneously the genre least actively pursued by writers in recent years. Instead of prospering as a specific genre in its own right, elements of hypertext have opened up new forms and genres. Complex multilinear narrative structures have for example become standard fare in long-form episodic television series. Some essential aspects of hypertext such as fragmentary narratives, user-activated navigation, and launching of hypermedia elements, spatial navigation, use of the interface as metaphor, and reflexive uses of the media environment are present in many contemporary genres of electronic literature such as locative narrative, CAVE and VR works, and interactive installations. Hypertext fiction may not have swayed the culture to accepting nonlinear storytelling on the computer and the network as a successor to printed books, but it has served as a foundation for many new types of literary work in digital media. As we will see in the following chapter, even hypertext *per se* has not entirely faded away, as it has recently become entwined in a hybrid form of interactive fiction.

4   Interactive Fiction and Other Gamelike Forms

Computer games and electronic literature share a rich common history. Computer games are clearly the dominant form of contemporary entertainment produced within digital environments and are the sites of some of the most developed thinking about the potentialities of computation for narrative, interactivity, and multimedia. Computer games are also, at this point in history, the focus of the largest popular entertainment industry, dwarfing even the film industry. As we'll discuss in this chapter, at least one genre of electronic literature, interactive fiction (IF), is directly derived from some of the earliest games made for personal computers – the "text adventure" games of the 1980s. Games such as those of the *Zork* series (first version developed at MIT in 1978–79) were very popular as personal computers began to enter American homes and schools during the 1980s. These games had no graphics but described a scene textually. The player would interact with the game by typing simple commands, such as "go east," "take sword," or "kill the troll with the sword."

For many of my generation, these adventure games provided our first experience of interacting with a computer program. During the course of the 1980s, as the processing power of personal computers increased, and graphics cards became a component of the standard PC setup, the market for text adventures shrank drastically, but a core group of enthusiasts kept the form alive even after the dissolution of Infocom, the largest commercial developer of the games. A community of "amateurs" coalesced around the genre, developing its own creation and distribution platforms, competitions, publications, and databases. This community of authors and developers in essence became its own audience. This amateur IF community has now persisted far longer than its commercial progenitor and has arguably produced more sophisticated literary work. Even as it has lurked in the background of commercial game development over the course of the intervening decades, IF has also remained a touchstone for developers striving toward rich language-based experiences within computer games, complex non-player characters (NPCs), and connections between spatiality and storytelling.

If interactive fiction is the genre of electronic literature most explicitly embedded within a gaming context, other types of games and the cultures that have formed around them also provide form and fodder for the creation of electronic literature. A number of compelling works, such as Jason Nelson's *Game, Game, Game, and Again Game* (2007) have been produced using gaming platforms and have explored the conflicting goals and desires that drive literary and gaming experiences. Digital artists such as Cory Arcangel have appropriated game platforms as artistic media, for example by hacking the classic Nintendo *Super Mario Bros* game to remove all the graphics and sprites other than the clouds to produce the artwork *Super Mario Clouds* (2002). Visual and interactive design conventions and the iconography of computer games are in a deeper sense part of the vernacular of contemporary culture. Works of electronic literature often engage digital culture critically and so there is no avoiding the tropes and conventions of contemporary computer game culture. In studying electronic literature, we are often called to think in terms of border zones between established forms of cultural practice. Electronic literature can be thought of as situated somewhere between a number of related practices and cultures, including print literary culture, arts practice, computer science, and performance. Computer games provide electronic literature with one such border zone.

Interactive fiction and the IF community

Compared with the communities driving other genres of electronic literature such as hypertext fiction and kinetic poetry, the interactive fiction community developed largely independently of academic environments and formally organized groups such as the Electronic Literature Organization or the E-Poetry Festivals. This is not to say that critics and researchers have not paid attention to the genre: the first PhD dissertation written about interactive fiction was Mary Ann Buckles' *Interactive Fiction: The Computer Storygame "Adventure"* (1985). A number of works of new media theory such as Espen Aarseth's *Cybertext*, Janet Murray's *Hamlet on the Holodeck* (1997) and Marie-Laure Ryan's *Avatars of Story* (2006) have addressed individual works of interactive fiction or considered its formal qualities in comparison to hypertext or other forms of digital narrative. Nick Montfort's *Twisty Little Passages* (2003) was the first book-length study of interactive fiction and covers the genre more extensively than any other. IF author and developer Emily Short has published a number of academic and popular articles about IF, and researchers such as Mark Marino, Van Leavenworth, Jeremy Douglass, and Clara Fernández-Vara have written about IF in dissertations, journal articles, and books. But the creative practice of IF development itself is characterized by affiliations of enthusiasts who share works, infrastructure, reviews, and archives within a community of practice. Interactive fiction provides us with one of the best examples of a creative community developing outside of a commercial market or academic environment. The IF community originated in an almost completely network-based fashion, via online mailing listservs, through online archives, and through online competitions. The process of resuscitating the adventure game format from the ashes of an abandoned computer game industry was a complex, collective, network-based endeavor – in part this was because of the fact that it was necessary to reconstruct the software platforms used to develop IF in order to make the form available to creators.

Many of the theorists who have written about interactive fiction have drawn connections between it and more conventional literary genres. Mary Ann Buckles compared the form to the detective novel. Montfort emphasizes IF's relationship to the riddle, and to the Oulipian idea of "potential literature" in considering interactive fiction programs as "potential narratives" (p. 26) – systems designed to produce an array of narrative outcomes dependent on interactions with the work. Montfort usefully considers the nature of works of interactive fiction as "*programs, potential narratives, worlds* and *games*" (p. 24). The *reader* of the narrative produced by interactive fiction is also the *player* of a game. In the rest of this discussion I'll dispense with the distinction between reader and player as Montfort does through the use of the term *interactor* (p. ix), which more appropriately describes the human role in the production of IF as a literary experience.

As a genre, interactive fiction can be identified by certain common elements and conventions. Interaction in the majority of the works in this genre takes place through a text parser, a conversational interface. The interactor is prompted to make certain decisions and responds by writing directives to the parser (e.g. "Go north.", "Get lamp.", "Kill the thief.") As Montfort wrote, the majority of these works are *worlds* in the sense that they are modeled environments the interactor navigates. The unveiling of the narrative experience takes place as the interactor moves from room to room, cavern to cavern, street to street, so the world is largely defined by spatiality. As the interactor moves through these environments, he or she interacts with objects and characters within the space, and those interactions determine how the story will unfold.

Most works of IF are *games* in the sense that the interactor is working toward a definable outcome – that is, the majority of these works can be "won" or "solved." One of the main activities of the player is puzzle solving. Montfort invokes the riddle as IF's closest literary cousin because riddles are defined by a reasonable challenge to their readers – all of the information necessary to solve a riddle is included in the text provided (p. 4). The principal challenge to the reader of interactive fiction, and its central pleasure, is to find a solution, to achieve the satisfaction of a successful session of deductive reasoning.

The interactor is usually positioned and addressed in the second person in IF and is therefore positioned as a player character in the text. While in some works, the player character is essentially a blank slate, a simple subject position from which to navigate the text (we know and learn nothing of the background of the player character in the classic *Zork* series), in other works the player character's backstory and orientation are of particular importance. In Adam Cadre's *Varicella* (1999) the player character is Primo Varicella, the Palace Minister of an Italian court, a distinctly Machiavellian character whose primary activity is dispensing with any aspirants to the throne who might stand in the way of his own hold on power. In *Varicella*, the interactor can adjust the player character's conversational tone, for example to be servile, hostile, or cordial, producing different outcomes not only on the basis of what is said but also how it is said. In some works of IF, such as Jon Ingold's *All Roads* (2001), which places the player character on the gallows in the opening scene, the primary puzzle itself is coming to a better understanding of how the character arrived in his situation to begin with.

The complexity of non-player characters in interactive fiction varies a great deal from work to work. While in some cases, non-player characters (NPCs) are little different from objects, flat constructs that are simply described to the reader or used as mechanical game elements (for example the thief in *Zork* functions as a device that steals items from the player's inventory and as an obstacle but does not generate much meaningful conversational interaction with the player). Non-player characters in Emily Short's works, such as *Galatea*, can by contrast be much more dynamic. In Short's works, the parser is conceived of not only as a device for delivering directives to the system but also as a conversational interface for interaction with non-player characters. Developing dynamic characters that can come across as realistic conversation partners during the experience of the work is a significant and important challenge for authors of interactive fiction. One of the main limitations of the genre is that the text parser often has an extremely limited vocabulary – the initial pleasure of the text parser is the illusion it creates that we can actually converse with the program in natural human language. The actual experience of interacting with IF can however sometimes seem more like conversing via telegraph with a precocious chimpanzee who has worked out a compass and the possession of objects than conversing with an adult human. Works that are able to rise above the linguistic constraints of a text parser's limited vocabulary are rare but all the more pleasurable for sustaining the illusion of conversational interaction.

Interactive fiction can seem hermetic in the sense that the use of the text parser interface and many other aspects of the form have been driven by conventions that date back to the first example of the genre. Enthusiasts of the form learn to communicate with the system in a very specific way, develop strategies, and recognize tropes familiar from reading other works of interactive fiction. Of course, the wonderful thing about conventions is that as soon as they are established, artists set about challenging and subverting them, or perhaps even casting them aside. Consider the fact that Twine, a platform that has as much in common with hypertext authoring software as it does with other IF authoring platforms, if not more, has in the 2010s become the most popular environment for IF authoring. Conventions can only survive for so long, for better or worse.

An *Adventure* begins

The first work of interactive fiction was *Colossal Cave Adventure.* Its first iteration was developed in 1975–76 by Will Crowther, a Cambridge, Massachusetts-based programmer who was part of the team who developed ARPANET, the original network infrastructure on which the Internet is based (Montfort, 2003, p. 86), and subsequently expanded by Don Woods (Crowther & Woods, 1977). Crowther turned his programming skills toward a game about cave exploration after his divorce in order to entertain his children when they visited him (Nelson, 2001, p. 343).

Crowther was a caver, who helped to map a network of caverns in Kentucky (Jerz, 2007). He used that experience as the basis for the network of caves described in *Adventure.* The game itself provided a relatively simple experience of navigation and puzzle solving. Players attempted to retrieve objects from within the cave environments and win by completing their collection – a kind of textual geocaching.

Crowther originally developed the program for his own kids to play, but in 1977 he posted it on an ARPANET bulletin board, where others could download it and subsequently modify it. This is an important fact and compelling to consider in the light of the evolution of the field of electronic literature. Although commercial and institutional efforts were important for the development of both interactive fiction and hypertext as forms, the real expansion of the field took place after the widespread adoption of the World Wide Web, and the most important distribution channel for electronic literature has been the network, where authors often publish their own work and enable users to experience it online or download it for free.

Crowther himself described *Adventure* as fairly rudimentary, "just some rather simplistic logic and a small table of known words – of course backed up by some very clever thinking," (Jerz, 2007, p. 20) but he expressed delight that many of the people who played the game thought that there was some complex AI at work enabling players to interact conversationally with the program – an effect very similar to that described by Joseph Weizenbaum when users first interacted with the chatbot *ELIZA* (1966), seeking privacy for their interactions with a virtual psychologist who was after all only a simple program emulating the talk therapy technique of mirroring, responding to the interactor's input with different linguistic formulations of the same text (Weizenbaum, 1976).

Crowther's game set out many of the elements that would become standard components of interactive fiction. The original version of *Adventure* could recognize 193 words and provided players with instructions to direct it with commands of 1 or 2 words (Jerz, 2007, p. 30). The essential activity of the game is moving through space and working out some basic puzzles. Crowther did not set out to simply replicate the experience of caving, but also introduced some magical and fantastic elements. The cave is populated with adversaries such as a dwarf, a dragon, and a snake.

The most popular version of *Adventure* is considered to be a co-authored work by Crowther and Don Woods. After Woods downloaded *Adventure* from APRANET and played it, he forked the code and expanded considerably upon the original work. While he kept Crowther's "maze of twisty little passages all alike" he also included a "maze of twisty little passages, all different." Woods added a number of significant elements to the game, such as a pirate who appears at random to steal the treasure the player has gathered, and objects with tracked states, and a water bottle that can not only be drunk from or emptied, as in the original game, but also refilled with water or oil, and inserted a number of new puzzles. Graham Nelson highlights Crowther and Woods' distinctly different approaches, "one intent on recreating an experienced world, the other with a really neat puzzle which ought to fit *somewhere*" (Nelson, 2001, p. 345). As Jerz demonstrated by actually traversing the physical cave system that Crowther explored in Kentucky, the geography of the world originally conceived by Crowther was based fairly faithfully upon his caving experiences in the Bedquilt region of Colossal Cave, while Woods expanded upon the fantastical context of the game.

Zork and the computer game industry it spawned

Many adaptations and follow-ups to the Crowther and Woods version of *Adventure* were developed in short order after *Adventure* was released on

ARPANET. A group of MIT students including Tim Anderson, Marc Blank, Bruce Daniels, and Dave Lebling (who referred to themselves as the implementors), developed *Zork*, the most influential successor to *Adventure*. *Zork* was originally developed in 1977 as a mainframe program running on a PDP-10. Its creators credited both *Adventure* and the popular dice-and-paper roleplaying game *Dungeons and Dragons* as their inspirations. The original program was augmented extensively over subsequent years and ported into several platforms. The PC version of *Zork I: The Great Underground Empire* (Blank and Lebling, 1980) was the first software title published by Infocom, and the first commercially successful game made for personal computers.

In his extensive reading of *Zork* and the cultural contexts surrounding its creation, Montfort establishes that the team who created *Zork* were not cavers like Will Crowther, but instead based their underground landscape both on the framework of the caverns of the original *Adventure* and on a cave system they were more accustomed to navigate in their daily lives – the warren of corridors, basements and sub-basements of the MIT campus (Montfort, 2003, p. 104). In addition to finding plenty of inspiration and a number of tropes and in-jokes specific to MIT there, the team also improved considerably on the game mechanics, literary content, and technical aspects of the text adventure genre. While the parser of *Adventure* would only work with commands of one or two words, the grammar of *Zork* was substantially more complex, able to distinguish verbs with prepositions, recognize direct and indirect objects, and to allow some verbs to take multiple objects. The authors also took particular pains to provide witty responses when an interactor used an object incorrectly or used vocabulary the system could not recognize, making the experience of interacting with the text parser less mechanical and more engaging.

Zork's authors made an important improvement to the treatment of *actors*. While in *Adventure*, the adversaries the interactor encountered were essentially single-function objects used to present challenges to the player, in *Zork* the non-player characters take on more dimensions, allowing the player character to interact with them conversationally in ways that have non-trivial impact on the game. The character of the thief in *Zork*, for example is more complex than his counterpart, the pirate, in *Adventure*. He is described in many different ways in the output provided by the program, for example as "seedy-looking," "lean and hungry," "a man of good breeding," "a pragmatist," in ways that provide the interactor with a clear impression of a character of a particular type. The player's interactions with the thief are also consequential in different ways over progressive stages of the game. The thief must be killed in order for a player to complete the game, but before that the player must have an interaction with the thief involving the exchange of a jewel-encrusted egg. The work of not simply providing the villain as an obstacle but also using language to establish the villain as a character with some degree of depth and distinct character traits makes the game more interesting as a literary artifact.

In 1979, three of the original implementors of *Zork* were founding members of the software company Infocom. The company was not established exclusively as a game company – its founders only knew that they intended to generate income by developing, selling, and distributing software. Nevertheless, since three of the founders had developed *Zork* and had it on hand, interactive fiction seemed like a good place to start. The company would become a major success for a short period of time, with revenues of over $10 million dollars and more than one hundred employees by 1985, but would essentially be defunct by the end of the decade (Briceno et al., 2000). Infocom was not a large company in comparison to today's multinational game companies, but its cultural impact was very significant during the early days of home computing. At one time, a quarter of the U.S. homes with computers had purchased an Infocom product (Nelson, 2001, p. 356). The rise and fall of Infocom maps onto the early history of the PC. When the first home computers were sold, they had an almost exclusively textual interface and were not well suited to graphic applications. *Zork* was an application that demonstrated capabilities of the personal computer both as a gaming machine and environment for aesthetic, interactive literary experiences. But once graphic cards of steadily increasing speed and processing power became part of the standard PC setup, graphical games very quickly began to dominate the market.

During the 1980s, Infocom released 35 works of interactive fiction in a wide range of styles, including a number of text adventures in the general vein of *Zork* – games set in caverns and dungeons, where the primary objectives were to solve puzzles while navigating through space in order to gather treasure and reach some final objective – but also works that explored other genres. Titles such as *The Witness* (1983), *Sherlock: The Riddle of the Crown Jewels* (1987), and *Deadline* (1992) dealt in the conventions of the detective story. Works such as *Planetfall* (1983), *Suspended* (1983), and *Trinity* (1986) engaged with the tropes of sci-fi. Some of the Infocom games, such as *Leather Goddesses of Phobos* (1986), *Nord and Bert Couldn't Make Head or Tail of It* (1987), engaged in over-the-top comedy, self-parody and (in the case of *Leather Goddesses*) soft-core titillation and bondage. Some of the most popular works produced during the Infocom era, particularly *The Hitchhiker's Guide to the Galaxy* (1984) and *Mindwheel* (1984, published by Synapse), involved collaborations with writers known for their work in print, Douglas Adams and Robert Pinsky. *The Hitchhiker's Guide to the Galaxy* was a novel before it became a game, and a radio play before it became a novel. The game was not a simple adaptation of a work between media but in the process of its translation to digital media, an entirely new work that, while structured around and including elements of the book, was also adapted to the conventions and gameplay of interactive fiction.

Reflecting on how Infocom not only had a shared platform but a distinctive house style, Graham Nelson notes that "by inheritance of parsing code from one game to another and by a shared in-house testing team, the strongest unity of style between the Infocom games is that they seem told by essentially the same narrator" (Nelson, 2001, p. 354). Nelson observes that though *The Hitchhiker's Guide to the Galaxy* and *Wishbringer* (1985) were market bestsellers at the time they were released, by the 1990s games such as Brian Moriarty's *Trinity* (1986) that were more "bookish and purposeful" were more respected within the IF community (p. 354). *Trinity* centers on the development and history of the atomic bomb and ranges across historical test sites at Trinity, in Nevada, Siberia, and the Eniwetok Atoll, as well at the site of the bombing at Nagasaki, and future scenarios in low Earth orbit and in London. *Trinity* shared a trait with early hypertext fiction in the fact that it was densely threaded with intertextual references, particularly to British children's literature such as Lewis Carroll's *Alice* books, P. L. Travers' Mary Poppins books and work by J. M. Barrie.

Infocom failed after a decline in sales in the late 1980s and after it had largely shifted corporate attention to its only business product, the database software "Cornerstone" (1986), which turned out to be a costly flop. In 1986, Infocom was sold to Activision, where it essentially withered on the vine, despite the release of some titles until 1989, after which Activision focused its attention exclusively on graphical games (Nelson, 2001, p. 357). Activision released the omnibus *Lost Treasures of Infocom* (1991) collections during the 1990s, keeping text adventures in circulation for another generation of PC gamers.

An amateur interactive fiction community takes shape

Although Infocom and other commercial interactive fiction publishers were largely out of commission by the late 1980s, discussions on online bulletin board systems such as CompuServe were just taking off, providing interactive fiction enthusiasts a venue to share ideas and programs. While some hobbyists developed rudimentary adventure games in BASIC, it wasn't until purpose-specific non-commercial interactive fiction game design platforms were released that a community of amateur interactive fiction developers began to take shape. In 1987 TADS (Text Adventure Development System) was released as shareware, providing IF writers with a system for writing games. In 1993 the first version of Inform, probably the most successful IF platform and the most similar to Infocom's development system, was released by Graham Nelson. Another technical innovation just as vital to the spread of IF was Nelson's development of the Z-machine standard. Infocom developed the original Z-machine for its text adventure games. Nelson reverse-engineered the Infocom system so that Inform could also compile Z-machine files. The virtual machine separates the game file from its implementation on a given system, so that it is possible to port the same code to a Z-machine implementation in that platform. Developers don't need to worry about creating different versions of games for Mac, Windows, or Unix. They can just create the game in Inform and let the interpreters for a given platform do the heavy lifting of preparing it for a given system. Graham Nelson and collaborators released Inform 7 in 2006, and it is still used to write interactive fiction. The platform is intended to bring interactive fiction writing closer to natural language writing.

Nick Montfort and Emily Short track the development of the amateur IF community in "Interactive Fiction Communities: From Preservation Through Promotion and Beyond" (Montfort and Short, 2015). Specific Usenet newsgroups dedicated to interactive fiction were created in 1992, and the Interactive Fiction Archive was established in the same year, founded by Volker Blasius at the German National Research Center for Information Technology. Andrew Plotkin and Paul Mazaitis set up IFArchive.org on the Web in 1999. Originally a mirror of the German site, it became the main repository of interactive fiction related materials. The IF Archive is an extraordinary resource, including not only game files, but also books, articles, software platforms, emulators and utilities, mailing list archives, and essentially anything else participants in the IF community have considered worth saving. The combination of an active online discourse community and an archive for the preservation and distribution of the games made it possible for a field of creative practitioners to develop completely outside of a commercial market. In 2003, the IFDB was founded and continues to be a vital resource. The IFDB is a Wiki-style game catalog and recommendation engine. Community members can add game listings, write reviews, and exchange game recommendations.

Competitions have been important in sustaining the interactive fiction community, beginning during the 1980s and early 1990s, when some took place on BBS systems such as CompuServe. A revival of interactive fiction competitions occurred starting in 1995. Annual IF competitions have been a core focal point for the community ever since. The XYZZY Awards and the IF Comp are the two most consistent competitions in the field. The IF Comp has probably been the most influential and generative over time. An important aspect of IF Comp is that it includes a time constraint – judges of the award are told to play the game for a maximum of two hours. This results in games that are meant to be more playable in a short period of time and less sprawling than some more voluminous works. The IF Comp provides authors with an audience and opportunity to venture down particular stylistic avenues they may otherwise not have explored. If the most extensive works of interactive fiction are comparable to novels, the works submitted to the IF Comp are the equivalent of short stories. The awards are judged through an open process online – each judge agrees to read and score at least five works. Participating judges often write reviews of work as well, so the competition also helps to develop the archive.

Thousands of works of interactive fiction are available in the IF archive. I'll discuss a few representative works here but within the very deliberative, discussion-oriented IF community, little consensus can be found as to which works are essential, as every year, rafts more of them are created. IF remains very much an amateur, hobbyist-driven phenomenon. While many authors still create fantasy or role-playing style works derived from the genre's origins in the Infocom games, there are also some serious literary artists within the IF community who have put considerable time and effort into developing engaging work in the genre.

Worlds, puzzles, characters, and wordplay in contemporary interactive fiction

In 2015, Victor Gijsbers organized a community vote for the "Interactive Fiction Top 50 of All Time." Given that only thirty-eight participants' votes determined the list, it can hardly be seen as the last word on the canon of interactive fiction, but it at least gives an indicator of some of the works and authors that have been valued by the community over time.

Topping the 2015 list is *Photopia* (1998) by Adam Cadre, winner of the 1998 IF Comp and XYZZY Award. *Photopia* prioritizes storytelling over puzzles. It is a short work, which takes about a half hour to navigate and read. Although the interactor must work out a few elementary puzzles in order to complete the game (mainly of the simple pick-something-up/put something down variety), it has an essentially linear structure and is relatively simple to navigate. The most important action in the game is using the "talk to" command to engage with the other characters. *Photopia* is comparatively complex from the standpoint of narrative style. While the action is focused on one central character, Alley, the author employs shifts in point-of-view and in time frame between a "real world" and a series of imaginative story environments. These small dream worlds are each named after a color (red is a Mars-like extraplanetary environment, while yellow is a golden beach). Shifts in the color of the texts and the background mark ontological shifts in the story: the real/present world has black text on a white background while the other texts are colored. These environments are poetic in the sense that each in some way serves as a metaphor for a character's relationship with Alley, who will die in a car crash during the course of the story. The narrative shifts through these metaphorical environments and different periods of Alley's life. Jordan Magnuson observes that *Photopia* is important in the history of interactive fiction because it "experiments with nonlinear presentation of time, menu-based conversation, and constrained game-play to support a specific plot" (Magnuson, 2009). *Photopia* is more linear than most works of interactive fiction in the sense that the reader's navigational choices and puzzle solving are trivial to the progression throughout the work. Some reviewers praised the piece for its emotional impact, while others decried its lack of adherence to the conventions of interactive fiction, as its puzzles serve as momentary gestures to encourage engagement with the story more than anything else.

Spider and Web (1998) by Andrew Plotkin moves its reader to a dungeon of a different sort than those usually associated with IF. The interactor is cast into the role of a prisoner undergoing an interrogation. A large part of the interactor's activity is gradually revealing his own story while engaged in a cat-and-mouse game with the interrogator. It is a spy drama that reflects cold-war conflicts and ultimately puts the player into the uncomfortable position of making decisions that could bring about a war. Unlike *Photopia*, however, the game's tolerance for inexact responses to questions is low and the narrative is difficult to traverse without the exact solution the system expects. Until the player gives the interrogator (who knows more about the player character than the player does) the sought-after information, she is repeatedly sent back to the place she left off. The player character's relationship to the interrogator mirrors the frustrations of trying to deliver the exact wording of a puzzle's solution to the text parser. As in many works of interactive fiction, the pleasure of *Spider and Web* is not that of smoothly flowing through an engaging narrative, but instead the click of a well-made box.

Just as there is a tension in hypertext fiction between narrative immersion and the interruption and branching potential narrative promise of the link, in interactive fiction there is a tension between the difficulty of puzzles – many games are valued because they are *hard* and therefore deliver a challenge to the gamer as competitor – and narrative engagement. Finding the balance between the ludic pleasures of solving well-made puzzles and the pleasure of the text associated with reading a very good story is a real challenge for the developer/writers of interactive fiction.

Jon Ingold's *All Roads* (2001) places the interactor in a particularly uncomfortable starting position – on top of a scaffold, about to be hanged. As the clock approaches the appointed hour and the trapdoor is about to drop, the interactor enters the darkness. He will fall into the darkness many more times, escaping from a situation long enough to unweave another fragment of his history – as we eventually learn – as an assassin. *All Roads* provides a compelling story situation through a cycle of return to crucial moments between life and death, through shifting point of view, and through the slow reveal of the circumstances that led to the situation at the scaffold.

Emily Short is one of the most prolific authors of interactive fiction. Some of her notable works include *Galatea* (2000), *Savoir-Faire* (2002), and *Counterfeit Monkey* (2012). Short's debut game *Galatea* is probably her best-known work, at least outside of the IF community. In addition to winning an XYZZY award for best non-player character, *Galatea* was published in *The Electronic Literature Collection, Volume One* (2006) and is one of the first works of interactive fiction that many readers from the broader electronic literature community encounter. *Galatea* has an explicitly literary theme. *Galatea* is one of the most non-player-character (NPC)-driven works in the genre. As the interactor, you encounter and have a single conversation with a marble statue commissioned by the late artist, Pygmalion of Cyprus. The game is multilinear in the sense that rather than moving toward one definable outcome, a "win" state, the conversation can end in a variety of ways. Along the way and through replay, the interactor can learn a great deal about Galatea's story and her relationship with her creator, so that the objective of the work is primarily to unwind that story, but rather than solving object-based puzzles to unveil aspects of the backstory, as in *Spider and Web* or *All Roads*, the play is much more about finding the right tone and approach to entice Galatea to reveal story to you. The NPC is a good deal more complex in *Galatea* than in the majority of works that preceded it: she has hundreds of lines that can be delivered, and tracks the conversation, remembering what has already been said and reacting positively or negatively to certain cues in the text parser. *Galatea* is a storytelling system more than a game. Unlike many games, where the pleasure is derived from a progressive march toward a final situation, *Galatea* is much more about incremental replay. An end state can be achieved in a matter of minutes, but the interactor will derive more satisfaction from replaying the game a number of times, both to understand more of the story and how it can be told in different ways and to experience Galatea's reaction to different topics and actions. Rather than dealing primarily with directional navigation or object acquisition, key commands in Galatea such as "ASK ABOUT," "TELL ABOUT," and even "THINK ABOUT" emphasize narration and memory. Interactive fiction is often by necessity stylistically sparse. Efficient prose is valued, as long narration slows the pace of interaction. This often results in characters that are more one-dimensional than developed; outlined rather than fully fleshed. But by emphasizing character over plot, and conversation over puzzle solving, *Galatea* makes a significant contribution to a literary aspect of interactive fiction often neglected by other authors.

Short's achievement with *Galatea* in developing a rewarding conversational experience with an NPC was one among many as she has extensively explored the potentialities of many different affordances and technical aspects of the form. Her *Savoir-Faire* (2002) is in some ways a more traditional text adventure than *Galatea*, in the sense that the interactor's main activities are navigating spaces and gathering treasures, but the work is driven by a compelling story situation and a richly imagined world. The work is set in eighteenth-century France. As the player character, you have returned to your family estate, in order to ask your family for money you need to pay some debts. You find the house oddly abandoned. *Savoir-Faire* is set in a magical world. Short includes a special command, "LINK," that unlocks the powers of Lavori d'Aracne, a magic that enables its user to link particular objects to each other if they share an operational logic. One can for example link a box to a door in order to be able to open it. The work also makes extensive use of the REMEMBER command. As the interactor encounters objects around the old estate, different memories that are attached to them, which often include crucial information about the puzzles within the game and the rules of operation of the magical system. So while the game moves toward a traditional end state, it is also a process through which the story of the protagonist's life and the history of his family are revealed.

In the end what makes many of Short's works so engaging is the fact that she writes well: her story situations are inventive, and her language is both lusher and more precise than that of many other IF developers. Her works are played as games but she is first and foremost a storyteller. Short is not really designing games to be won or lost, but worlds to be experienced, interacted with, and understood.

To step back a bit and try to characterize a general trend during the amateur era of IF, the affordances of the genre for story, for character, and for world building have come more to the fore. While navigational exploration and object-based puzzles never went away, at least for some of the leading authors working in the genre, the focus shifted from simple goal-oriented mechanics and stock situations to more fully imagined worlds and complex narratological experiments. In an interview with Illya Szilak, Short says that she prefers to "to see puzzles that contribute in a meaningful way to the themes of the story" in a process that "teaches the player something narratively significant about all the characters involved" (Szilak, 2013). As we have seen in the examples discussed, the reward for solving puzzles is more often than not the revelation of information about either an NPC or the player character, the protagonist directed by the interactor. In many of the richest works of interactive fiction, the puzzles serve to develop and enrich the story, and not the other way around.

That is not to say that puzzles have been neglected as an element of the genre. They are still considered an essential element of most interactive fiction. If, as a literature reader but a comparative novice in interactive fiction, I am more drawn to works that privilege good writing and engaging storytelling over difficult puzzles, seasoned IF players might tend to be dismissive of work that is less challenging in this regard. In my view, one of the signs of the growing aesthetic maturity of interactive fiction is the fact that the nature of many of the puzzles has shifted: while there are still plenty of examples of digging around in a pile of sand to find a key or looking under a floorboard for a box that requires a combination to open, many interactive fiction authors have broadened their idea of what might comprise a puzzle. The puzzle might for example involve deducing the precise conversational trigger required to get another character to reveal key plot information.

Some authors have also turned to wordplay as a form of puzzling. In Nick Montfort's *Ad Verbum* (2000), the player is an adventurer charged with helping to demolish the Wizard of Wordplay's mansion. To do that the player must endure a punning series of wordplay games, for example surviving a round of the insult-based game the Dozens, and work through a series of alliterative rooms that can only be navigated using words that begin with the same letters as those words used to describe the room. You can't "take the diaper" from the "Neat Nursery." Instead one must "nick nappy" in order to progress. In Short's *Counterfeit Monkey* (2012) wordplay is also the primary game mechanic. Over the course of the work the interactor uses a number of different tools that change the objects within the game through linguistic transformations – by removing, adding, changing, and rearranging letters. The interactor starts out with a letter-remover that enables her to for example turn a pint of apple into a potable pint of ale, merely by removing two letter Ps. This work highlights the fact that whatever else IF is, it is mostly text, and that the imaginary it invites us to inhabit is one that is almost exclusively produced through language games played by the interactor through conversations with the author, the software, and the platform.

Modeling ethical choice and moral complicity

Although most interactive fiction tends to stay clear of contemporary politics, there are some examples that engage with political reality. In *Rendition* (nespresso, 2007) the player character is a brutal interrogator torturing enemy combatants. The only interaction the game allows between the interactor and Abdul, the only non-player character in the work, is to physically abuse – punch, poke, kick – a specific part of Abdul's body. The game only allows the interactor to commit a specific act of violence once on a particular body part, and only permits the use of the same torture three times, in a parody of "rules of engagement." Eventually the victim gives up some information, but that information turns out to be false, as is often the case when information is coerced through acts of political violence. The game makes a simple but effective argument that torture is essentially ineffective. *Rendition*'s author described it as a "political art experiment in text adventure form." While neither the writing nor the "gameplay" (as such) of *Rendition* are particularly sophisticated, it does provide an example of interactive fiction as a kind of agitprop "serious game." In affecting the player's complicity in the act of torture, during a period when the use and efficacy of torture was a matter of contemporary debate, *Rendition* demonstrates the potential power of interactive fiction to be a medium of procedural rhetoric.

Aaron A. Reed's *Whom the Telling Changed* (2005) is an interactive retelling of the first half of the *Epic of Gilgamesh*, in which the nature of persuasion is a central focus. The interactor first shapes the role and the identity of the player character through the selection of a symbolic object and a beloved person. During the course of play the interactor, placed in the role of a villager whose people have gathered to hear the tale, plays a role in shaping the Sumerian people's decisions about war and peace. Using predefined keywords, the interactor attempts to influence others on how to interpret elements of the story being told and by extrapolation how to address their own attitude in debating the conflict within their own diegetic world.

Reed has put a good deal of effort into making the interface and flow of interaction in his works less challenging for IF novices. In his more ambitious novel-length interactive fiction work *Blue Lacuna* (2009), Reed uses a keyword approach to identify elements (objects, places, characters) that can be interacted with, which helps ease the delivery of the narrative. The story is that of a wanderer who (in the first part of the work) heeds an irresistible call to explore the world. At the outset of the work the player makes several choices (between making love and making art, between being a man or a woman, between being gay or being straight) that frame and shape the narrative that follows. The bulk of the work is set on the island, Blue Lacuna, where the player character finds herself after leaving her lover. There is one other occupant of the island, a madman or castaway named Progue. The process of interacting with *Blue Lacuna* is one of solving puzzles to better understand the mysteries of the island including a number of fantasy/sci-fi elements such as a swarm of intelligent bees or an egg-shaped spaceship, but also ultimately that of revealing Progue's history and relationships. So the reward for the ludic work of puzzle solving is a richer story and a more developed understanding of principal character and modeled world. The work applies a number of technical innovations, for example using generative and responsive room descriptions that change on the basis of factors like the time of day, weather conditions, and information that the interactor has already learned. Reed develops complex characters, who converse, remember, and form opinions. As in *Galatea* and *Whom the Telling Changed*, these interpersonal interactions are non-trivial but have important outcomes in the story. Reed also introduced a "drama manager" that analyzes how the interactor is moving through the work and introduces hints within story elements to help people who are stuck to continue through the work. The "story mode" of the work provides a satisfying experience for novice interactors, while interactive fiction aficionados can confront the puzzles in the work at a higher degree of difficulty. Astrid Ensslin describes Reed's efforts to simplify the reading experience as "reverse ergodicity: where program code is used in such a way as to facilitate rather than disrupt or complicate the reading process in nontrivial (ergodic) interactive systems" (Ensslin, 2014, p. 114).

Interactive fiction is a genre of electronic literature that has evolved (as of this writing) over the course of almost forty years. From its beginnings with *Adventure*, through the commercial period of popular text adventures published by Infocom and others, and through to an amateur period remarkable both for its longevity and its refinements and innovations, interactive fiction has been a superb example of a community-driven form of electronic literature. It has not only refused to die, but also over time developed a much richer corpus and legitimacy as a literary art form. IF also demonstrates how digital literary genres are shaped both by the technological platforms and the social contexts in which they are produced.

Inform and many of the other platforms used to write interactive fiction were directly based on the systems and information structures used to produce the Infocom games. And the conventions and elements of Infocom games shaped a particular community's expectations and interactions with interactive fiction, from the text parser interface to the use of the compass and the basic syntax of interacting with the system. Those systems and conventions were expanded and refined, and particular subgenres (e.g. the cave adventure, the space opera, the historical drama, the conversational fiction, the one room work) were explored extensively. But the popularity of a newer web-based platform, Twine, has to some extent disrupted that lineage of conventions.

Hypertext + Interactive Fiction = Twine

While Inform 7 allows for complex parser-based interactive fiction, Twine is a platform released by Chris Klimas in 2009 that hearkens back to hypertext conventions of the 1980s and 1990s. Twine was designed with Choose-Your-Own-Adventure stories, branching path narratives, in mind. It offers a similar set of features to the Storyspace software used by some of the authors published by Eastgate, such as conditional links and the ability to track choices made by the user. Twine is not parser-based, but instead hypertextual. In contrast to the complexity of parser-based interactive fiction authoring tools, which tend to have a fairly steep learning curve, Twine has a user-friendly browser-based authoring environment. Authors do not need to touch any code in order to start creating in Twine. The platform is also open source. As Twine author Porpentine puts it, "Twine simply exists and doesn't belong to anyone except everyone" (Charity Heartscape and Short, 2012). She also notes the extensibility of Twine, which allows authors to add functionalities using HTML, CSS and JavaScript, and the usefulness of the node map view that provides a visual interface showing the structure of the work as it is being written. While works produced in Twine are hypertext at their core, many of the authors in the community that has developed around the platform consider and describe their works as games or as interactive fiction, and have engaged with the interactive fiction community extensively, for example entering works in the IF Comp and XYZZY awards, and in some cases winning. After hypertext was considered all but dead as a genre of electronic literature, it appears to have suddenly risen from the ashes clothed in the garb of interactive fiction.

Branching path narratives and the historical antecedent of Choose-Your-Own-Adventure (CYOA) books have long been referenced in discussions of hypertext, but in reality, few authors of hypertext written from the 1980s to the early 2000s wrote CYOA-style works, where readers explicitly choose from a set of predefined options to determine story outcomes, whereas this is the default mode of Twine-based works. By 2014, almost as many games entered in the IF Comp were choice-based games rather than parser-based. If the aesthetics and structural concerns of parser-based and choice-based interactive fiction are fundamentally different and the two communities sit somewhat uncomfortably in the same box, Twine games have clearly colonized at least a patch of interactive fiction territory. While the underlying principles of Twine are based on hypertext, many Twine games have also adopted conventions from interactive fiction, such as the second-person form of address to the player character, spatial navigation through the narrative, and a sparse, economical style of writing.

The Twine community has also developed its own identity as a place of avant-garde experimentation with language, gender, and identity. Twine is particularly popular with young authors who are arguably the first generation of "digital natives." This is electronic literature that emerged first not in online magazines, academic gatherings, festivals, or online databases, but instead on Tumblr feeds.

Hypertext and interactive fiction had a baby and she named herself Porpentine Charity Heartscape. In 2017, the Whitney Biennial included a seven-piece exhibit of Porpentine's works (Heartscape and Chan, 2017). Her works have a kind of rawness and a punk edge that calls to mind the work of Kathy Acker. Porpentine is a transwoman. Many of her works address gender, the body, fear, and subject position in worlds that present us with metaphors of displacement, whether in a sadist's pit or an alien body.

In *Howling Dogs* (2012) Porpentine presents us with a bleak picture of existence. The player character lives in a cell-like environment. The only escape on offer is a virtual reality system that places the player in variety of dark fantasy environments. As Porpentine writes, the system offers "false catharsis in the form of these victories – but at the end of the day you're still in the black room" (Heartscape and Short, 2012). Porpentine weaves the biological, the mundane, and the drudgery of ordinary life into the surreal unfolding of her often-painful hypertext fantasia. When there is a bed it is there for you to sleep in. In *Howling Dogs*, you need to eat by getting a nutrition bar that varies only slightly in its flavor in successive meals, and you need to drink before each session with your virtual reality device. Porpentine describes the work as a metaphor for a situation of many living as "refugees in their own country," destitute, and "less and less capable of caring about yourself," able to afford only the bare minimum: "Terrible food and some kind of glowing screen, and when you look away from the screen, you're still in the same place."

The fantasies offered by the VR system are hardly escapist in the sense that they focus on painful episodes and uneasy subject positions. In one of the VR episodes, the player character is enlisted to strangle an abusive partner. In another she is cast into the role of Joan of Arc in the last moments before she is burned alive. Porpentine's prose is taut, sharp, precise, and visceral. She uses the second person in a similar way to most interactive fiction, but in Porpentine's stories, the "you" often sees the world from a precarious position, as some kind of moral or physical violence often lurks on the immanent horizon. When violence takes place, it is not the easily dismissed cartoon carnage of video games. In one scene in *Howling Dogs*, the player character is described as "sopping with blood, shouting, bellowing, ramming your weapon through rib cages, twisting, shredding hearts into flimsy strips that hang from chest-holes like tinsel wigs." The text of the link that follows is "You bring back a couple fingers for your bone-sparrow to nibble on." It is not enough simply to describe the player character vanquishing an opponent: the player participates instead in killing as psychosis, playing a murderer who not only throws herself into surreal acts of butchery, but also collects flesh trophies to bring back as snacks for her creepy familiar.

In an interview Porpentine says, "I really hate this world and so when I make something I'm making something I can bear to live in" (Iadarola, 2017). In *Their Angelic Understanding* (2013) the player character lives in fear as the enemy of angels, whose visitations are not heavenly but tortuous violations. She has been scarred and wounded by an angel, and no one came to her aid. She is unconsoled, deeply conflicted, feeling somehow complicit in her own violation: "… I finally woke up, stupid stupid stupid, no one will save you, no one cares. / No one cares when an angel touches you. / I realized what I had to do. / I had to sacrifice my desire to be thought of as a good person." She lights off on a surreal journey to confront those who have hurt her. At one point she has to clean the streets of amputated hands that fall ceaselessly from the sky, covering every surface. She has to play a cruel game of endurance in which she and her opponent must clutch red vampire tiles that cut their flesh and suck blood from their hands. Again, the writing is suffused with a sense of displacement that seems related to a sense of being born in the wrong body, such as "i keep my hands in my lap where i can see them/ and the other moms will never know/ how much I want to rip their wombs out/ and fix my big horrible problem."

At the beginning of *With Those We Love Alive* (2014) the reader is asked to "Please remember: nothing you can do is wrong." This is both a technical commentary – in Porpentine's work, you do not need to solve puzzles in order to progress, you merely need to follow your chosen path – and a commentary on the nihilistic questions raised within the work itself. *With Those We Love Alive* strives to bring the reader into the work in an embodied way, both by asking readers to physically inscribe themselves with symbols (spiroglyphs) from the text of the work and by using the interface of the Twine game. When you sleep the screen goes dark. When you are asked to hold your breath, the words disappear from the screen for an interval before you are directed to exhale. The work also includes an evocative soundtrack by Brenda Neotenomie. Like many other elements of the work, the soundtrack has the effect of reaching outside of the divide between the person and the screen. The story almost seems to want to crawl out of the machine and wrap itself around the reader. The element of enlisting the interactor to actually mark their flesh, to choose parts of their body and touch them with pen and ink, brings the reader into sensuous intimate contact with the work. It calls to mind Shelley Jackson's *Skin* project (2003) – a story which was actually written on the skin of "words" – reader participants who agreed to have one of the words from the story tattooed in their body in exchange for the story itself: Jackson only revealed the full text of the story to her "words."

In *With Those We Love Alive* Porpentine places the player character in between a mundane and often painful reality and a fantasy world that seems to promise some kind of escape but more often only heightens a sense of precarity. When the player character first visits a balcony where she can scan the horizons for signs of life below, she sees several different vistas, but none of them are particularly calming or beautiful in any conventional sense. We witness, "Rat kids […] digging up lung fish for their meal, lithe little claws cracking mud cocoons to pull out the soft fleshy coil inside." The player character is employed making weapons and other objects for the Queen, often using bones and other remnants of humans the Queen has killed. Porpentine's dark vision meditates on the problem of complicity. At one juncture, the interactor has to choose whether to be a person, part of a community, or to remain separate and alone. In order to be part of the human community, the player character has to stomp to death "princess-spores" that the Queen has spawned. The Queen herself is an evil hunter of humans, but in order to join the human community, the player character must participate in a metaphorical act of genocide. One of the few pleasures in this world for the protagonist is to visit the dream distillery – a place where the dreams of sleepers are harvested as products for the use of others. So even this escape comes at the cost of complicity. As Emily Short notes, the work presents us with a bleak picture of the possibilities of human connection and community: "participating in community and joining in connection with other humans is inextricable from participating in systemic violence and oppression. It is only possible to retain one's empathy and the ability to exercise individual conscience if one at the same time remains alone and capitulates in no shared ethos at all" (Short, 2014).

Porpentine explores the narrative possibilities of several hypertext techniques conceptualized as far back as Ted Nelson's *Computer Lib/Dream Machines* (1974) but not often utilized in literary web hypertexts before Twine. She uses "stretchtexts" with links that expand upon the text currently on the screen with new lines or paragraphs inserted between the lines when the link is clicked. Links are often used to provide variable choices to the reader or alternate depictions of the same scenes or events. Clicking a link will often change adjectives or character traits. Her works also use timing delays (pauses before the next text is pushed to the screen for dramatic effect) and visual representations of time and action through color choices and fonts. Porpentine is a talented dystopian writer who has thrown herself into the serious exploitation of the affordances of a constrained system. She has taken the children's literature genre of Choose-Your-Own-Adventure and carved it into a vehicle for dark existentialist poetry.

If Porpentine is the most notorious Twine author, she is certainly not alone in a robust and thriving community of mostly young authors who have published hundreds of works. One Twine game, *Depression Quest* by Zoe Quinn (2013), sparked the Gamergate controversy. *Depression Quest*, a game designed to faithfully communicate the first-person experience of depression, received a fair deal of attention for its unusual approach and subject matter. A group of (primarily male) gamers attacked Quinn, charging that her relationship with a journalist had brought the game undue attention, and attacked the very idea that such a work could be considered a game. Some of these trolls then "doxed" her, releasing her personal information, and launched a torrent of vicious tweets about what they tagged #gamergate (Parkin, 2014). The #gamergate tweet storm snowballed into major controversy, not as much about journalistic ethics as about misogyny within the contemporary computer game industry and fan community.

In addition to *With Those We Love Alive*, two other Twine games included in the *Electronic Literature Collection, Volume 3* (2016) are representative of somewhat more playful and parodic impulses, if not fueled by as incendiary a literary vision as that which drives Porpentine's work. In *The Hunt for the Gay Planet* by Anna Anthropy (2013) the player character is a sci-fi explorer of extraplanetary worlds, who is often frustrated in her attempt to locate the gay planet of Lesbionica. When she finally gets there, she discovers Lesbionica ruled by a despot who has made a deal with the Federation to keep all the lesbians on one planet. The player character overthrows the despot and frees the lesbians to explore other parts of the universe. *The Hunt for the Gay Planet* is a parody that does not take itself particularly seriously, but the parodic sci-fi frame does provide the author with an opportunity to make fun of the rhetoric of exclusion in a heteronormative world. *Quing's Quest VII: The Death of Videogames!* (2014) is another parody, developed by Dietrich Squinky for Ruin Jam 2014, an event organized in response to post-Gamergate tensions over gaming culture identity and accusations by right-wing gamers that feminists and diversity advocates were out to ruin the game industry. The game features a spaceship named the "Social Justice Warrior" piloted by a player character who came from the planet Videogames but who was exiled after an invasion by the Misogynerds. The game also plays with retro-gaming nostalgia by using early computer-game 8-bit style graphics and references. Both games are examples of how parody can be used in games to make effective rhetorical points, even in a retro-oriented form that does not take itself too seriously.

The popularity of Twine games and the ease with which a generation of authors has adopted the platform and built a readership is an exciting development. A few years before Twine, most of the talk about hypertext fiction was done in the past tense. By creating an open-source and open-access platform based on earlier models of hypertext authoring software, and importantly by promoting an easy-to-use web-publishing-first model that is easily woven into social networks, Twine has tapped into the energies of millennial online writing communities, including many writers who had heard neither of hypertext nor interactive fiction when they started creating in Twine, but who may have for instance participated in fan fiction communities or shared independent games or animated gifs on Tumblr.

Games as literary platforms

This chapter has tracked a line of practice in interactive fiction from its origins in *Adventure* through the Infocom era, the rise of the amateur culture of IF, and into Twine games scene, which intermingles elements of hypertext with elements of interactive fiction in a non-parser-based form. But not all electronic literature that engages with the form, tropes, interface, and mechanics of computer games has emerged from this stream. Rather, as computer games have become a dominant cultural form, they have not only affected technological platforms but also cultural identity. Certain games have become common cultural touchstones, referents that generations widely share. At this stage, many of us are more likely to have played the same computer games as our contemporaries than we are to have read the same novels, or even to have watched the same television shows or films. Games become focal points of nostalgia, generating associations with childhood and the domestic sphere. They have also produced a visual language of familiar icons. Space Invaders, Pac-Man, Mario and Luigi, Donkey Kong and many other sprites are familiar to us even in silhouette. One might go so far as to say that computer games have served to shape and reinforce ideology and worldview. There is a reason why the American military produced the game *America's Army* (United States Army, 2002) to use as a recruiting tool, and a reason why American soldiers in conflicts in Iraq and Afghanistan often came back from missions to trailers on the base to play first-person shooters to "wind down." Games are powerful tools of simulation – not only in the sense that they model world environments, but also because they can shape understandings of the world outside the game. A number of electronic literature authors has developed works that explore the metaphors, form, and interfaces of games and uses game environments as material or medium.

Arteroids (2002) by Jim Andrews is a poem for the Web, developed in Shockwave, in the form of the classic video game *Asteroids*. The reader/player of *Arteroids* is called upon to make poetry suffer. Piloting a red "id entity" around the screen, the interactor executes texts, lines of poetry, which play the part of asteroids in the game. When words and phrases are hit, they explode into circular sprays of letters. Andrews describes the interaction as "cracking open language" in the same way as William S. Burroughs described the effects of using the cut-up technique on audiotape. Andrews plays in particular with the materiality of digital expression. When audio, image, movement, interaction can all be edited and inscribed in the same way as language, at what point can we draw a line between image and text, poetry and pixel? Andrews writes "*Arteroids* shifts the focus between game and play, between text as readable literary object that gets its primary meaning from the meaning of the words to text as meaning via sound, motion, and destructive intent. When does "poetry" mean poetry, and when does it mean arteroid? It is a question of velocity, density, and other such concerns of visual (even multimedia) rhetoric, of emphasis and intent" (Andrews, 2002b). The work has a "game" mode and a "play" mode. At the higher levels of the game mode, the text is functionally unreadable, while in the play mode aspects of the text and the interface are configurable. The work is ultimately a meditation on how we make meaning from language and from play and, like much of Andrews' work, calls upon us to consider how poetry might function not only through semantically meaningful language, but also through single letters, through gestures, through space and time, and through embodied interaction.

Natalie Bookchin's *The Intruder* (1999) is a retelling of the Jorge Luis Borges story of the same title through ten computer games. Borges' story is a brutal tale of jealousy and misogyny. The "intruder" of the story is a woman whom two brothers obsess over and treat as their possession. They mistreat and objectify her as she functions as a pawn in the game that the two of them are playing with each other. One of the two brothers ultimately kills the woman in order to clear the tensions between the brothers. Bookchin combines elements of Borges' story with simple games to perform a critique both of the brothers' casual attitude to their abuse and murder of the woman and in a larger sense to the cultural values embedded in the games themselves. In order to advance through the story, the interactor must "win" a series of elementary games modeled on classic video games. In playing the games – for example a version of *Pong* in which the paddles are used to swat a figure of the woman back and forth – the interactor is drawn into a complicit role in the objectification and abuse of the woman. As N. Katherine Hayles notes, this uncomfortable positioning can serve to heighten the affect produced by the work, "Because the games compel the user to enter dynamically into the production of text, they serve to connect the user in surprisingly powerful ways to the narrative" (Hayles, 2000). Bookchin's work also comments on the militaristic origin and nature of many archetypal video games. Given the incredible new powers of expression offered by digital media, is there anything natural about the fact that many of the most successful examples of computer games are essentially modeling war, that killing and destroying often define relationships in games? *The Intruder* is an example of what Astrid Ensslin in *Literary Gaming* describes as "antiludic design" that "uses elements from videogame architectures such as interface items, rules and feedback mechanisms, or even complete minigames (puzzles, jigsaws, etc.) to critique structural, thematic, and cultural aspects of games and gaming" (Ensslin, 2014, p. 90).

In *The Princess Murderer* by Deena Larsen and geniwate this antiludic design manifests in a rough adaptation of the story of Bluebeard. In three different sections of the story the reader is alternately cast as suspect, victim, and witness to the killing spree. As the reader/player (addressed as in the second person), you are told that with each of your clicks, a princess dies, and in one strand of the story, the number of princesses decreases with every click. This text thus also plays with the relationship between interaction and complicity. There is no clear "win" state. While playing the role of voracious and misogynistic killer piling up the princess bodies would clearly not be satisfying to any but the most sociopathic of players, there can also be "too many princesses" in the castle, at which point the player needs to kill more in order to proceed. You can win neither by following the default path nor by trying to resist. In traversing the work, we also encounter a number of meditations on the relationship between texts, images, bodies, and coded behaviors. The work performs a meta-critique of games, in particular of the way many games represent women as objects and trivialize violence. At one point the text describes "life and death" as "a Boolean choice." The text doesn't really offer a way out of the cycle of violence, reinforcing the idea that within the game (or the culture), roles and identities are pre-defined. In this game, you are boxed in. As the authors describes the situation: "All you want is closure. All they want is you, enclosed." Ensslin reports that there is one strand of the narrative which does present an alternative – a version told by an Amazon queen who has come to take revenge on Bluebeard, but it does not appear on every reading of the text: "the text is hidden in such a subtle way that it may be seen as a reference to hacking, modding, and other subversive practices in game culture, in which cheat codes are used, for example, to access user-generated gaming content or to facilitate or speed up progress" (Ensslin, 2014, p. 100). Larsen and geniwate suggest that gender roles, in popular media such as computer games, have been so predefined that they are encoded into the structure of the game, and of society itself.

A number of Jason Nelson's works, including *Game, Game, Game and Again Game* (2006), *I Made This. You Play This. We Are Enemies.* (2008), and *Nothing You Have Done Deserves Such Praise* (2013) are presented in platform game format. Nelson is a poet of the interface. The way that we move through a Nelson piece, its visual design, quirks of interaction, and mechanics are treated as poetic elements as important as the language itself. Nelson isn't particularly interested in making a "good game" as much as he is in using games as a platform to speak in a contemporary digital vernacular that is part poetry, part digital ephemera, part game, part outsider art. From the first screen of *Game, Game, Game and Again Game* it is clear that the work is breaking both with our expectations of what writing should be and of what games should be.

Game, Game, Game and Again Game (or *Belief systems are small clumsy rolling-type creatures*) adheres to the gameplay style of platform computer games, such as *Super Mario Bros.*, but presents us with a world of crude hand-drawn sprites and obstacles. The subject of the game is essentially metaphysics. Each level deals with a particular theological or ideological approach to life. On the Capitalist level, for instance, the player leaps onto dollar signs and encounters short texts having to do with obsessions for certain shiny objects (a brand-new bicycle) and fetishistic consumerist desires. The hand-drawn elements in Nelson's works are an essential part of their charm. While commercial game interfaces tend toward a kind of glossy surface polish, Nelson's drawings, hurried, wild, and garish, are like the crayon scrawling of a precocious child. The images are not about photorealistic perfection, but human imperfection: a hand was here and left its fingerprints all over the place. The interface seems somehow broken on purpose, oriented against seamlessness. Nelson also frequently uses recordings of his own voice to reiterate the human intervention in the game environment. When our avatar falls into a pit, we hear Nelson's singsong voice chanting, "Come on and meet your maker!" The platform game serves as a stand-in for the bigger game of life and the absurdity of the belief systems we construct in order to make sense of existence and mortality. If we are going to deal with teleology, why not do so through a platform game that offers us plenty of bottomless pits and lava flows on which to test our theories?

I made this. You play this. We are enemies. is both a meditation on the agonistic relationship between game developers and game users and a deconstruction of the relationships between web users, developers, and web design conventions. Nelson has said that the inspiration for this work came from hate mail he received from religious fundamentalists who were reacting to *Game, game, game and again game*, which made Nelson think about the relationships people form with websites they visit, and the ideologies and attachments that are both embedded in the websites and that people project onto them. The game world is composed of messy doodles and texts layered on top of platform levels based around some popular web sites (Level 1 is Google, Level 2 is Yahoo, Level 3 is Fark). The result is a cross between a sophisticated semiotic commentary on contemporary digital culture and the ravings of a conspiracy theorist. Conspiracy also forms the basis of *Evidence of Everything Exploding* (2009). Where *I made this...* used popular websites to establish motifs, the levels in this game are built upon a collection of odd documents, such as a page of an old dictionary, an announcement of a Dadaist festival, a NASA moon flight plan, and Bill Gates' "hobbyist letter", which have no readily apparent connections between them. Along the way, the reader launches various written and spoken texts related and unrelated to the background material: a snatch of a Robert Frost poem attached to the dictionary, a bit of a Malcom X speech juxtaposed with a Dadaist environment. Attempts to "read" the game, to find meaning in these juxtapositions, mimic exactly the sort of conspiracy-theory activity the game is about and for which the infinitely interconnected Web provides a fertile breeding ground. *Nothing You Have Done Deserves Such Praise* (2013) meditates on the nature of computer games and the psychology (or perhaps sociopathology) they represent. The game parodies the cycles of positive reinforcement that game designers use to hook gamers on their product, the trophies and badges and bonus points that are awarded to players for trivial acts. The game ridicules these absurd Pavlovian mechanisms, while the background illustrations of human anatomy serve as reminders of human mortality, gestures of memento mori.

Deviant: The Possession of Christian Shaw (2004) by Donna Leishman illustrates one of the central distinctions between electronic literature and print literature *per se*, in that language is often not the only or even the dominant way of communicating an interactive story. In *Deviant* a complex and difficult situation, rich in narrative content, can be explored interactively by engaged users primarily through interaction with environments and characters, but largely without a great deal of intermediating language. The reader navigates *Deviant* in much the same way as an online visual puzzle game. Clicking on windows, trees, flowers, or a book will activate story elements and progress the narrative nonlinearly. There is only a small bit of text hidden in the work; otherwise the ambient narrative unfolds through the reader's exploration and activation of visual elements in the landscapes she encounters.

Dwarf Fortress (2006), a popular single-player text-based game by Tarn Adams and Zach Adams, may itself be said to generate a kind of literature. *Dwarf Fortress* is a simulation game – players attempt to manage an expanding population of dwarves while building an ever-expanding fortress. The game is generative in the sense that randomized situations and events have a determinative effect on play as it unfolds. The game is entirely text-based but also graphical – the program uses ASCII text to visually represent the game state. Although little processing power goes into the graphics, the game is processor-intensive because of its intensive procedural generation. As Josh Diaz notes, "each dwarf is described with a unique set of psychological attributes, and has an indication of their current mood, based on factors like the availability of work, the decorum of the fortress, and their relationships with other dwarves; dwarf children, as they age, are educated into religions, cultures and professions. These systems are inter-related, with effects from one affecting another, and allow for a huge range of player experiences" (Diaz, 2009, p. 19). The game inevitably ends in failure. *Dwarf Fortress* produces a transcription file that provides an account of occurrences in the game, akin to medieval chronicles, describing things like the birth and death of dwarves, rough winters, starvation, etc. in a simple linear progression without any clear narrative indication of causality. In the hands of the players, these chronicles become what game scholars Salen and Zimmerman (2004, p. 383) refer to as "emergent narratives" – tellable series of events that emerge from the player's interaction with the generative system. The literary aspect of *Dwarf Fortress,* and what makes it interesting as electronic literature phenomenon, is that a large community of players adopted these rudimentary accounts into more extensive fictions, which they share with other players online. The *DF Community Games & Stories* bulletin board now includes over 150,000 posts, primarily of these elaborated stories. Stephanie Boluk and Patrick Lemieux (2013) note: "textual artifacts produced in response to the game could be called dwarven epitaphs, ludic obituaries created to memorialize the death of play. *Dwarf Fortress* transforms from a world generator into a story generator."

With the rise of massively multiplayer online games, we find games that are not based solely on individual play but are instead richly imagined and extensively developed virtual worlds (see Corneliussen and J. W. Rettberg, 2011). Because they are social spaces, these games can also function as performance environments. Alan Sondheim and Sandy Baldwin are two authors who have exploited game spaces and virtual worlds in the creation of artistic experiences. In Baldwin's model of the first-person shooter game *Half-Life*, *New Word Order: Basra* (2011), the player shoots away letters from phrases of a Billy Collins poem. Sondheim's work often includes interventions in virtual worlds such as Second Life, in which thematic generated and modified texts from Sondheim flood the chat channels as grotesque, deformed, and mutated bodies twist in virtual space. Baldwin also experimented with anachronistic performances in massively multiplayer online games such as a performance that recreated the 1912 West Virginia coal miners' strike and the Battle of Blair Mountain using the *Lord of the Rings* online game, with dwarves playing the part of striking miners, as other players carried on with the game around them.

In Michael Mateas and Andrew Stern's *Façade* (2005) the interactor participates in a one-act drama in the form of a visit to the apartment of a couple of old friends who are in the midst of a critical marital argument that could spell the end of their relationship. *Façade* is similar in many ways to interactive fiction, although it is presented in a graphical interface rather than at a command line. The user/player/reader of this work responds to the characters in the drama, providing typed responses to Grace and Trip, the conflicted married couple at the center of the work. *Façade* is considered groundbreaking both for its comparatively convincing natural language processing and for its conception of "interactive drama" tied very closely to classic Aristotelian theories of drama. Interactive drama may well develop into a compelling genre in its own right, as interactive voice interfaces such as that of the Amazon Echo become more prevalent (see chapter 7) and conversational AI commonplace. One can imagine a version of *Façade* in which the interactor speaks to the other characters in the drama, rather than typing to them. Works of this kind are certainly on the way. Although

Façade was clearly an interactive narrative artwork, it was also a computer science research project that resulted in a number of publications on natural language processing and expressive artificial intelligence.

This chapter has focused on games that sit outside of the mainstream commercial game industry and are self-consciously constructed as poetic or narrative works. This is not say there has not been narrative innovation in AAA commercial games. On the contrary, in recent years a number of major titles have been released that are driven by strong narrative content as much as they are by game mechanics. *Portal 2* (Valve, 2011) players for example explore evocative environments and solve puzzles to uncover the details of a complex plot. Games such as *Gone Home* (The Fulbright Company, 2013) and *What Remains of Edith Finch* (Annapura Interactive, 2017) adapt the adventure game conventions and spatial exploration of interactive fiction in developing richly imagined narratives of mysterious family histories. *Firewatch* (Camp Santo, 2016) places the player in a first-person role of a fire lookout trying to locate two girls who have gone missing after launching fireworks and igniting a forest fire. The game is much more about interpersonal relationships and existential choices than it is about winning or losing. The increasingly popular "mystery adventure narrative" genre provides many examples of games that are much closer to novels that the player explores than they are to first-person shooters.

Games as digital vernacular

Interactive fiction provides an instructive example of how an enthusiastic user community can develop and sustain a digital literary form outside of traditional commercial publishing environments. Interactive fiction demonstrates what an important role networked creative communities play in emergent digital forms. Interactive fiction adapts particular elements of traditional fiction (such as character development, different models of temporal framing, and second-person point of view) to a ludic textual environment. Interactive fiction also demonstrates the importance of platform to the formation of genre, as the affordances and constraints of given platforms such as Inform and Twine have material effects on the nature and structure of the works produced using them.

Games are arguably the most predominant form of storytelling in contemporary digital media, and some games have become shared cultural referents. Literary and performative takes on digital games can serve as lenses to defamiliarize and critique both contemporary computer games and culture more broadly. These literary games demonstrate the blurring of genres and movement of conventions and ideas between genres common to many types of electronic literature. Computer game conventions have become a form of digital vernacular, the gestures and tropes of which are available to other art forms.

5   Kinetic and Interactive Poetry

Digital poetry has a rich and varied history. Chris Funkhouser describes digital poetry as "not a singular 'form' but rather a conglomeration of forms that now constitutes a genre even though the creative activity itself – in terms of its media, methods, and expressive intent – contains heterogeneous components." He asserts that a "poem is a digital poem if computer programming or processes (software, etc.) are distinctively used in the composition, generation, or presentation of the text" (Funkhouser, 2008, p. 318). In chapter 3, we considered one major strand of poetic practice in combinatory and generative poetry, which dates back to the early history of computing. But the ability to recombine and generate texts with algorithms is not the only aspect of digital media that has attracted poets to create work in computational environments. In this chapter we consider some other significant aspects of digital poetry, most importantly kinetic, multimedia, and interactive digital poetry. These forms of digital poetry have rich relationships with antecedent movements, particularly those that are concerned with the materiality of the text as image, with the granularity of language, and with the relationship between poetry, sound, and music. Animation and interactivity have consequences not only for our experience of the text as read, but also for our understanding of letters and words as manipulable material objects.

Characteristics of kinetic and interactive poetry

Kinetic and interactive poetry explore the specific multimedia capacities of the contemporary computer as a poetic environment for both composition and reception. Just as concrete and visual poetry and artist's books use the space and material properties of the printed page to foreground aspects of the relation between text and image, digital forms reconfigure the text as moving image in space and time and thus work with registers of signification more familiar to visual and performance art. Words and letters are not only carriers of meaning but material objects that themselves have variable properties. Movement in digital poetry functions as a metaphorical figure with as much semantic intent and affect as the words.

Time and movement

Kinetic poetry by definition deals in time-based poetics: its main distinctive characteristic is that texts change through animation, and that animation itself conducts meaning. Álvaro Seiça notes that in kinetic poetry, "spatial and temporal dimensions bridge notions that go radically beyond the print paradigm – in which content and representation prevail, and, at best, form suggests. In kinetic poetry, space and time present themselves, they materialize, but they also represent" (Seiça, 2018b, p. 51). In addition to the text, visual, and audio components, time and motion are signifiers. N. Katherine Hayles notes that the "time of a poem can be considered to consist of the time of writing, the time of coding, the time of production/performance, and the time of reading" and that each of these events can be understood discretely (Hayles, 2009, p. 182). Hayles emphasizes the fact that any kind of digital text might be better understood as a process rather than an object, given that its very legibility depends on a machine performance in response to code. The poem is experienced as the performance of the code within a given configuration of a given platform rather than as the code itself. Because any experience of a poem is constrained by these contingencies, as Seiça remarks, we might consider the poem itself to be deobjectified, variable, and conditional (p. 104). John Cayley observes that code drives "the temporal atoms of literal signification" (Cayley, 2009, p. 382) which in turn restructure the human experience of time. This idea is important for our understanding of kinetic poetry. The text in performance accrues a temporal dimension that is encoded and manipulable. Time can also be used as a variable element. In Cayley's *Speaking Clock* (1995) and *Wotclock* (2005), the time of day registered from the reader's machine has material effects on the language displayed. In the case of *Speaking Clock* the words of a combinatory poem take the place of numerals on a conventional clock, producing poetry that responds directly to the reader's temporal situation.

The materiality of language

Many works of kinetic poetry share concerns with the Lettrists in their focus on language at a granular level. A good portion of kinetic poetry is richly multimedial. Synesthetic effects are often important to many works when sound, motion, text, and typography are in complex interaction with each other, or when the embodied interactor uses physical gestures to manipulate text within an interactive textual installation. Interactive digital poetry further considers the relationship between reader and text as a recursive feedback loop, the relation of physical gesture to poetic trope, and the position of reader as embodied actor. For example, in Stephanie Strickland's *V: Vniverse* (2002) the poem is kinetic not in a Lettristic sense that the letters move on the page, but because the reader's movement across points of constellations in a field of stars determines which tercets will fade in and out of view, and the structure of the poem therefore takes shape as it is read.

A typology of kinetic typography effects would not be easily achieved, in part because there is no common vocabulary to describe individual movements of words or letters on the screen. Even if one did attempt to name and map every possible gesture or form of movement of letters, there is no clear adherence of these movements to specific poetic effects. Letters falling, fading, twisting, turning, layering, or overlapping on the screen can mean many different things. The texts, visuals, audio, and interactive elements contextualize the given motion effect. Although it is certainly possible to attempt to read the kinetic typography effects of a given poem, as Alexandra Saemmer does in a reading of gestures in Brian Kim Steffan's *The Dreamlife of Letters* (Saemmer, 2010), the same movements would likely have completely different effects the next time they were used in a different poem.

The interactive dimension of digital poetry is distinct from the kinetic dimension. Not all kinetic poetry is interactive and not all interactive poetry is kinetic. But interactivity is a common dimension of many digital poems produced in recent years. In this case, the poem involves another dimension of performance: the performance that is required of the user in order to operate the text machine. Hayles describes the performance of an interactive poem as a series of feedback loops: "The machine produces the text as an event; the reader interacts with that event in ways that significantly modify and even determine its progress; these readerly interventions feed back into the machine to change its behavior, which further inflects the course of the performance" (Hayles, 2006, p. 187). These feedback loops range from those that are essentially trivial (in some kinetic poems, mouse clicks simply activate the next section of text) to the determinately consequential (in some works, the user actually writes the text that is manipulated by the program).

Digital poetry in relation to literary and artistic traditions

Digital kinetic poetry provides text as time-based moving image, often with a sound dimension, and is often interactive and responsive as well. The ideas of poetry as material image, auditory materiality, and interactive potentiality are not essentially new to poetry in digital media but have developed in conversation with several twentieth-century literary movements. Indeed, poets such as bpNichol and Ottar Ormstad bridge between concrete poetry in print and digital poetry. This section considers the relation between digital poetry and related movements such as Concrete Poetry, Lettrism, Futurism, Visual Poetry, Sound Poetry, as well as related practices in cinema.

Concrete poetry

Language is not a formless thing, not a transparent and immaterial method of transmitting ideas from one human mind to another. When we speak of "English" we are referring both to a practice of spoken communication and to a written language. The spoken and the written language are related but they are not the same thing. In writing, language has a material form that occupies space within a visual field. Written language is symbolic – we produce letters on the page that are representative of words that are representative of thoughts we hope to share – but it is also visual, and its visual form has aesthetic and semiotic effects. If we write the same love letter in flowing cursive writing, or type it out on an Olivetti, or print it off in Comic Sans, or cut its letters out of magazines and paste them on a sheet of paper, or cast its words into a 3D virtual reality space, the same text, the same words, become radically different things, which will be experienced and interpreted differently by their reader. Spoken language also has material form. The same word whispered, or shouted, or growled can have a substantially different effect. It can be spoken through a bullhorn, or a computer voice simulator, or by Leonard Cohen, or Denzel Washington, and in the process change material form. We hear a difference, and we can also see it when we look at sound spectrograms in contemporary audio software.

Concrete poetry is based on an awareness of and interest in the material nature of language, its shapes and forms, and the aesthetic and semantic effects made possible by manipulating language as a material. Mary Ann Solt describes concrete poetry as poetry with a "concentration upon the physical material from which the poem or text is made" and references Mike Weaver's distinction between three types of concrete poetry, "visual (or optic), phonetic (or sound) and kinetic (moving in a visual succession)" (Solt, 1968). All three of these types of concrete poetry are well represented in digital poetry, most often in conjunction with each other.

There are examples of poetry that use the shape and arrangement of the words to convey or reinforce meaning dating back as far as ancient Greece. Simmias of Rhodes wrote poems in the shapes of wings, an egg, and a hatchet (Higgins, 1987, p. 20). Shape poems or pattern poetry were a popular form during the Renaissance. George Herbert's "Easter Wings" and "The Altar" (Herbert, 1633) are examples of English Renaissance metaphysical poetry in which the forms of the poems echoed their titles to serve as a visual correlative of the content of the poems. American modernist poets such as E. E. Cummings and Ezra Pound worked with the arrangement of letters on the page, for example in Cummings' poem "l(a" (1958), the poet breaks the word "loneliness" with the phrase "a leaf falls," into nine lines of two to five letters cascading down the page, using the vertical space of the page to bring the reader into the moment of a leaf's descent and to underscore a feeling of solitude.

Concrete poetry became recognized as an international poetry movement during the late twentieth century. Brazil and Portugal were particular centers of activity in the 1960s, though European poets were also engaging with similar forms at the same time. The term concrete poetry itself was defined by the Noigrandes poets of Brazil as poetry in which "graphic space acts as structural agent" (Perloff, 2004, p. 175). In their "Pilot Plan for Concrete Poetry" (de Campos, A. et al., 1958) the Noigrandes put forth perhaps the simplest definition of concrete poetry with their statement that "Structure=Content." The layout and typography of a concrete poem shape the meaning of the words contained in it as much as the semantic import of the words themselves. The arrangement of the words or letters on the page in modern concrete poetry is most often conceptual and abstract, and the use of space takes up a good deal of semantic weight. As Rosmarie Waldrop writes "both conventions and sentence are replaced by spatial arrangement" (Perloff, 2004, p. 175).

Augusto de Campos' "ovo novelo" (1956) (Bohn, 2011, p. 125) is a classic example of a concrete poem in which the visual form (it is shaped like an egg) corresponds to the verbal content. The poem is about human conception and birth, part of a four-poem cycle of circular poems that deal with human birth and rebirth. Although the poem is shaped like an egg and begins with the lines "egg/ ball of yarn" it is not only working on the visual level – there is also quite of bit of wordplay and alliteration involved in the work, and it is made to be read out loud as well as seen: the use of concrete form is not its only register of meaning.

"Silencio" (1954) by Eugen Gomringer and "Apfel" (1965) by Reinhard Döhl are two often-cited examples of twentieth-century concrete poetry. In "Silencio" the word "silencio" is repeated three times in the first and last two lines of the poem, but in the middle line it is missing from the second position, leaving a block of silence with an empty space in the middle. Roberto Simanowski writes, "all other words are just a preparation because the gap conveys the message that, strictly speaking, silence can only be articulated by the absence of any words… Certainly, the message is to be seen but it will only be revealed on the fundament that one did read the surrounding words before" (Simanowski, 2004). The visual form also may remind us not only of silence but also of *silencing*. The empty space only has the effect of representing silence because of the words around it – just as it is the case that one is only silenced in an authoritarian regime if others are complicit. In Döhl's "Apfel" the word "apfel" (apple) is repeated on the page in an apple-like shape. The words are put in the material shape of the thing they represent. It is only when the reader actually moves from seeing the shape to the written language that she spots one "wurm" amidst the lines of "apfel."

bpNichol's work bridges print and digital concrete poetry. He published a number of concrete poetry chapbooks and anthologies of work by himself and contemporaries. In an afterword to the anthology the *cosmic chef: an evening of concrete* (1970) bpNichol described the works in the book as representing an approach of "boderblur": "everything presented here comes from that point where language &/or the image blur together into the inbetween & become concrete objects to be understood as such" (bpNichol, 1970). bpNichol's interest is this process of transformation eventually led him to write some well-known examples of early computer-animated poetry in his *First Screening* (1984), which we will consider in more detail later in the chapter.

bpNichol's contemporary Steve McCaffery was one of a group who focused on using the typewriter for concrete poetry. The term "dirty concrete" has been used to describe his and bpNichol's break with the Noigrandes and other concrete poetry traditions. Much of McCaffery's work dips in and out of legibility. Words are typed over each other in order to support patterns or images that the letters form on the page. There is often a kind of conversation or dialectic struggle between writing as pure image and readable text. In his work *Carnival* (McCaffery 1973a, 1973b), published in two panels (1967–70) and (1970–75), the reader had to unbind the book object and arrange the pages on a grid in order to see the work in its intended format. McCaffery encouraged his readers to "consider the page not as a space but as a death occurring in the gap between 'writing' and 'wanting to say'" (Perloff, 1998). The panels in *Carnival* depict carnival masks through typed texts, but they also constitute a deconstructionist take on language and meaning-making, as texts rise in and out of intelligibility, are cut and interrupted, or flow off into rivers of type. While in creating the first panel McCaffery used a typewriter exclusively, in the second panel he integrated Xerography. He was exploring the affordances of each of these technologies of inscription, pushing their limits and using them to achieve aesthetic effects beyond those for which they were usually intended. McCaffery is also known for virtuosic readings of his work, in which the struggle between intention and communication manifests in words that degrade into unintelligible sounds or individual letters. McCaffery's use of concrete forms on the page extends to the material qualities of voice and sound in performance.

At least one concrete poet, Ian Hamilton Finlay, literally worked in concrete as well as other media. He and his wife Sue Finlay constructed the garden of Little Sparta at his home on an estate outside of Edinburgh, over the course of decades. Very short poems are stamped into concrete and stone sculptures, which play with themes from the ancient Greek and Roman classics, as well as French Romanticism. In one section of the garden, large boulders each have one word carved in them, together quoting a short phrase by one of the leaders of the French Revolution, Louis-Antoine St Juste. Taken together the stones read, "The order of the present is the disorder of the future" (Campbell, 2012). The stones are at the summit of a hill in the park, in a meadow of tall grass, which, if left untended, would overgrow and hide the stones. In his "Detached Sentences on Gardening" (2012) Finlay wrote "Certain gardens are described as retreats when they are really attacks." His statement refers both to certain aspects of the garden itself, which comment on war in a variety of ways, as well as a protracted battle Finlay had with local authorities about the tax status of the garden, but the garden itself also represents a kind of aesthetic attack on the idea that poetry can exist only on the printed pages of a book. Jenny Holzer also made a number of language art works in stone and on many other non-print surfaces such as park benches, cinema marquees, and digital billboards on Times Square. Her media art installations often involve texts scrolling across LED signs, emphasizing the movement of unconventional forms of text in unexpected places in public environments.

Symbolism, Futurism, and Lettrism

In his *Un coup de dés jamais n'abolira le hasard* (*A Throw of the Dice Will Never Abolish Chance*) (1897) Stéphane Mallarmé used varied typography, white space, and even the folds of the book to enable the reader to recombine different associations among the fragments of the text. The work is often cited as an antecedent to hypertext, as the relation between the fragments is not clearly dictated by the author but primarily constructed by the reader. Chris Funkhouser credits "the variations in typography, the integration of blank space, and the liberal scattering of lines" (Funkhouser, 2007, p.11) often found in digital poetry as derived from Mallarmé's work and claims Mallarmé "gave poets permission to arrange poetry using inventive graphical methods" (Funkhouser, 2007, p. 87). Johanna Drucker points out that Mallarmé was appropriating design techniques that were already established in the graphic design of newspaper advertising of the period, and turning them to poetic expression (Drucker, 1994, p. 56). In some ways this appropriation anticipates kinetic poets who used Shockwave and Flash during the 1990s and 2000s, whose work was often developed in conversation with designers working in commercial forms.

Italian Futurism was an early twentieth-century poetry and art movement associated with the rise of fascism, which emphasized speed, technology, youth, violence, as well as the machines and industrialism of modernity. The leader of the futurist movement (and one of the authors of the first Fascist Manifesto) was the poet F. T. Marinetti. In the *Manifesto of Futurism* (1909), Marinetti attested that he was inspired to start the movement after a car crash in 1908 that threw him out of the Fiat he was driving head over heels into the ditch (Marinetti, 2002, p. 290). Marinetti used the space of the printed page to create a sense of speed and motion, and to foreground "parole in libertà" (word autonomy), abandoning meter and line to focus on juxtapositions of single words or letters with each other in the typographic space of the page. His *Zang Tumb Tumb* (1914) is a book-length work about the siege by the Bulgarians of Turkish Adrianople in the Balkan War, which Marinetti had witnessed as a war reporter. His inventive typography uses textual elements in different fonts arranged in different sizes and shapes on the page to represent the noises, speed, and chaos of battle. Marinetti wrote that he was calling for "a typographic revolution directed against the idiotic and nauseating concepts of the outdated and conventional book," a revolution "directed against what is known as the typographic harmony of the page, which is contrary to the flux and movement of style." If Marinetti's ideology was disturbing, his uses of letterforms on the page to represent movement, speed, objects, and ruptures were influential for a number of subsequent literary movements engaged with the materiality of the written word. Marinetti also performed the work as sound poetry, presenting both language and sound as concrete materials that could more effectively represent ideas by using space, time, and shape, than they could be in regularly formatted print books.

Lettrism (or Letterism) was a movement based on idea that the poem of the future would be purely formal, and devoid of semantic content. Romanian theorist Isou (Isodore Goldstein) established the movement in Paris during the 1940s. Lettrism carries forth one of the core ideas of the Dada, that by the twentieth century, language itself had become corrupt and was in need of deconstruction. Isou distinguished between "amplic" (amplique) and "chiselling" (ciselante) phases of the history of poetry (Cooper, 2012). He described an amplic phase of poetry stretching from Homer to Victor Hugo during which the blueprints for what a poem could be, set out in the ancient classics, had been exhausted, concluding the phase. This was to be followed by a chiselling period, during which poets such as Charles Baudelaire and Tristan Tzara would deconstruct and break apart the conventions of the prior amplic period. Only when that act of deconstruction was complete could we re-encounter language and begin to reconstruct literature at its most essential level. For Isou this meant that the basis of the new poetry would not be words, but letters encountered as objects and sounds encountered not as semantic form but pure auditory experience. Initially Isou's Lettrism was more influential as theory than as an artistic movement, but it did give rise to a focus on language at the granular level of the letter that many concrete poets picked up on and that supplied inspiration for a strand of practice in digital poetry. These digital Lettrists are concerned with signification, but signification achieved through letters and their movement in time and space, not necessarily through the formation of words, phrases, or lines. Digital poet Natalia Fedorova contests the idea that digital Lettrists abandon meaning in their engagement with language as material, arguing that the "complete annihilation of semantic meaning is neither possible nor desirable" and that the point is instead "to turn letters from the transparent carriers of meaning to objects" (Fedorova, 2017, p. 140).

Visual poetry

Building upon the work of the concrete poets, the poets associated with Vispo (which, like sound poetry, is perhaps better understood as a set of associated practices than as a movement) have continued to explore the treatment of the letter as visual material throughout the late twentieth century and into the present. Vispo has extended from the granular treatment of letters to non-letters that reference the symbols and practices of writing. It seems a project to extend and complete the project of the Dada. In *The Last Vispo Anthology*, Nico Vassilakis writes "You are looking at an alphabet after it's exploded and word/letter cohesion is broken. What you're looking at is the trajectory of the verbo-visual extending into asemic language compositions" (Vassilakis, 2012, p. 8). Asemic writing moves beyond even the restriction of using letters as individual units, by using "letter-like" writing that is untranslatable because it purposefully conveys no linguistic meaning but instead gestures toward legibility.

A number of poets have explored writing in different forms of material media. Maria Damon creates visual poetry in cross-stitch. Artists such as Cy Twombly, Max Ernst, and Derek Beaulieu have produced works of asemic writing which reference language as a kind of negative space or variable component, an illegible language which is inscrutable or almost-present, coming into being. In W. Mark Sutherland's work "Negative Thoughts," white blobs set against a black background in the upper left side of the page move toward legible letters on the bottom right, suggesting the transition from unformed thought to legible letter (Sutherland, 2010, p. 50). Mikeal AND combines legible letters with invented ideograms. The connections between Vispo and some strands of digital poetry are explicit. There are a number of authors and artists such as Jim Andrews, Ted Warnell, Maria Damon, and Miekal AND, whose work bridges Vispo (reflected in works in print or other media) and digital poetics. Funkhouser notes that by the 1980s, visual poets were already using digital tools, as "digital processes become overtly implemented in static visual poems" (Funkhouser, 2007, p. 86). For poets centered on letterforms, making images that suggest language and the formation of language in space, the transition from visual poetry on the page to the screen made clear sense.

Of the antecedent movements and practices discussed here, visual poetry has the clearest direct relationship to kinetic poetry made for digital environments. Considering the relation between writing and technology, visual poet Derek Beaulieu writes "I propose a poetic where the author-function is fulfilled both by the biological 'author' of the text and the technology by which it is created" (Beaulieu, 2012, p. 74). Beaulieu may not be referring specifically to digital work, but his observation underscores the fact that especially when poets are working with software, the tool itself is an authored system and its constraints to some degree determine the range of effects poets can produce using it. We collaborate with our technologies by inescapable default.

Visual poets share with kinetic poets a concern with language in motion. Nico Vassilakis writes, "Seeing is believing that alphabets are in motion and in a moment come together to form a word. Otherwise, letters are everywhere at once, hovering in consideration" (Vassilakis, 2012, p. 9). These moments of transition between letters and words and communicable thought are represented both in Vispo imagery and in the letters and words moving across the screen in kinetic poetry. We observe language coming together and falling apart in a never-ending process, or struggling between that which can be articulated and that which can merely be gestured toward.

Manuel Portela sees this concern with the instability of language as extending to kinetic poetry as "specific forms of animating texts symbolize both the instability of signifiers and the instability of meaning" (Portela, 2010). Visual poetry, and much kinetic poetry that follows, is concerned with the dual nature of language as both material object and simultaneously as always-emerging thought, never quite fixed.

Sound poetry

Sound poetry is another strand of practice that has had important influence on digital poetry. The tradition of sound poetry dates back to the Russian and Italian Futurists and the Dada at the Cabaret Voltaire. Steve McCaffery describes the Russian Futurists Khlebnikov and Kruchenykh's manifesto *The Word as Such* (*Slovo kak takovoe*) (1913) as "the first decisive break with language's symbolic relation to an object, with the consequent disappearance of the thematic and the minimization of the semantic levels" (McCaffery, 1978). Italian Futurist F. T. Marinetti extended his concept of "parole in liberta" in performance as an attempt to replicate in sound the typographic innovations of his poetry. The work of the Dada is the main foundational touchstone for many contemporary sound poets. In Dada sound poetry we hear an extension of their focus on breaking down prior notions of what constituted poetry and their project of deconstructing boundaries between genres of artistic practice.

Hugo Ball first presented his sound poem "Karawane" in 1916 at the Cabaret Voltaire in Zurich. Ball's performance was typically Dada in its absurdity: he performed the work while dressed in a cardboard costume that resembled a lobster. "Karawane" is a poem of invented nonsense words that Ball described as a work of "Lautgedicht" (sound poetry). The printed version of the poem is concrete in the sense that Ball used different typefaces to represent different types of enunciation, though not in a way that would be clear to a reader who had not heard it read aloud. The poem has no meaning in itself except for its embrace of non-meaning. Ball said that he did not want to use "words that other people have invented … I want my own stuff, my own rhythm, and vowels and consonants too, matching the rhythm and all my own" (Ball, 1916). This approach was described as "bruitist" sound poetry, which works primarily through onomatopoeia for its effect. Tristan Tzara launched another strand of Dada sound poetry with his "simultaneous poems" – these involved several people reading at the same time, often in different languages, with different intonations and rhythms. The effect is cacophony. While individual words might have some meaning, as a whole the listener hears babble. Both approaches are in keeping with the Dadaist interest in rejecting nationalist modernism, and creating poetry and artwork that is essentially anti-art.

Talan Memmott paid tribute to Ball's work with his digital work *The Hugo Ball* (2006), a multimedia remediation of Ball's sound poem "Gadji Beri Bimba." When the interactor moves the cursor over a ball-shaped face, it begins chanting phrases from the poem, which are also represented as visual texts. Davin Heckman describes how Memmott breaks "the text down into hypothetical syntactic elements, pairing these elements with visemes (animations that match the phonemes), and recombines these pieces according to a hypothetical grammar (an algorithm)" (Heckman, 2010).

With his sound poem "Ursonate" Kurt Schwitters, who played roles in Dada, Surrealism, and Merz, began a practice of developing scripts for sound poetry with notation similar in some ways to musical composition. Schwitters described "Ursonate" as a sonata of four movements, with an overture and finale, as well as a cadenza in the fourth movement (Schwitters, 1922). This form of scripting or notation was influential for contemporary sound poets, who most often score their pieces before performing them. There is a clear relation between this type of scripting and the performance of computer code.

If Dada was recognizable as an artistic and literary movement, sound poetry might be better described as a practice with a discontinuous history. Steve McCaffery writes, "there is no 'movement' per se, but rather a complex, often oppositive and frequently antithetical interconnectedness of concerns – attempts to recover lost traditions mix with attempts to effect a radical break with all continuities" (McCaffery, 1978). It is however clear that many writers and artists who worked in avant-garde practices with visual language, from Dada to the Fluxus, were also interested in sound poetry as an auditory extension of their treatment of language as material rather than as an explicit carrier of meaning that can be easily parsed. Dick Higgins (1980) writes that sound poetry is "inherently concerned with communication and its means, linguistic and/or phatic. It implies subject matter; even when some particular work is wholly non-semantic, as in the microphonic vocal explorations of Henri Chopin, the non-semantic becomes a sort of negative semantics – one is conscious of the very absence of words rather than, as in vocal music, merely being aware of the presence of the voice."

Contemporary artists such as Jackson Mac Low, John Cage, and Christian Bök have paired sound poetry with different sorts of constrained composition, conceptual writing, and algorithmic thinking. A number of contemporary sound poets have also crossed over into digital practice. The

Finnish poet, translator, and publisher Leevi Lehto for example is known both for his robust performances of sound poetry and for his development in 2002 of the first "Google Poem Generator" (Lehto, 2006). Jörg Piringer presents a case of a contemporary Lettrist and sound poet who works extensively both in live sound performance and in digital poetry with interactive and generative works that bring together human and machine vocalization and Lettristic treatment of language.

Moving letters in film

Kinetic poetry did not arrive suddenly with the digital age. There is a substantial history of typographic animation in film, both in films that were produced explicitly as poetry projects and perhaps even more importantly kinetic text used in other film contexts, such as titles sequences.

Marcel Duchamp's *Anemic Cinema* (1926) is a playful example of early kinetic poetry produced by filming a set of spinning rotoreliefs (swirling kinetic drawings) alternated with spiraled and rotating texts, including puns and alliterative texts. The juxtaposition of the hypnotic kinetic drawings and the spiraling texts reinforces the material relationship between image and text. The texts are as much images as the drawings, and the line drawings and spinning text are in some sense interchangeable in their synchronized motion.

Filmmaker Len Lye was working with written poetry moving in space in films dating back to the 1930s. His films are experimental, each featuring a different interaction of motion, color, letters, words, music, filtering effects, collaged imagery, and effects particular to the physical media Lye was working with, such as scratches made directly onto the celluloid film. What is remarkable about such films as *Trade Tattoo* (1937) is not that their effects seem strange or dissimilar to contemporary audiences, but rather that they seem so familiar. His films look like contemporary video art, extensively processed on the computer. A number of Lye's films look as if they might have been produced last year. But the layering, filters, and kinetic text effects were all produced by Lye in the 1930s, using analogue processes.

John Cayley (2005) notes the importance of the work of film title sequence artist Saul Bass, who during the 1950s developed the titles for film classics such as *The Man with the Golden Arm*, *Psycho*, and *North by Northwest*. He writes that Bass "gave us the first literal performances of this necessary and vital interplay between language-as-visual-form and language-as-symbolic-representation." For Cayley the fact that the letters in Bass' animations were treated both as carriers of semantic intent and as visual material artifacts is what makes them essential antecedents to kinetic poetry. Letters are both symbolic representation and specific visual forms to be treated as aesthetic objects in their own right. The movie titles, like digital kinetic poetry, are on a "continuum that is played out in literal time-based art, a continuum of rhetorical possibilities and signifying strategies that cross and recross from visual to linguistic media and back, in evocative iterative performance, without ever losing a grip on their specific materialities." Letters have their own ways of signifying through visual attributes, movement, and time. The double nature of text, as symbolic and representational on one hand, and letter and word forms as material objects in their own right on the other, remains a central concern of poets working with kinetic text in digital media.

Early work in digital poetry

The various twentieth-century avant-garde movements developed traditions in visual poetry, sound poetry, and video poetry, engaging in processes of continual reconceptualization of the relationship between lines, words, letters, space, time, motion, and semantics. The addition of the personal computer and global network to the toolbox of poets interested in this form of textual materiality results in forms of kinetic poetry that are not essentially new, but rather the continuation of processes rooted in the earlier avant-garde. Lori Emerson describes digital poetry as a "rematerialization of language in the digital realm" (2008). The digital turn might in fact mark the point at which these forms have ceased to be avant-garde, as moving letters, inventive typography, integrated imagery, and even nonlinearity are common aspects of everyday textuality in contemporary media ranging from television to the Web. The same motion graphic techniques that are used to create a digital poem might be used for instance to sell an automobile or advertise a restaurant's menu. While Mallarmé and Marinetti's approaches to poetry may have shocked the audiences of their day, contemporary digital poets are simply accessing and engaging with a contemporary vernacular of letters moving in space. Given the comparative ease of achieving multimedia effects on contemporary computers, it is no surprise that many poets have integrated visual imagery, motion graphics, sound, computational effects, and interactivity into their practice.

During the 1960s, working at Bell Labs, Kenneth C. Knowlton worked with artists Lillian F. Schwartz and Stan VanDerBeek in producing a number of computer-animated works including the *PoemField* series (Knowlton and VanDerBeek, 1966). The computer graphics/poetry videos were produced in BEFLIX, a bespoke domain-specific language for computer animation that Knowlton developed at Bell Labs. The videos use the computer to bring together some basic text animation, flickering light fields, and instrumental and computer music, often to psychedelic effect. Marc Adrian's *Computer Texts* (1968) used randomly selected elements not only at the level of words but also at the level of typography. The program pulled texts from a database and delivered its texts to a grid. The words varied in size and were sometimes layered on top of each other. Adrian produced computer poems not only to be printed but also developed a way for the computer to print directly onto film (Funkhouser, 2007, p. 95). During this period a number of concrete poets also migrated from print to video formats. E. M. de Melo e Castro's abstract video poem *Roda Lume* (*Wheel of Fire*) (1968) is one influential example, produced using video equipment at Rádio Televisão Portuguesa (RTP) studios.

Digital tools such as word processing and image manipulation programs had an effect on the production of static works of concrete and visual poetry as well as kinetic or dynamic works. Funkhouser points to Lillian Schwartz and Ken Knowlton's "Observances" (1969), a printed poem that layers an abstracted face onto a page of text by altering the contrast through the weight of the printed text – perhaps the first example of ASCII art. Funkhouser observes that the work uses the computer as a tool to "extend the level of the ideogram to the pictographic" (Funkhouser, 2007, p. 104). More recent works such as David Daniels' *Gates of Paradise* (2000) extended the type of concretist shape poetry produced earlier with typewriters even further due to the more precise control of typography and layout rendered possible by the computer. Daniels said that "no one could write the shapes I write without a computer" (Daniels et al., 2004). Computation and digital media tools have become essential means of production even for concrete and visual poets producing work specifically intended for the print media environment.

Eduardo Kac's "Holopoetry," produced during the 1980s and 90s, provides another take on expanding the vocabulary of concrete poetry and exploring the materiality of text as a "photonic" object. Some of his holopoems were produced via conventional holographic photography, with later examples produced through computer generated 3D graphics. Kac describes holopoetry as an exploration of "motion, displacement, and metamorphosis" (Kac, 2007, p. 65). His hologram poems are kinetic in the sense that as the reader moves around the hologram in 3D space, the positioning and materiality of the letters and words, and their relations to each other also move and change. In "Maybe then, if only as" (1993) as the reader moves around the hologram, letters in words such as "where, here, we, are, were" shift in and out of the given words, reformulating our understanding of the poetic "line" when it is functioning as a cluster of words, floating in space, different from every angle. Richard Kostelanetz also created holopoetry, but outside of Kac's practice (and due not in small part to the complexity of the technical process) holopoetry did not become a widespread genre, though it has served as inspiration for later digital poetry that traffics in 3D typography, such as works developed for CAVE environments.

During the 1980s and early 1990s, kinetic poetry made the transition from print and film to computer screen in a number of different contexts and languages, with significant kinetic poetry being produced by writers and artists such as Silvestre Pestana (Portugal), Roger Laufter, Michel Bret, Jacques Donguy, and Tibor Papp (France), Marco Fraticelli, bpNichol, and Geoff Huth (Canada), Ana Maria Uribe (Columbia) and João Coelho (Brazil), among others. The French journal *alire*, first published by the L.A.I.R.E collective of Philippe Bootz, Tibor Papp, Frédéric Develay, Jean-Marie Dutey and Claude Maillard in 1988, was an important venue in the history of French digital poetry, with a number of its issues featuring kinetic poems (poèmes animés) and inventive use of computational techniques in their production.

As personal computers became more available to artists and writers, software platforms were increasingly important to establishing the range of formal qualities available to authors of kinetic and interactive digital poetry. In some cases, discourse communities and affiliations of writers and artists formed around particular platforms as much or more than they formed around any particular aesthetic or ideological agenda.

Kinetic and interactive poetry in technological context

The evolution of forms of kinetic and interactive poetry is deeply related to the development of the multimedia capacities of the contemporary computer. We can see shifts in the types of kinetic and interactive poetry that writers and artists have created that roughly correspond to the history of human computer interfaces and to the adoption and popularity of particular software platforms – for example BASIC, HyperCard, Shockwave, Flash, and Processing. This section will situate digital poetry from a platform studies perspective and explore the extent to which we can consider genres of kinetic and interactive poetry to be technologically determined by the constraints and affordances of the platforms used to create them. As discussed in the introduction to this volume, platform studies provide a useful tool set for the analysis of digital poetry, because individual platforms have built-in constraints and affordances that to some extent limit and shape literary practices produced within them.

BASIC

BASIC is a computer programming language originally developed during the 1960s, intended to be easy-to-use and to initiate computer users into the procedural logic of coding. It may seem difficult to believe now, in our contemporary age of computers as sleek user-friendly consumer devices, but when personal computers were first marketed to the public, there was an expectation that people who purchased computers would also want to learn to program computers themselves. I can still remember when I first used a computer at my junior high school during the early 1980s. The first thing we were taught to do was not to play games, or to use word processors or PowerPoint, but to write simple programs in BASIC. There are few of my generation of computer users who do not remember writing a loop program that would fill the screen with our own names, scrolling endlessly past the cursor.

bpNichol's *First Screening: Computer Poems* (1984) is a set of twelve kinetic poems Nichol produced on an Apple IIe computer using the Apple BASIC programming language. bpNichol distributed the work on his own imprint (Underwhich) in 100 numbered and signed copies on 5.25-inch floppy disks. After bpNichol's death, *First Screening* was the subject of a remarkable archival project put together by Jim Andrews, Geof Huth, Lionel Kearns, Marko Niemi, and Dan Waber. In their introduction to the project, the authors write "O ye digital poets: the past of the art is in your hands and it is you who must recover and maintain it" (Andrews et al., 2007). The project demonstrates one of the principal challenges of electronic literature: works are produced within platforms that are not fixed and unchanging. Digital poetry depends on software and hardware platforms that are subject to rapid cycles of obsolescence. The *First Screening* project represents an effort to use multiple archival strategies to assure that the work is not lost. The project includes a video file walkthrough of the work, an emulated version (simulating the actual conditions of the Apple II original), a JavaScript version, and a HyperCard version. The HyperCard version is at this point virtually impossible to run directly. It was ported from the Apple II BASIC version in 1992 by J. B. Hohm, which kept the work in circulation through the 1990s. Unlike codex books, most forms of electronic literature require migration from media to media and platform to platform in order to survive.

First Screening provides evidence of the fact that even under very limiting platform constraints, poets can achieve kinetic effects that have significant semantic and aesthetic impact. *First Screening* is enlivened by bpNichol's wit and wordplay, expressing itself through moving text. Several of the poems make use of simple looping effects. In "Islands" one single-spaced repetition of the word "ROCK" is surrounded on both sides by a double-spaced line of three repetitions of the word "WAVE." The scrolling effect creates a visual sense of approaching and subsiding waves and the isolation of the island. In "<u>sun</u>" the word "SUN" first rises over an underscore with the text "(field)" beneath it in the center of the screen. The word "HOE" then moves from right to left across the screen. By spacing one space back after each two spaces forward, the word replicates a hoeing motion. As it moves through the underscore, the "HOE" is transformed into "HOE rizon." In "OFF-SCREEN ROMANCE" the words "FRED" and "GINGER" dance about the screen, sometimes closely and other times coming apart. The dancing motion makes it clear that the words reference Fred Astaire and Ginger Rogers. Each of the twelve poems in the suite explores, in a different way, how motion can be used to achieve wordplay effects. While BASIC is a very limited programming language that did not provide for complex typographic effects, *First Screening* demonstrates that even such a limited tool can provide for a great variety of approaches to animating poetry.

HyperCard

Apple released HyperCard in 1987. It shipped free with all Mac computers sold at the time and was one of the main selling points of the Mac. The application was designed to bring the power of scripted behaviors to average computer users who did not have any prior programming skills. HyperCard was fundamentally a database program, but one with a flexible and graphical interface that could be modified by users. HyperCard included its own scripting language, HyperTalk. Users could essentially use HyperCard to develop their own applications. While most users produced simple "stacks" at the level of recipe catalogs and rolodexes, those who dipped more deeply into HyperTalk could develop more sophisticated applications. If HyperCard was essentially a hypertext system (as discussed in chapter 3), its extensibility made it attractive to visual and language artists working with computation as well. HyperCard was popular during the late 1980s and 1990s, but Steve Jobs dropped development of the project after 2000, and Apple completely abandoned it after 2004. HyperCard was nevertheless influential on subsequent computer user interfaces, including the first browsers for the World Wide Web. Features like bookmarks, history, tables, graphics, and extensible coding were present in HyperCard before they became standard features of web browsers. Although HyperCard's graphics capabilities were limited by those of the systems on which it was designed to run and it did not include motion graphics capabilities, later versions of HyperCard did allow for video and for more sophisticated programming effects. Several of CD-ROM publisher Voyager's electronic book projects, such as their version of Art Spiegelman's *MAUS* (1994), were produced in HyperCard.

A number of digital poets, such as Jim Rosenberg, Jean-Pierre Balpe, Eduardo Kac, and others experimented with using HyperCard for digital poetry. John Cayley's early works are among the most influential works of kinetic poetry produced in the platform. Cayley's works often merge kinetic elements with sophisticated computational effects. His *Windsound* (1999), originally developed in HyperCard, was the winner of the 2001 Electronic Literature Award for Poetry. *Windsound* is a meditative poem that runs as a 23-minute text movie experience. The work is a play between the author's own reflections and his translation of a Song period classical Chinese lyric, "Cadence: Like a Dream" by Qin Guan (1049–1100). *Windsound* makes use of a technique the author described as "transliteral morphing" (Cayley, 2006). Heather McHugh (2001), judge of the 2001 Electronic Literature Award, described the technique: "Material both visual and vocal, both structural and semantic, is constantly dissolving and re-solving, and giving rise to a host of readerly impressions. Fields of floating phonemes and morphemes sometimes seem to assemble into patterns – form meaningful phrases and sentences – only to morph away again, before our ears and eyes." In this case, the kinetic aspect of the work is not that the letters move about in the space of the screen, but instead that they move iteratively through letters toward new phrases with new meaning. The movement is one of language rising to the surface, becoming intelligible, fading away and rebuilding itself anew. *Windsound* is not primarily concerned with the movement of letters in space, but instead the movement of letters toward and away from intelligibility. In the original version of the work, the transliteral morphs and textual transitions were generated differently with each run of the program. HyperCard was well suited to Cayley's work at the time, primarily because of its extensibility, which enabled him to develop some fairly complex scripted behaviors and run them within the HyperCard application. Some aspects of multimedia, such as text-to-speech, were also integrated within the work.

HyperCard was better for scripting than fluid animation. Timeline-based platforms would ultimately be more important for the majority of digital poets specifically concerned with text animation in the late 1990s and 2000s.

Director, Shockwave and Flash

Director, Shockwave, and Flash share a common lineage as multimedia software platforms. These tools share in common a timeline-based development environment, and are shaped around a movie-based production metaphor: the developer is positioned as the "director" of the application development. Macromedia (and subsequently Adobe) Director originated with a Mac application, Videoworks, in 1985. The program could produce black and white animations on the original Macintosh screens. In 1987 the product was rebranded as Director 1.0. In 1988, with the release of Director 2.2, a custom scripting language, Lingo, was added and the platform included a facility for extensibility via "Xtras." Before 1993, Director was solely an executable application development environment.

Director quickly became an industry standard for multimedia development. The majority of the multimedia CD-ROM games and other entertainment and educational multimedia titles produced for the Macintosh were developed using Director. In 1993, Macromedia released Shockwave Player, which made it possible to use Director to create multimedia applications for the Web. Director and Shockwave made for a powerful and feature-rich combination for early developers of multimedia web content, and a number of important digital poetry projects were produced in Shockwave format. At the same time the Director/Shockwave pairing had some significant drawbacks. The footprint of the Shockwave player itself was quite large, posing challenges during a period when bandwidth was typically much lower and download times much longer than they are today. Shockwave applications were also typically fairly large and required significant load times. Digital poetry pioneers such as Jim Andrews, Philippe Bootz, Simon Biggs, Geniwate, and William Poundstone produced much of their work in Shockwave.

Jim Andrews' *Nio* (2001) is an example of visual poetry produced in Shockwave that merged together a Lettrist approach to visual language, sound poetry, and interactivity. The work provides its "wreader" (Andrews' term) with a toolset for poetic exploration. No words are involved in the piece, but the wreader is invited to interact with elements including lettristic animations, sound files, and sequence. In the first verse of the piece, the wreader layers audio and animations. In the second, the wreader can both layer and sequence the animations. Though no representational language results from the process, the work produces a highly interactive aesthetic experience. In my experience of teaching electronic literature, *Nio* serves as an excellent boundary case, a clearly poetic work that pulls directly from avant-garde literary tradition while challenging conventional definitions of poetry.

At the time that *Nio* was produced, Director was the tool of choice for complex interactive multimedia work. It could not at that point have been produced using Flash. The competing (if owned by the same company) standard of Flash was released in 1996 after Macromedia acquired FutureWave Software and its FutureSplash software. Although as development environments Director and Flash were based essentially around the same filmic metaphors, Flash was developed more specifically with the Web in mind. Some Director features were sacrificed with Flash, but its footprint was much smaller, so both the Flash player and applications could be downloaded and interacted with more quickly. Later versions of Flash (from Flash 5 onward) also integrated ActionScript, allowing for scripting behaviors comparable to Lingo. Flash was stripped-down and lightweight in comparison to Director but its smaller footprint allowed for mass adoption as the World Wide Web took off. While both platforms were used throughout the 2000s and early 2010s, Flash took hold much more extensively as the tool of choice for web animation, digital art, and digital poetry. Adobe acquired both Director and Flash, but over the course of the 2000s gradually shifted the focus of their development efforts to Flash.

Like Director, Flash was based on a timeline model, featuring a stage, keyframes, and "tween" animations of vector-based graphics. Tweens allow animators to quickly define transitions without actually having to draw the frames in between, vastly reducing the amount of effort required to produce an animation. Salter and Murray note that Flash changed not only the practice of creating animations for the Web, but our cultural expectations of animation in a broader sense: "The accessible metaphor of the timeline, with its reliance on keyframes and processing rather than labor and data-intensive methods of traditional animation, transformed the expectations associated with both production and distribution of animation" (Salter and Murray, 2014, p.41). One attraction of Flash was its cross-browser and cross-platform compatibility. As long as the Flash plugin was installed, designers didn't need to worry about accommodating browser-specific standards in order to achieve the effects they desired. Flash was very much a visual-designer-oriented tool. Rather than sketching a prototype that would look different when implemented on different browsers, designers could simply design their work once: as long as Flash was running, their work would look essentially the same regardless of which browser implemented it.

Flash was a popular tool among poets schooled in concrete poetry who wanted to move into creating work for digital media (a fairly instinctive step in a form concerned with representing letters in transition). Tweening and other designer-friendly tools built into Flash made the leap from visual poet to kinetic poet a rather short hop – no formal training in animation was required to set letters moving in space. If hypertext fiction was the most prominent genre during the 1990s, the decade of the 2000s was dominated by kinetic poetry produced in Flash. The *Electronic Literature Collection, Volume One*, published in 2006, included 26 works developed in Flash out of a total of 60 works in the volume.

In their book on Flash, Anastasia Salter and John Murray note that when new media artists and authors used Flash, they often "took the affordances of the platform and the expectations users brought to Flash works and subverted them, or broke out of the affordances and created new systems for their art" (Salter and Murray, 2014, p. 15). Because Flash was quickly and widely adopted across the Web for the production of banner ads and commercial pop-up animations, early on the platform was associated with advertising and other "flashy" and often superficial forms of engagement: eye candy. While some poets leapt into this emerging visual vernacular of the commercial Web, others chose to go against the grain of those expectations.

Although ActionScript coding allowed for a greater range of interactive behaviors in later Flash work, many of the most-referenced works of digital poetry are non-interactive works that make more basic use of the timeline and animation. Brian Kim Stefans' *The Dreamlife of Letters* (2000) (presented by "reptilian neolettrist graphics") is a Flash piece very much in line with a concrete poetry/Lettrist tradition. Stefans produced the poem by processing an essay written by poet and feminist literary theorist Rachel Blau DuPlessis. Stefans first alphabetized DuPlessis' text and then reconstructed that word list into a series of concrete poems. Unsatisfied with these poems in a static representation, he then animated the series together as a Flash poem that runs as an 11-minute Flash poetry film. The strength of the work lies in Stefan's recognition of the power of movement of letters within the two-dimensional space of the screen itself as a device for clever wordplay and thought-provoking arbitrary juxtapositions of words. The letters in the piece, composing words derived from a text concerned with gender and the imagination, seem to have their own Freudian dream lives, rife with double-entendre. In comparison to many works of digital poetry, *The Dreamlife of Letters* is both technically simple and stylistically austere, but by carefully limiting his use of multimedia effects, Stefans invites a more concentrated focus on how the movement of letters can carry as much metaphoric weight as the semantic intent of the words they form together.

Young-Hae Chang Heavy Industries' (YHCHI) poems similarly use a very limited set of Flash's capabilities in a highly effective way. The two artists in the collective, Young-Hae Chang and Marc Voge, use the capabilities of Flash primarily to sync texts (usually black text on white backgrounds) with musical soundtracks. Texts are usually displayed as single words or short phrases shown in quick succession in a single typeface in a large font. The use of typographic effects is minimal and controlled, but the pace at which the words are displayed is often very rapid, pushing at the limits of how quickly we can read and absorb the meaning of the words. Though the actual movement of letters on the screen as individual objects is comparatively minimal, the speed of jump cuts between words and phrases, in concert with energetic jazz soundtracks, produces a sense of hyperkinesis and a nearly overloaded field of verbal and visual information. In her essay on YHCI's *Dakota* (2002), Jessica Pressman notes that YHCHI resist "the alignment of electronic literature with hypertext, evade reader-controlled interactivity, and favor the foregrounding of text and typography, narrative complexity, and an aesthetic of difficulty" (Pressman, 2014. p. 81). Pressman reads *Dakota* in the context of its relationship to Ezra Pound's *The Cantos* I and II (1934), itself in part an adaptation of Book 11 of the *Odyssey*. In *Dakota*, Odysseus' journey to the underworld is recast as a drunken teenage road trip, with Elvis playing the part of Tiresias. Pressman claims that in reinterpreting Pound in new media, YHCHI "lay claim to an ancient cultural past as scaffolding to support a contemporary literary moment and recuperate the relevance of literature in it" (p. 316) in the same way as Pound used an ancient text to make a claim for the relevance of his modernist approach. Although *Dakota* rejects interactivity, multilinearity, or particularly flashy visual effects, it manages to engage readers in spite of (or perhaps because of) this limited technical range. The words, the sound, and pace of the piece are enough to redirect and focus attention more powerfully than a work that uses multiple modalities to pull the reader's attention in other directions might have.

The years of what Manovich (2002) called "Generation Flash" brought animation conventions and heightened interactive multimodality to the Web, but forums on the Web also brought creative community to the software platform and a sharing economy that resulted in the transmission not only of ideas but also of visual and interactive effects across sectors. Designers, marketers, coders, and artists working with Flash shared snippets of code on bulletin boards, discussed works-in-progress, developed tutorials, and so forth. The Flash community that developed wasn't so much about any kind of shared artistic, economic, or aesthetic agenda as it was about the affordances of the platform itself. Donna Leishman describes the networked community as "instrumental in fostering a particular state of creative mind. For Flash it provided a simultaneously discursive and practical open sharing of ideas and code… in principle free from geographic politics and/or the traditional logistics of production and distribution" (Leishman, 2012).

For about a decade, digital poetry and Flash went hand in glove. Kinetic and interactive poetry also did a great deal to bring attention to electronic literature outside of academic communities and into broader visual arts and design contexts. In comparison to genres such hypertext, poetry generators, or interactive fiction, kinetic and interactive poetry are more amenable to gallery display and exhibition. The balance of digital poems produced in Flash are perceived as visual artworks as much as they are read for the semantic content of the words or letters with which they are composed. Many Flash poems are also brief and linear, which makes them more readily appreciable in a short period of time.

During its relatively short active life on the Web (2000–04), the online journal *Poems That Go*, edited by Ingrid Ankerson and Megan Sapnar, had a significant impact. More than 50 digital poems, the majority of them produced in Flash, were published in the journal. The works collected there demonstrate a broad range of approaches to using Flash software in the production of kinetic poetry.

During the first couple of years of *Poems That Go*'s existence the majority of the works published were essentially non-interactive, often merging moving text with soundtracks and representational imagery. *Murmuring Insects* (2002) is representative of a number of poems in the journal that used existing texts as a basis and recontextualized them through design elements. The text of *Murmuring Insects* is a translation of a poem by Otagaki Rengetsu (1791–1875). The text includes three brief sections: air, earth, and water, and the text of the three sections together reads: "In the sky/ flocks of departing geese/ In the weeds/ murmuring insects/ tears like dew/ well up in my eyes." On the title page the work is described as being "in memory." Ingrid Ankerson's design reframes the 200-year-old text, and the resulting kinetic poem is a lament. Produced immediately after the 9/11 terrorist attacks, the poem integrates audiovisual elements from television news reports of the event and layered images, such as one of the twin towers at the moment one of the planes struck, and the face of a fireman. In the "water" section of the poem, the words "tears like dew" in the shape of the fireman's eye transform into "well up in my eyes" and then fall to form an image of the moon in the sky. The visual presentation of the poem, the movement of words in space, and the integrated media elements lend the poem a powerful contemporary affect it would not have if simply read on the page.

Interactive elements became more prominent in later issues of the journal, although for the most part interactivity was used in a subdued and controlled way. *Breathing/Secret of Roe* (2003) is a two-part video poem with a depressive side and a manic side. Both poems obliquely describe a traumatic event in the life of the poem's focalized speaker. The soundtracks, images, and the presentation of the texts of the two parts of the poem underscore the mood of each section. In the first section of the poem, "Breathing," we are presented with a minimally decorated white screen. On the left side of the page, we see a half-visible outlined shape of a woman standing next to a doorway, while on the left side of the screen we see blurred and shimmering lines of a poem, which are unreadable until we mouse over them, one line at a time. Both the content of the soundtrack and the legibility of the text are determined by where the reader positions the mouse. If we position the mouse over the doorway, we hear an echoing whisper of a man's voice, though what he is saying is impossible to discern. As we move the cursor to the individual lines of text to bring them into focus and make them legible, an ominous soundtrack plays. The lines of the poem themselves, such as "I am in the wrong place room city / she isn't really reading / suddenly my life tilts," describe a depressive personality. Beneath the image of the woman on the far-left side of the window, words cycle at a high speed one at a time, together reading, "sometimes you are the only truth." There is a sharp contrast between this hyperkinetic line flickering past and the lines on the right that we must slowly bring into focus. When the reader moves the mouse over it, the line links to the second part of the poem, "Secret of Roe." This part of the poem is a manic composition. The same image of the girl's body appears but this time in front of her, one man is restraining another, in a fight or perhaps a seizure. The soundtrack includes a driving electronic rhythm, and an echoing voice reading the poem in an urgent voice. Text from the lines of the poem flickers rapidly in two separate layers and fonts on the screen, challenging legibility and producing a sense of violent rupture that corresponds to the fevered energy of the poem itself.

The interactive sound capabilities of Flash are also represented by several poems in a later issue of the journal. *[soundpoems]* (2002) by Jörg Piringer and *Conversations* (2002) by Jason Nelson are each concrete poems in the form of interactive sound mixing devices. Piringer's piece includes two sound poem devices. In "Interactive soundpoem one" the user pulls small red tokens, each representing a sound, into boxes on the screen, sequencing phoneme-sized clips of sounds including k!, ch, uh, ür, um, bi, me, and rr into a composition. In the first poem these sounds are machine generated.

"Interactive sound poem two" is similar, except that the user selects boxes to sequence sounds produced by human vocalization, and the sounds can be changed and reversed (e.g. ax, xa, to, ot). Neither poem approaches comprehensible language in total though both devices encourage interaction with sounds that can be extracted from human language. In Nelson's *Conversations*, spoken language can be understood, but the voice tracks are set up to layer on top of one another, mimicking the sort of nearly understandable cacophony of overheard conversation in a crowded room. The user mixes eight voice tracks, each of which are segments of interviews concerning topics including injuries, robots, and consumer products. The user controls both the comparative volume and the left-to-right stereo placement of the sound. As in many of Nelson's works, the imagery and icons used as controls for the piece are playfully absurdist.

María Mencía also worked with the audio capabilities of Flash to explore interactive sound poetry and intermodal practices. Her *Birds Singing Other Birds' Songs* (2001) provides sound mixing capabilities and merges typographic concrete poetry with sound that explores linguistic communication without using actual words. In this case, the sounds of eight birds were transcribed and then sung by human voices. Hitting the play buttons on any one of the eight tracks both launches the audio loop and sends a typographic animation of the transcription of the birdsong flying across the screen in the shape of the bird whose song it represents. The work provides us with a beautiful and playful meditation on the different types of signification involved in our linguistic engagement with the natural world.

Flash was a flexible platform that enabled poets who were not necessarily proficient in coding to work with animation and media elements on a comparatively simple timeline interface. Works produced in Flash emphasized visual design elements and interface design, and a time-based approach. Flash however had a number of built-in constraints. The program separated source files (in editable FLA format) and playable output (in SWF format), so critics and other readers of digital poetry are by default unable to look "under the hood" to see how the work was constructed. This is particularly important in the electronic literature community, where writers often learn methods and technique by studying others' source code. Flash was a proprietary standard, which makes it difficult to port out to other formats. Finally, Flash had a number of security vulnerabilities, and a number of current browsers block Flash files by default. Adobe is in the process of completely abandoning support for the Flash format. Although as of this writing, users can override browser settings to enable the Flash player, it is quite likely that within a matter of a few years, a great deal of kinetic poetry produced in Flash format will be obsolete and inaccessible, creating a large gap in the archive.

Processing

Processing is a non-proprietary platform that some authors have used to produce digital poetry. Processing is an open-source programming language with an integrated development environment. First initiated in 2001 by Casey Reas and Benjamin Fry, the platform was developed specifically with the electronic arts in mind and intended to teach artists the fundamentals of computer programming for a visual context. Processing offers authors the ability to quickly preview the work while they are developing it, to export to a number of different formats, and to extend the platform with a wide variety of libraries, such as Daniel Howe's RiTa library for working with natural language in programmable media. Processing.js is a related project that allows authors to write code in Processing, which can then be interpreted in JavaScript and displayed easily on the Web. A more recent project, p5.js is a complete reinterpretation of Processing in JavaScript. Because Processing is open-source software with a large user base, works produced in the platform will likely not have the same preservation issues as those produced in Flash. Processing is also designed with easy code sharing in mind, making it easier for artists to learn from each other's work.

Although not as much digital poetry has yet been developed in Processing as in Flash, some significant works have been produced using the platform. Mary Flanagan's *[theHouse]* (2006) is one example of a poem that takes advantage of 3D capabilities of Processing in a spatialized text work. The text of *[theHouse]* is written on cube-shaped "rooms" which emerge to create "houses" among the intermingling texts. The subject of the poem itself is a relationship between two people that is coming apart within the confined environment of a shared domestic space. The reader interacts with and realigns the texts in a type of physical struggle that echoes the interpersonal struggle described in the text of the poem.

Peter Cho's *Wordscapes & Letterscapes* (2002) are two sets of 26 pieces each, which the author describes as "typographic landscapes." Both are gems of clever design and typographic wit. In *Wordscapes*, we select a letter of the alphabet circulating in the space of the screen before us. Each letter connects to a short sketch based on a word beginning with the letter we select. The sketches are interactive – as we move the cursor, the word forms react to our touch. The interaction of each piece is based on a playful presentation of the word selected: As we move the cursor we sail through the sky with "Aloft," as we navigate "Vanish," the letters hide and fade before our eyes, "Worry" presents us with pulsing lines reminiscent of vertigo, and

"Xenophobia" attempts to avoid our cursor at all costs. The companion work *Letterscapes* is similar but even more granular. The letters here are encountered as entities in their own right, but our interactions with the letterforms pull them out of their usual composition – they break into 3D objects of diverse geometries.

Works of kinetic poetry produced in Processing are emblematic of a wider trend in digital poetry: poets creating work in digital media have been drawn increasingly closer to the code. Flash was essentially a designer's platform. Although some coding was often involved in the form of ActionScript, the development interface was largely intended as a design tool for non-coders. Processing is intended conversely to bring artists in at the level of code and increase their programming competency. Processing is also popular for digital poets working with physical computing, as it can fluidly communicate with Arduino. This increasing procedural literacy will likely result in a more dynamic field that produces works that will be easier to port and to archive.

HTML5, CSS, Canvas, JavaScript

While text animation and motion graphics were not only produced in Director or Flash, during the 1990s and 2000s drawing and animation were not possible directly in HTML. Shockwave and Flash players were necessary plug-ins in order to experience works produced in Flash and Director. That changed with the release of HTML5 in 2014. Using the Canvas element, CSS, and JavaScript libraries such as textillate.js, animate.js, and lettering.js, many of the text animation effects of Flash are now accessible to digital poets working in HTML, and video and audio are now supported directly in HTML. As Adobe has abandoned its development and support of Flash, digital poets are also migrating to the Web's core open standards. Award-winning electronic literature authors who made their name producing work in the Flash platform, such as Alan Bigelow and Jason Nelson, have migrated to HTML and JavaScript. Although Director and Flash were hugely important in terms of bringing interactivity and polished design to kinetic poetry on the Web, the move from Flash to open standards bodes well for the future of the genre. Work based on open standards is not tethered to a corporate agenda that can result in an entire platform becoming abandoned and make the work more difficult to access and preserve. Open standards also typically result in open code, in the sense that critics and other authors can access and read both the surface text and the code that underlies it.

Reading through platforms

I've provided an introduction to kinetic poetry in relation to the platforms in which the works were developed. This is in some ways an arbitrary way to organize a discussion of kinetic poetry, as the platforms used to produce digital poetry do not have a strictly determinative effect on their content or style. As evidenced by the discussion of Flash works above, within any given platform there is potential for a great range of approaches. But platforms do constrain the *range* of multimedia and interactive capabilities available to the digital poet. More limited capabilities do not necessarily negatively affect the quality of the work. In terms of the reader's engagement with the text of a given poem, more limited registers of information may in fact shift the focus of the reader's attention from a configurative mode (in which the bulk of attention is focused on navigating an innovative or challenging interface) to an interpretative mode (in which the reader's attention is focused on the writing and its interaction with space, time, the user's feedback, and the interface).

The impact of platforms on the work of digital poets is cultural as much as it is technological. Design ideas, techniques, libraries, and bits of code shared within the communities that form around particular platforms have effects on the look and feel of work produced by members of those communities and so often affect common visual styles and modes of interaction within a contemporaneous period. From the standpoint of preservation, whether a platform is open or proprietary may be the most important factor as to whether or not poems produced within it can survive.

Balancing movement and interactivity in digital poetry

Chris Funkhouser distinguishes between "projected" kinetic poetry – in which the movement of letters and words and their interaction within the audiovisual environment of the work are the site of the aesthetic experience of the work, and "participatory representational strategies" (Funkhouser, 2012, p. 14) which demand not only the readers' attention, but also their input to configure the system, or even to write its text. Although interaction and interface innovations have certainly been important for kinetic poetry, interactivity is nevertheless absent in many of the most celebrated works of digital poetry. Some works in fact grapple with problems that negotiating an interface can pose for poetry – while interactivity itself becomes a form of meaning-making, in some cases interaction can pull attention away from the intent of the language.

Some quite minimalist kinetic poems are among the most effective. *Ah* (2002) by K. Michel and Dirk Vis ruminates on time, Einstein, and the way that idle moments of wandering thought might bring about certain types of epiphanies. For the most part, we encounter the text as a single line, scrolling rapidly to the left off our screen and out of our field of vision. As the words move across the screen, they cross over and occlude one another. Periodically however the line will break and "ahs," "ohs," "lalas," and other ambiguous expressions of the thought process will break out of the line and float in arcs across a wider visual field. While the line strings together lucid ponderings on physics and the psychology of closure, what the poem does most effectively is demonstrate how words moving silently through space can non-verbally effectuate the rhythms, flow, and stuttering of the human thought process. Subtitled "shower song," the poem is a visual representation of thoughts surfacing and wending their way through the mind.

Stephanie Strickland and Cynthia Lawson Jaramillo's *slippingglimpse* (2007) is an often-cited example of interactive kinetic poetry in which the movement of the text is mapped onto "chreods" on background videos – patterns in the water, representing feedback loops between the poem text, the image capture technology, and the patterns in the waves. The lines of the poems themselves are excerpted from interviews with artists who use digital image capture in their practice, woven in with texts discussing earlier image capture technologies. N. Katherine Hayles considered *slippingglimpse* in terms of "the non-conscious agent forming a creative coupling with human consciousness" (Hayles, 2008, p. 23), understanding the resulting process as one of distributed cognition. As many of the texts themselves describe relationships between humans and their digital tools, the machine reading of the chreods underscores the text's concern with those symbiotic relationships.

David Jhave Johnston's work is disarmingly uncanny, driven by a set of attractions he outlines in his theoretical work *Aesthetic Animism: Digital Poetry's Ontological Implications* (2016): Jhave defines digital poetry less formally and more conceptually as "a memory resource unit (inducing long-term potentiation from the cruft and spam of experience), GPU-accelerated lyricism (multimedia lamentations and celebrations), compression utility (compressing narratives into epiphanies), and translation algorithm (converting the cultural heritage of bards into interactive and generative formats)" (p. 4). Many of his works weave together video, animated typography, and generative text. Jhave is interested in a kind of animism in which texts are animated not merely in the sense of moving on the screen, but in themselves taking on some of the characteristics of living organisms interacting with other beings and objects. Jhave merges modalities in a way that he describes as TAVIT, "Text-Audio-Visual Interactivity," such that the interaction between these elements makes them impossible to consider separately from each other.

In *Sooth* (2005), a series of six interactive poetry videos, Jhave meditates on both the lyrical and the ecological in a set of works that are both about human relationships and about human relationships to the environment. The adulatory poems of *Sooth* are addressed from the poet to his lover in what seems a classical lyric subjectivity. The texts of the *Sooth* poems are overlaid on beautiful moving images of nature (e.g. ferns rustling in the wind, human bodies that in soft focus resemble a desert landscape, flowing water, or a fish moving underwater) and intimate images of the human form. The texts interact with the videos both in terms of their relation on the screen and in response to the reader's physical interaction with the text. The lines of poetry move in concert with the video images, for example swirling with the running water in "Root." Rita Raley observes that the relationships between media elements are "less contingent and more structurally and logically motivated" and so constitute "a distinctive media ecology" (Raley, 2011, p. 886). The interactions in the work, including those described in the poet's paean to his lover, those between the interactor's touch and the surfaces of the work, and those between the text and the landscapes of the poem, eventually transcend relationships between individual people and suggest a philosophy of the human's ecological intertwinement with the environment. The text of "Snow" reads "one merges into one/ uniqueness dissolves/ we are with ourselves/ absorptive particulates/ osmotic unions/ others identical to our own." Raley identifies these lines with both a breakdown of functional distinctions between media elements and a rejection of the anthropocentric idea that the human perspective is the only essential one.

Norwegian author Ottar Ormstad migrated his Lettristic concrete poetry practice from print to digital media. Since the mid-2000s Ormstad has produced animations, films and, with Taras Mashtalir, live performances that merge concrete poetry with time-based art. Ormstad often puts letters and words in cross-language play, as in *Lyms* (1999) where words in Spanish, French, German, English, and Scandinavian languages build up from their first letters, and are slowly grouped together by their shapes as visual forms rather than by their semantic intent. In Ormstad's collaborations with Taras Mashtalir (as half of the "OTTARAS" duet), liveness and sound performance become key aspects of the work, as Mashtalir live-mixes audio and video elements with Ormstad's readings of his poems, which themselves are musical elements, vocalizations more intended to be heard and experienced than scanned for meaning. The video elements of letters appearing and moving in space and forming words or word-like collections of letters are often grouped with atmospheric background video. In *Long Rong Song* (2015) and *Navn Nome Name* (2016) words with similar structures come together and are read together on the basis of their shape and sound.

In *Pentimento* (2012) by Jerome Fletcher, interaction with the poem takes place via a "scratching" behavior. The reader's action is one both of erasure and revelation. By peeling away layers of images, the reader reveals fragments of text and image as in a palimpsest. Bits of narrative about a famous artist and an act of betrayal, in addition to single words, are revealed and scraped away. The interaction in a way suggests the formation and passing of thought, or memory, or writing. The journey of the text is not one toward resolution, but constant movement of thought as a kind of ceaseless labor, each fragment being scraped away toward another without ever becoming completely established.

Many works of interactive poetry are concerned explicitly with the nature of human-machine interaction and with the contingencies of creation in a technologically mediated environment. Philippe Bootz's *Small Uncomfortable Reading Poems* (in French, *Petits Poèmes à Lecture Inconfortable*) (2012) is a set of four poems that meditates on the problems and frustrations of human/machine interface by providing the reader with tools that make reading the poems difficult or even impossible. In "brush to dust/blow the fiction" the reader must continuously move the mouse to dust off a generated fiction, but the dust itself reappears at virtually the same speed, enabling the reader to access only a few words at a time. In "plane poem" the reader must use the mouse as if it were a carpenter's plane, uncovering the poem with each scrape, but the surface reconstitutes itself at an increasing speed, so the reader must plane continuously faster and faster in order to achieve any kind of legibility. In "a poem to stir" the reader must manipulate a kinetic poem that is hidden beneath a layer. The reader must create circles to make space the poem can be seen through, horizontal lines to provide energy to the poem's movement, and vertical lines to order the lines. The trouble is that while all of these movements are necessary in order for the poem to be read, they are impossible to do simultaneously. The set of poems together comprises a meditation on the difficult relationship between the ergodic activity of performing the interface and the noematic activity of reading and interpreting the poem.

Ian Hatcher carries forth both sound and kinetic poetry in performance works such as *Drone Pilot* (2015b) and *Prosthesis* (2013). Hatcher mixes a unique style of performance vocalization with interactive media poetry.

Hatcher has trained his voice to function in a particular monotone that sounds as if it is representing an uncanny computational presence: the voice of the machine, or in the case of *Drone Pilot*, the voice of a networked techno-military artificial intelligence. The kinetic aspects of Hatcher's works often involve information flows that push at the borders of intelligibility. Hatcher describes *Prosthesis* as concerned with "identity, artificiality, feedback loops, and the self as multiplicity" and *Drone Pilot* as "concerned with telepresence and systemic violence." Both works deal with the uncomfortable situation of the human within a societal apparatus increasingly dominated by automated systems and machine intelligence. In the kinetic poem *[]/[Total Runout]* (Hatcher, 2015a) text scrolls past vertically at an unreadable speed, while the horizontal visual field contracts and expands. At points the reader can pick out individual words, but the text moves too quickly for human language processing, and sometimes contracts to a narrow band of letters. It seems to represent the timescale of machine data processing rather than that of human reading. Álvaro Seiça observes that for a human reader "the work only permits a time-lapse reading, in that glimpses of letters, syllables and words emerge as perceptible entities, from time to time" (Seiça, 2018b, p. 268). Seiça performs a "deformative reading" on the work, modifying the code to slow down the movement of text in order to bring the work into human legibility. The texts Hatcher remixes include appropriated texts from a WikiLeaked manual by the UK Ministry of Defense and essays on artificial intelligence, as well as some of Hatcher's own text. When he performs *[]/[Total Runout]* as part of *Drone Pilot*, Hatcher is able to read at an extremely high speed and mimic the visual movement of the text on the screen, although he is actually reading different sections of the text than those that are being reshuffled in a randomized order on the screen. The net effect is a presentation of the human as entwined with and occupied by machine intelligence. The performer is presented as an embodiment of the posthuman, a cyborg inseparable from the networked computational environment.

Amaranth Borsuk and Brad Bouse's *Between Page and Screen* (2012) takes the form of an augmented book of poems composed of linguistically playful epistolary exchanges between P and S, Page and Screen. The work's introduction describes, "a series of letters written by two lovers struggling to map the boundaries of their relationship, do not exist on either page or screen, but in the augmented space between them opened up by the reader." The printed book includes simplified fiducial markers that work like QR codes. When readers load the Flash application and put the book in front of a webcam, they see the poems spring to life in the image shown on the screen of themselves with the book in their own hands. As readers move the pages of the book, the poems float in space and move with the page. The texts can be rotated on a 3D axis, can spin on the page, or zoom off into space toward the camera. Several of the poems, such as the poem "Circe" that is shaped like a pig, take conventions of concrete poetry into an interactive and haptic augmented reality environment.

Letters moving in space and time

Kinetic and interactive poetry provide clear examples of genres and practices that flow comparatively seamlessly from twentieth-century avant-garde writing movements into a technologically mediated present. The digital poetry corpus weaves various traditions ranging from concrete poetry to sound poetry and animated typography into a multimodal tapestry of new forms. We can see in digital poetry the aesthetic effects of a kind of democratization of media as poets access digital tools that enable them to engage with modalities beyond text and new methods to explore the poetic limits and capabilities of images, sound, time-based poetics, programmed processes, and interactivity. The movement from concrete poetry on the page to kinetic poetry on the screen has further migrated from the computer screen to mobile environments, augmented reality, and virtual reality. Kinetic and interactive poetry are often woven in to other genres of practice in electronic literature. In haptic works such as the 2014 Robert Coover Award-winning *P.o.E.M.M. (Poetry for Excitable [Mobile] Media)* cycle by Jason Lewis and Bruno Nadeau (2014) the movement of the poem responds expressively to the reader's touch. In chapter 7 we will discuss installations such as *Text Rain* (1999) by Romy Achituv and Camille Utterback and the CAVE work *Screen* (2003) by Noah Wardrip-Fruin, et al., in which kinetic text becomes responsive to the reader's own movement.

Perhaps we have always imagined our letters as objects, as material forms in constant movement, pulling themselves together into thoughts, words, and poems. Kinetic poetry enables us to see and experience this process, which has until now lived in our imaginations, before our very eyes.

6   Network Writing

Network writing is electronic literature created for and published on the Internet. It may require readers to visit multiple sites to experience the narrative, it may interrogate the nature and materiality of the network itself, it may use the Internet's potential for collaboration, or use the network as a site for performance.

For much of the world, networks are a condition of contemporary life. Their ubiquity has changed the nature of our communication, our styles of writing, and perhaps even the way that we structure our thought. A great deal of our contemporary written communication and social interaction is mediated on networks and shaped by networked interactions. Networks are both technological and social structures. For electronic literature, networks are both platform and material. As technology has led to rapid societal change, one of the most logical extensions of the project of electronic literature is to serve as a locus of reflexive critique of the position of the human within the technological apparatus.

Authors working in digital media are able to create critical digital media, which demonstrates the character and the problems of network society in ways that critical work or fiction in print could not: by embodying and simulating the effects of the network within the communication technologies of the network itself. This chapter will consider various practices of network writing that share an interest in the material properties of the global network and the writing environments it affords. While this constellation of practices is admittedly less squarely defined than some of the other genres addressed in the book, as it includes several subgenres with their own specific approaches to the network, there are clearly important strands of electronic literature that primarily engage with the architecture, code, and social structures of the network itself.

The Internet is a fully multimodal medium. Unless I change the default application settings on my mobile phone, when I open Facebook, video clips will launch themselves and start playing, with obnoxious audio tracks blaring full-blast as I scroll down the feed past them. The bells and whistles are in full effect. Video, audio, images, animations, various other elements increasingly compete for our attention, but the main component of our experience of the network nevertheless remains text. We compose and receive our emails and instant messages; we post our tweets and screeds on social networks. We read. We write.

There is no doubt that our immersion in this ocean of diverse textual forms has changed the nature of contemporary literacy. Reading and writing skills have not necessarily increased – certainly recent elections have provided ample evidence that critical reading skills may be on the wane, even as network-based political propaganda is on the rise. The fragmented and distracted nature of networked communication – continuous feeds and notifications chirping from multiple windows, on multiple devices – has in some ways degraded our experiences of reading and writing. One need not be a luddite or curmudgeon to recognize problems that networked communications pose: phatic likes in the place of developed interpersonal communication, memes in the place of reasoned argumentation, aimless browsing in the place of immersive reading, perhaps even dialogue with scripted bots in place of interaction of human interlocutors. Yet for all of the negative aspects of network discourse, a greater proportion of people spend more of their time writing and reading now than ever before.

The production and consumption of text has been radically democratized, even as vast multinational corporations, governments, and various ideological factions wrestle to profit from, influence, and instrumentalize the flows of network writing. We may or may not appreciate this new populist literacy, but we are called to better understand it. One of the roles of contemporary electronic literature is to provide us with self-conscious literary artifacts, processes, and performances that defamiliarize network-writing practices and provide us the critical distance necessary to better situate our own engagement with them. In this sense, many works of electronic literature can be understood as interventions.

This is not to say that most works of electronic literature are meant to serve as digitized critical theory. On the contrary, many works of electronic literature embrace the multimodal, distributed, and scattered nature of network discourse. Some projects have exploited the fact that the World Wide Web is not in effect a single channel in the creation of a type of work that Jill Walker (2005) described as "distributed narrative." Elements of a project might be located across different social networks or other websites and include narrative components situated in the physical world. Network writing also encompasses elements of what Christy Dena (2009) has described as *transmedia* narratives, storytelling endeavors that plant blogs, games, and social network activity across the network in support of a narrative that crosses between all of its media manifestations. Alternate reality games (ARGs) often also involve bits of writing, clues and puzzles that are spread across websites, bulletin boards, and social networks in support of games that suggest secret layers and plots hidden beneath surface reality. ARGs are not typically solved by individuals working alone, but by communities of players sharing clues and solutions online.

Rapid changes in *styles* of discourse are not only disruptive, they are also thrilling for writers, as they open arenas of creative practice. Electronic literature authors are presented with a plethora of new media environments, each with their own media constraints and affordances, idiosyncrasies and cultural contexts. And with each new medium they encounter, writers are given the opportunity to answer the question "But how do I write in it?" How can I write a time-based novel that unfolds over multiple email accounts? How can I write a simulation of a social movement that takes place on a social network? How can I use YouTube as a medium for poetry about how YouTube is shaping identity? How can I enable a collective performance through tweets? How would Melville retell *Moby Dick* if the only media at his disposal were filtered photos on Instagram? Literary encounters with network styles can be simultaneously critical and comic, as there are few things funnier than recognizing absurdity within our lived present.

Play is an essential aspect of electronic literature: that includes both playing with new media environments in order to explore their potential for storytelling and poetics, and perhaps even more importantly, playing well with others. The network enables modes of collaborative creation not easily achieved in literature made for print. One type of networked writing that exemplifies the collaborative potentialities of digital media is collective narrative: works that are written by groups of people operating together, taking advantage of networked communication technologies to create works, structured in a variety of different ways, which could not have been produced by any single individual alone but are instead the product of collective activity. Collective narratives have ranged from small groups working together within a shared narrative environment, such as *The Unknown*, attempts to develop novels written by large groups of people, such as *Invisible Seattle* (Seattle, 1983) or the wiki novel *A Million Penguins* (Mason and Thomas, 2007), database works that welcome input from readers, such as Judd Morrissey's *The Last Performance* (2007), and a number of "netprov" projects organized by Mark Marino, Rob Wittig, and others during the 2010s.

This chapter considers how twentieth-century art movements concerned with materiality, discourse networks, and collective writing anticipate some of the practices in network writing, before considering network styles and forms such as codework, Flarf, home page fictions, email novels, fictional blogs, Twitter fictions, online writing communities, collective narratives, netprov, and works of electronic literature that critique the power structures of the contemporary network itself.

Antecedents to network writing

Network writing shares concerns with a number of twentieth-century literary and artistic movements, emerging from modernism and postmodernism, which demonstrated an interest in interrogating the formal and technical qualities of the medium in which they were produced within the art object or work of writing itself. In modernist painting movements such as abstract expressionism, we saw a shift away from representation toward work that exploited the material properties of the materials used for their own effects. Jackson Pollock's action paintings were not about *depicting* anything through paint. They were about what happens when paint is cast onto the canvas with particular gestural movements: dribbles, splashes, smears, the application of human energy to pigments and canvas. The fact that these paintings are not representational enables the viewers to encounter them as objects and as images in a different way, one in which the materials, technologies, processes, and bodily actions involved in making the art object are foregrounded much more than any particular indexical referent or sensation.

In her *Writing Machines* (2002), N. Katherine Hayles proposed the term "technotext" to describe a work of writing that interrogates the inscription technology used to produce it. This would include for example artist books that interrogate the materiality of writing, such as Tom Phillips' *A Humument* (1970). Philips purchased a copy of an obscure 19th Century novel by William Mallock, *A Human Document*, using only the criteria that the book cost less than three pence, and then painstakingly "treated" the pages of the book by covering over most of the original text with images. The images serve to obscure portions of the previous text and to highlight others, developing a new text and narrative through the erasure of the old. The images however also develop and reveal the book as a platform for visual art with specific material properties of its own. On the book's first page, the uncovered text, joined by "rivers" of uncovered white space reads, "The following I sing a book a book of art of mind art and that which he hid I reveal." The creative act of Philips' work, of "revealing" what had always been a potential text within the untreated novel, is also that of encountering the book as an artistic object, rife with potential rerenderings. The page with words on it, when torn from its context as a page in a novel, is a radically different material than the blank page. While any two readers could read the same book and walk away with two different interpretations of the story, Philips' work (including multiple retreatments of the same page of the novel) suggests that every page of every book embeds a multiplicity of semantic networks that can be revealed by encountering the page as manipulable visual object.

Johanna Drucker's artist's books often play with the effects of typographic choice on the aesthetic and semantic experience of a given text. One page of her work *The Word Made Flesh* (1989) reads "The tongue lies on the table, writing, writhing, spelling out the breath of its efforts in an unseemly desire to be seen." The mixed typography includes an oversized "T" that might indeed suggest a tongue excised from a mouth and laid on a table, and emphasizes the fact that there is considerable distance between the word as thought, the word as spoken, and the word materialized through typography on the page. The printer's table, with type spread out upon it, is a site upon which meaning is wrestled with and contested. A designer can through book layout and typography radically change the nature and meaning of a text. Consider what might happen to the meaning of Hitler's *Mein Kampf* if it were printed as a series of aphorisms on Hallmark Greeting Cards, or Martin Luther King's "Letter from Birmingham Jail" if it was spelled out in a set of colorful children's blocks. By writing (in part) about inscription technologies, letters, and writing using inventive typography and letterpress printing, Drucker embodies in the art artifact the theoretical issues that her work wrestles with. In a number of forms of network writing, in particular "codework" by authors such as Mez, Talan Memmott, Alan Sondheim and Ted Warnell, electronic literature authors similarly engage with the technologies of inscription at their disposal – in this case technologies complicated by their multilayered nature as computer code – to wrestle with the ontology of digital writing.

We have previously (chapter 3) considered the relationship of hypertext and metafiction. Metafiction interrogates ideas of authorship, narrative structures, assumptions, materials, and traditions within fictions that navigate these concepts within their own frame. We also see the metafictional impulse within many forms of network writing, as authors interrogate the materiality of the network as both writing environment and social sphere. Talan Memmott framed much of his early work as "Network Phenomenology." He described this work as investigating "in hypermediated ficto-critical terms, the ways in which identity is constructed, desire conducted, language altered, and self extended through the network" (Memmott, 2011). Works such as *Lexia to Perplexia* (2000) and *Translucidity* (2001) operate less as fictions in any conventional sense than they do as critical interventions that demonstrate the experience of network-mediated consciousness. Texts that engage with topics such as the fragmentation of identity and the externalization of memory and desire are rendered in Memmott's works as visual, interactive phenomena. We confront the problems of being a human component of a network interface through our encounters with difficult interfaces. Memmott's network phenomenology text machines are metaphors for our relations with devices, that themselves manifest as interactive devices.

Collective forms of writing on the network also have literary precedent. The Mass-Observation movement, which began in the UK in 1937 and continued until 1945, could be a source of inspiration for works of network writing that involve large groups of contributors. The movement, organized by Charles Madge, a poet and journalist, Humphrey Jennings, a surrealist painter and documentary filmmaker, and Tom Harrisson, an anthropologist, set out to create a portrait of British society based on the observations of hundreds of citizen observers. The Mass-Observation movement proposed the assembly of "an anthropology of ourselves" through the contributions of individuals from across the UK who would regularly send in detailed reports on minutiae of their ordinary lives. In a letter to *The New Statesman and Nation* announcing their endeavor, the organizers proposed that with these contributions they could study phenomena such as:

> Behaviour of people at war memorials. Shouts and gestures of motorists. The aspidistra cult. Anthropology of football pools. Bathroom behaviour. Beards, armpits, eyebrows. Anti-semitism. Distribution, diffusion and significance of the dirty joke. Funerals and undertakers. Female taboos about eating. The private lives of midwives. (Crain, 2006)

Although it was in essence an ad hoc anthropology research project, the Mass-Observation movement was dreamed up by artists and poets and for the most part executed in the spirit of an experimental art project. For a book project about the day of King George VI's coronation, *May the Twelfth: Mass-Observation Day-Surveys 1937 by Over Two Hundred Observers* (Jennings and Madge, 1987), the collection of data took place via three different methods: 43 people wrote day-surveys (diaries of their own activities and observations), 75 people filled out questionnaires, and a dozen people covered the coronation itself in reportage style. Jennings and Madge explained the collection method in filmic style, with focus in "close-up and long shot, detail and ensemble" (Crain, 2006). The book that resulted from the project is a representation of the event and the society in which it took place from a panoramic perspective that moves across London with wandering eyes and ears catching overheard snatches of dialogue along the way. Like any collection of observations, the book was an edited linear rendition, a *cut* in the film director's sense and therefore a single filtered representation. One wonders what other versions might have resulted if it were presented as a database, or a hypertext. The Mass-Observation movement produced a number of other works including the 1939 text *Britain*, which focused on public opinion about Prime Minister Neville Chamberlain, and the 1943 book *The Pub and the People: A Worktown Study* (Mass-Observation, 1987), which focused on people's behaviors in their local drinking establishments. The Mass-Observation organization received some government contracts during World War II, even as critics attacked their methods as unscientific. The founders of the group quit during the war, and the organization was eventually transformed into a market-research firm. During the 1980s the project was revived at the University of Sussex, which maintains an archive of papers from the original project and collects information from new mass observers (Mass-Observation, 2017).

The Mass-Observation movement is useful to consider in terms of collective narratives. Its method of collecting writing from a large group of people through directive-based writing diaries and questionnaires, then remixing those responses into coherent collective narratives, provides an instructive antecedent to network-based collective narrative. We will later consider the *Invisible Seattle* project and other, network-based, projects intended to result in literary works produced by large groups. The main distinction between the type of mass writing conducted by the Mass-Observation movement was that their output (including films in addition to books) was destined toward one fixed printed report, or one version of a film, while database structures can allow for the output of the same pool of writing in many different arrangements.

A number of electronic literature projects can be understood as performances online, or as performative interventions. These can be understood in relation to different traditions of live performance. When a networked performance about social network exploitation of users as unpaid content providers unfolds on Twitter streams and Facebook posts – as in Rob Wittig and Mark Marino's netprov *I Work for the Web* (2015b) – it calls to mind theatrical traditions such as Agitprop or the Theatre of the Oppressed, as this type of performance is political theatre, taking place before an audience on the network within systems that are themselves parodied in the performance. Netprov in particular has a very specific and intentional relationship to the tradition of improv comedy that emerged out of venues such as The Second City theatre in Chicago. Artists such as Judd Morrissey and Mark Jeffery also make very specific connections between performance writing activities that unfold on the network and time-based performances that take place live onstage (Rettberg, 2010).

The Internet is the most important contemporary communications network, but earlier discourse networks, such as the postal system, have also been used for literary art. During the 1960s, New York-based artist Ray Johnson began sending collages, drawings, annotated newspaper clippings, and found objects and images to other artists – some of whom were his friends, others simply celebrity artists whose addresses he looked up. Along with these strange little works of art, he often also enclosed interactive instructions and invitations to reply ("Please add and return to Ray Johnson") with further works of art. Many of the artists he corresponded with responded in turn and a network known as "The Correspondence School" developed around the activity. Some of these works functioned like surrealist exquisite corpses, as each correspondent added new elements to the same drawing or collage that he or she had been sent. The Correspondence School exploited the specific materialities of the postal system in interesting ways that challenged an art world increasingly dominated by a big money agenda. Johnson promoted art as a democratic phenomenon. Works of mail art are essentially de-commodified. They are dropped into a postbox as casually as a Christmas card, and function as personal gifts within a gift economy. There is no guarantee that the artist will receive anything in return. The letter and the envelope are reconceived as arts media, and the postal system as a kind of open gallery. Mail art represents a rejection of the gallery system and the conventional art economy. Ray Johnson himself stopped exhibiting art commercially in the middle of his career, essentially rejecting the gallery economy altogether. For the Correspondence School, art was the exchange of ideas as material objects sent through the post from one artist to another.

Mail art is an important antecedent for network-based electronic literature in a number of ways – the recentering of value from market-driven to networked sharing represents one important aspect of that. The other is the idea that commerce-driven communications technologies – the postal service is used for many purposes, but few are more central than the delivery of bills and advertisements – can be configured as venues for art, that the network can itself take the place of the gallery. All forms of electronic literature are in some ways built around communities able to thrive not because of commercial success, but instead because the community has an interest economy of its own, an economy based on sharing, a networked gift economy. One piece of mail art made by Ray Johnson dated Nov. 12, 1983 is a hand-drawn letter that reads "Mail art is not a square, a rectangle, or a photo, or a book, or a slide. It is a river" (Johnson, 2017). The essence of this art practice, Johnson suggests, lies not in the art object as a commodity, but instead in the flow of ideas through space and time.

Forms and styles of network writing

From the 1990s until the present we have arguably seen the most substantial shifts in commonplace reading and writing behaviors since the invention of moveable type. The various communication technology platforms that now constitute our contemporary media ecology have each left their own distinct marks on our language and society. Some of these changes have been surprising: consider the fact that text messages have taken the place of many types of communication that used to be transacted on the telephone. People often choose to type short messages to each other on their phones over speaking with one another on the same device. Email has overtaken most forms of written postal communication, and online social networks have overtaken many other forms of social exchange. Electronic literature represents only a small subset of forms of writing that have changed radically online. Everyday textuality has also been deeply transformed in ways that affect everyone who regularly uses a networked computer, mobile phone, tablet, or any other connected device. For creative writers, each of these networked forms offers a new canvas for creative expression and reflexive commentary on different styles and practices of network writing.

Codework

Codework entails forms of writing that interrogate the double nature of writing produced on the computer and on the network as both surface writing and underlying code. Although codework does not necessarily depend on the Internet (some works of codework are intended to be experienced on a stand-alone computer) the majority of the best-known works are situated in relation to the network. In a 2001 special issue of the *American Book Review* on the topic, Alan Sondheim identified types of codework including works that use "the syntactical interplay of surface language, with reference to computer language and engagement," works "in which submerged code has modified the surface language," and "in which the submerged code is emergent content; these are both a deconstruction of the surface and of the dichotomy between the surface and the depth" (Sondheim, 2001).

Work by authors who play with the style of code in written language that is expressed for surface reading would fall into Sondheim's first category. A good portion of Mez Breeze's work (she is usually referred to as Mez) could be described in this way. Mez conceived of a style she called "Mezangelle" which the *Rhizome Net Art Anthology* (Anon, 2016) describes as "neologistic 'netwurked' language that treats code like malleable found material. It incorporates bits of code as well as coding structures – such as indentations, brackets, periods – to create new and unexpected meaning." Mez's own description of Mezangelle in the author's description accompanying _cross.ova.ing][4rm. blog.2.log][_ published in the *Electronic Literature Collection, Volume 2* is that it is "language evolved/s from multifarious computer code>social_netw orked>imageboard>gamer>augmented reality flavoured language/x/changes. 2 _mezangelle_ means 2 take words>wordstrings>sentences + alter them in such a way as 2 /x/tend + /n/hance meaning beyond the predicted +/or /x/ pected" (Breeze, 2011). Like several other artists who played with language and code in this fashion, Mez originally posted much of her work on mailing lists. Mez's essential technique is to use brackets, periods, slashes, and other punctuation to break words in unexpected ways that yield new meanings. Rita Raley (2002) described Mez's play with language as the creation of "complex combinatorial anagrams." Florian Cramer observed of this type of codework that, "computers and digital poetry might teach us to pay more attention to codes and control structures coded into all language" (Cramer, 2001). Mezangelle is as much about coded structures (including power structures and constructions of gender) embedded in normal language as it is about computer code. Many of Talan Memmott's early works, such as *Lexia to Perplexia* and *Translucidity* also played with code-like language in this way, if toward different ends. As Raley (2002) notes, Memmott was using his codework neologisms in "developing a language of network theory" through terms such as "cyborganization," "Narcisystems," and "exe.termination" to conceptualize the relation of the human subject to the network apparatus.

A good deal of Alan Sondheim's codework can be described as under his second category. Sondheim is a network performer. He is incredibly prolific, sending out writing almost every day on mailing lists and other online venues. Much of his writing has been modified in various ways through computational processes before he sends it out. Sondheim's *Internet Text* is a massive ongoing writing project that has spanned more than two decades. Sondheim describes it as a "continuous meditation on 'cyberspace,' emphasizing language, body, avatar issues, philosophy, poetics, and codework" (Sondheim, 2006). An archive of the project from 1994–2006 was published in *The Electronic Literature Collection, Volume One*, but as he continues to distribute his work on mailing lists, *Internet Text* continues to accrue on Sondheim's site (Sondheim, 1994). The codework appears alongside images, videos, and music files, representative of his polymath practice. A book of selected writing from the project, *Writing Under*, was published in 2012. The *Internet Text* is as much a durational performance as it is a "work." Consistent across the texts is an interest in the often-abject place of the human body and consciousness within a network apparatus and an oppressive society. Software, computers, and network protocols are not merely tools in Sondheim's work, they are prostheses in a different sense, as they augment, rearrange, and mangle human expression and often in the image work, human form. Glitched, twisted, twisting bodies contort in an impossible space in between the human and the machine.

In "The Code is not the Text (unless it is the Text)" John Cayley (2002) makes the point that much of the work discussed as codework is not actually code in the sense that computer code is generally addressed to the machine, and it has a substantive difference from human language because it is operational. You run a program in a way that you cannot run a printed poem. There are some exceptions to this rule, where artists and writers have created works that both produce a surface effect and are intended to function as literary works at the level of code. Cayley provides an example of a HyperCard poem he wrote that functioned both as a human-readable poem and as an operational program. Perhaps the best example of a program that was both operational code and aesthetic object is Carl Banks' *Flight Simulator* (1998) – a program that ran as a simple but functioning flight simulator. The main aesthetic achievement of the work was however located in the code. When users viewed the source code in a text editor, they found an ASCII artwork in the shape of a plane.

The net.art work of the JODI collective (Joan Heemskerk and Dirk Paesmans) is the classic example of the third type of codework identified by Sondheim. In their work, the code often interacts with the web browser and with network protocols in ways that modify or degrade the web pages over time. Code can sometimes be used to hijack browsers, for example, in 1996 with a web page that generated pop-up windows all over the screen until it overwhelmed the browser's memory capacity, causing it or the computer to crash. In http://wwwwwwwww.jodi.org/ (2001), partially operational code produces what appeared to be just garbled numbers and punctuation, but when users view the source code they find an ASCII art diagram of a nuclear bomb.

Codework is perhaps better described as an interest in a set of practices and concerns than as a genre. Talan Memmott described codework as an "Anti-Genre." Not a genre but "an evidentiary phenomenology of computer-based inscription" (Memmott, 2011, p. 31). If there is a commonality across different types of codework, it is this shared interest in the interface between human language and code, between text and operational instructions, and in the status of human expression in an environment mediated by code.

Flarf

Flarf was a movement, gathered as an online community around a listserv during the early 2000s, focused on exploiting the experience of language produced in the course of searching and navigating the Web. Flarf poetry celebrates the profusion of language unleashed into our lives with search engine technologies and the ever-expansive flood of algorithmically curated human discourse continually available to anyone with a web browser and an open search window.

Flarf embraces and parodies the arbitrary and idiosyncratic flood of texts that marked the adoption of the Internet into our lives, both the banal and the bizarre. Flarf and conceptual writing are both movements that make use of the Internet as a text-provision technology, if to different ends. Kenneth Goldsmith describes the distinction as follows: "Flarf plays Dionysus to Conceptual Writing's Apollo. Flarf uses traditional poetic tropes ("taste" and "subjectivity") and forms (stanza and verse) to turn these conventions inside out. Conceptual Writing rarely 'looks' like poetry and uses its own subjectivity to construct a linguistic machine that words may be poured into; it cares little for the outcome. Flarf is hilarious" (Goldsmith, 2009). Conceptual Writing is a movement that has much in common with Oulipo, in its love of constraints, and with conceptual art, in favoring the structured abstract expression of ideas through performances in writing. Classic examples of Conceptual Writing include Christian Bök's epic lipogram work *Eunoia* (2001) and Kenneth Goldsmith's *Day* (2003), a transcription of every word printed in *The New York Times* including the text of advertisements, as one long flowing text. Goldsmith teaches courses in "uncreative writing" – and argues that what the world needs now is not more language but reframing and reuse of discourse that already exists.

Flarf is a poetic reaction to the Internet. Flarf poets appropriate and reframe Internet search results into poetry by subjectively making use of and reframing Internet texts. Flarf embraces the absurd and plays with constructed notions of taste. Gary Sullivan describes the quality of "Flarfiness" as "something akin to 'campy,' but with somewhat different resonances. More awkward, stumbling, 'wrong' than camp" (Sullivan, 2014). The Flarf poets typically did not spend great pains carefully crafting language; they were in it for the laughs, the comic juxtapositions, the quick LOLs out there in everyday network writing. Flarf was about noticing what the Internet was doing to our experience of language and having fun with that. Take for example a stanza from Mel Nichols' "I Google Myself" (2009):

> I don't Google anybody else
> When I think about you
> I Google myself
> Ooh I don't Google anybody else
> At home alone in the middle of the night
> I Google myself
> and I like what I see
> Oh oh oh oh I can't stop Googling myself
> 1,690,000 results for Googling myself

Juxtaposing the lyrics of the Divinyls' 1990 pop hit "I Touch Myself" with ego-surfing, the poem underscores the shades of narcissism and onanism involved in the continuous availability of one's own information and reputation on the network.

K. Silem Mohammad's "Poems About Trees" (2009) deals with search results in a way typical of Flarf, operating with lines and phrases pulled directly from search results and remixing them into stanzas in semi-coherent form, as in its first stanza:

> I have written a couple of poems about trees
> poems about trees and snakes and lakes and birds
> poems about nature and life in New England
> I write crappy poems and eat babies
> if you like poems about trees you're in for a treat

The poem begins in a way that seems almost conventional, until we encounter the narrator's sudden appetite for babies. The sudden and arbitrary twist to absurdity is typical of Flarf. Gary Sullivan suggests that Flarf collaborates "with the culture via the Web, as an imperialist or colonialist gesture, as an unexamined projection of self into others, as the conscious erasure of self or ego" (Sullivan, 2006). Flarf is perhaps more than anything else a reflection of how a strange, alien but familiar, collective unconscious writes the language of the Internet.

The Flarfy impulse to feast on and restructure the torrents of language on the Internet is also reflected in the work of authors who wrangle texts from Google, RSS feed and Twitter streams into their work. Judd Morrissey often integrates writing gathered from live Twitter streams into his performance works. Jason Nelson's *Textual Skyline* (2012) uses RSS news feeds to create a digital poetry city. Nelson's Flash ActionScript code searched through designated news feeds for specific words or phrases that represented emotive states, and then built textual and visual elements of a skyline in response to those specific coded words. The Internet provides writers with a vast pool of continuously streaming texts to harvest, reshape, remix, and remold into new literary forms.

Stuart Moulthrop describes Flarf and related phenomena in terms of the relationship between interface and database: *"the work of citational composition may be regarded as creation of an interface to a database … *The poem in this view – quintessentially in the case of Flarf – may be thought of as one of these productions, a recorded or inscribed state of the interface"* (Moulthrop, 2018, p. 48). The role of the poet becomes that of editor and interpreter of the output of algorithms that filters the language of the Internet. The algorithm itself is available neither to the poet nor the readers, but remains shrouded and proprietary.

A number of Eugenio Tisselli's works deal with the materialities of code and network operations to modify the text of pages in textual artworks that played out as time-based performances. His *degenerative* (2005) and *regenerative* (2005) each engage with the network in terms of erasure and inscription. In *degenerative* every time a user visited the page, one character was removed from the text of the page until the process left an empty page. The author published an archive of screenshots illustrating the process of decay over a period of a few weeks. Tisselli's *regenerative* used a similar process, but each time an element was removed from the page, the script also attempted to scrape in some text from the referring page. The result is a jumble of broken HTML. In this case, both works are fundamentally about the network, and also about the fragile state of any site on the Web. It reminds us that the network is not a fixed and stable writing medium, but one in which human and non-human actors intervene. Anyone who ever had a WordPress blog attacked by hackers will feel a shiver looking at the broken HTML markup of *regenerative*, recognizing in it the signs of procedural intrusion. Davin Heckman and James O'Sullivan note that in *regenerative*, "the medium is the message. And the message is to make the operations of the code apparent, unavoidably obtrusive" (Heckman and Sullivan, 2018, p. 107). When we write to the network, we do so knowing that the network might eventually write back to us, or write over our writing. Bots that hack websites don't care whether they're attacking a novel or an ad for Viagra, for them it's all the same vulnerable code, ripe for infection.

Home page fictions

The "home page" is one of the lost forms of the early World Wide Web. When HTML was first presented to the world the first impulse was not only to view and consume web pages, but also to reciprocally create and present your own material, and your own identity, to the world. When people signed up for an Internet service provider for the first time, the first thing many did was learn some basic HTML and create a homepage, planting a flag on a small patch of the Web and claiming it as their own. These home pages became a genre of their own. Often poorly designed, gaudy, and idiosyncratic, home pages presented anyone on the Web with an opportunity to say anything they wanted to the world. And people were often confounded by that opportunity: Beyond "Hello world!" how could or should they use this vastly interconnected medium to represent themselves to the world?

Early examples of network writing include projects such as *To Be or Not Be Mouchette* (1997) by Martine Neddam and Rob Wittig's *The Fall of the Site of Marsha* (1999), which both played with the medium of the home page as the realm of fictional characters whose stories unfold on their own sites. *Mouchette* is presented as the domain of a troubled thirteen-year-old girl whose thoughts turn to self-destruction. Mouchette's home page and other sections of her site revolve around dark and angstful preoccupations. The site allows for a great deal of interaction, mostly through web forms. Mouchette's readers respond to polls with disturbing queries such as "What is the best way to kill yourself when you're under 13?" The site's author often then uses the content provided by users as the basis for short Flash animation works. The various sections of Mouchette's site play with early conventions of web design such as tacky repeating gif backgrounds, short web quizzes, photo galleries, and so on. Mouchette is an example of a "virtual character" – a fictional character presented on the Web as an actual person. Of course, Mouchette, twenty years after her first appearance on the Web, remains a thirteen-year-old for all time. A remarkable aspect of the project is that the author has continued to change and redevelop the work over a twenty-year period.

Rob Wittig describes his "perennial affliction: whenever I see written and pictorial communication in a new medium I have the overwhelming urge to pretend I'm some imaginary character and begin extravagantly misusing the medium's fledgling conventions" (Wittig, 2018, p. 114). Wittig's home page fiction *The Fall of the Site of Marsha* featured three versions of a home page dedicated to angels (the particular obsession of Marsha, the title character). One of the sites was provided as Marsha first published it, and two further hacked versions reveal the personal story behind the scenes of the published website. Marsha's husband, wanting to get out of the marriage, had hacked the page to make it seem as if the angels were after Marsha. His infidelities are revealed through the clues left in the vandalized site itself, after the angels turn into vandals. Wittig's fiction reveled in the garish, trashy, folky conventions of early web design with a work that serves both as a comic domestic fiction and a parody of poor design.

Email novels

Email is another genre of network communication explored by writers in the 1990s and early 2000s. Rob Wittig played with the emerging stylistic conventions of email in his novel *Blue Company* (2002). The work is focalized through Berto, an advertising copywriter sent by his employer back through space and time to fourteenth-century Italy as part of a campaign to change the course of history to bring about circumstances more beneficial to their corporate client. Berto smuggles a laptop back in time to compose emails from afar to the woman he is enamored of in his own present time. *Blue Company* was sent out to its initial subscribers in serial form in e-mail messages over the course of a month. Wittig took advantage of the real-time correspondence of the fiction in relation to the time scale in which it was read. Because events in the fictional world were unfolding at the same pace as readers were receiving the episodes of the novel in their in-boxes, Wittig was able to play with pacing in a different way than typical in a print novel. When characters in the novel waited, the readers also waited. When a tournament was taking place in the novel, readers received updates on the score over the course of the day.

Shortly after the end of the distribution of *Blue Company*, I followed up with a sequel of sorts, *Kind of Blue* (Rettberg, 2002), which made use of characters from Wittig's novel but recast in a different time frame. In *Kind of Blue*, Berto has not been sent back in time but into a mental health institution where he is struggling with his delusions, as the rest of the cast struggle with the new conditions of life unfolding in a paranoid, terrified, and conspiratorial post-9/11 society. Rather than writing in one epistolary voice as in *Blue Company*, in *Kind of Blue* the story unfolded via emails between characters and was closely tied to events unfolding in the news on the same time scale (for example a foiled terrorist incident at LAX and ongoing announcements of increased security measures) as the readers were receiving the episodes in their email stream. Both *Blue Company* and *Kind of Blue* were published as online archives after their initial distribution through email.

Jill Walker (2005) identified "distributed narratives" as forms that engage with network communications platforms as modes of distribution. She considered three conditions of distributed narrative based on a reconstruction of Aristotelian unities, describing works that were distributed in space, or distributed over time, or in which authorship was redistributed between writers and interacting readers. In *Surrender Control* (2001), an SMS interactive performance piece by Tim Etchell, participants received directives such as "Think about an ex-lover, naked and tied to a bed." or "Write the word SORRY on your hand and leave it there until it fades." periodically over SMS. It was up to those participants to decide whether or not to obey the order, but that aspect of the performance would not be realized unless they did. In the sticker novel *Implementation* (Montfort and Rettberg, 2004) participants (or implementers) were physically mailed fragments of a novel in eight installments of thirty business-sized shipping labels, each of which comprised a different narrative episode in the work. Implementers were asked to put these stickers up in public places and photograph them, and to consider how this placement in the world framed and situated the writing on the sticker. Photographs submitted by implementers were then gathered in online databases where web readers could access them, and eventually a coffee table book with photographs of the entire novel gathered in photographs taken around the world (Montfort and Rettberg, 2012). In Bob Bevan and Tim Wright's *Online Caroline* (2001) readers answered survey questions about themselves that generated an online profile used to personalize emails from the principal character of the work, Caroline, who is the subject of a disturbing experiment. The website changed each time the reader visited it both on the basis of their time-based position in the story and on choices they make in response to the ongoing narrative. The majority of the narrative is delivered through web cam videos of Caroline, and comported in the personal, confessional style of some "vloggers" (video bloggers).

Fictional blogs

Weblogs, described by Walker as "frequently updated website consisting of dated entries arranged in reverse chronological order, so the most recent post appears first" (Walker, 2005, p. 45) were the successors to the homepage, and were during the period before social networks the most popular form of independent personal writing on the network. Blogs were the product of software platforms such as WordPress, designed for content management and distribution, and networks such as Blogger.com. The syndication of content by technologies such as RSS and interlinking of blogs via "blogrolls" enabled these personal writing media to develop audiences and writing networks of considerable scale. Perhaps because the weblog form lent itself both to first-person perspective and to narrative, in the sense that individual weblogs took form over time, developing specific interests and life stories over time, it worked well for fictional as well as non-fiction narratives. Justin Hall's *Justin's Links* (Hall, 2004) was a particularly engaging personal blog started when Hall was a college student in 1994. Over the course of twenty years, as Hall writes in the introduction to a documentary film he produced about his experience (Hall, 2015), he "documented family secrets, romantic relationships, and my experiments with sex and drugs." Hall wrote about and shared intimate experiences from dealing with the death of his father to considering and planning personal relationships and breakups. A considerable audience gathered around Hall, following his story as a kind of serial drama, and followed his life lived in public on the Internet. If sharing emotional states, personal triumphs, traumas, and grief has become standard fare in the age of social networks, at the time Hall first took a turn towards personal writing on his blog, it was still relatively rare for a writer to reveal himself so nakedly on the Web.

Fictional blogs appeared in many different forms and guises. Some are best described as hoaxes, while others have been carefully planned as novel-length fictions. The examples of the Kaycee Nicole case (Swenson, 2001) and *lonelygirl15* (Becket et al., 2006) discussed by Jill Walker Rettberg in *Blogging* (2014, p. 228) are two examples of fictional blogs that could be read alternately as fiction and hoax. Kaycee Nicole was a young blogger who used her blog to describe her fictional struggle fighting leukemia in what turned out to be a desperate and cruel hoax. Her story extended out from her blog to chat rooms and web forums and even out into personal friendships in real life. Her mother Debbie subsequently started her own blog describing her experiences as a caregiver. After the reported death of Kaycee Nicole, readers discovered that both Kaycee Nicole's and Debbie's blogs were written by a woman who was neither a teenager nor dying of leukemia. As the story of the hoax unraveled, Kaycee Nicole's friends and audience were devastated by the way the fraudulent story had played upon their emotions.

Lonelygirl15 is a project more explicitly planned as a fiction. The project unfolds in a series of web cam videos in vlog form on YouTube. *Lonelygirl15* first seemed to be a normal confessional vlog revealing the typical angst and concerns of a home-schooled teenage girl, "Bree." Her story soon however took some unanticipated turns involving cult activities guided by her restrictive parents, who planned to include her in some ritual involving strict dietary requirements and learning an ancient language (J. W. Rettberg, 2014).

Further examples of blog novels include works written across multiple blogs written by characters interacting with each other, and even, in the case of Jean-Pierre Balpe's work, blogs and social media accounts written by characters who are themselves poetry-writing generative textbots.

Twitter fiction

In chapter 2, we briefly addressed Twitter bots, a popular form of text generators that write short constrained texts to Twitter on a timed basis. Bots are also forms of network writing, dependent in some ways on their timed appearance within the flow of other networked discourse for their impact. Twitter has been used for a number of other types of network writing, such as Netprov, discussed below. A number of people have also played with reformatting existing texts into Twitter streams that unfold on a timed basis. An early example of this was Ian Bogost and Ian McCarthy's *Bloomsday on Twitter* (Bogost, 2007), an interpretation of the Wandering Rocks episode of *Ulysses* that unfolded as a performance of tweets from named characters in the novel over the course of the day. A number of well-known print novelists, such as Jennifer Egan, Philip Pullman, and Margaret Atwood have written works that unfolded on a twitter stream (Goldhill, 2015). Twitter is a social network that was based around a writing constraint of 140 characters per tweet (now doubled to 280), and so posed interesting challenges for novelists and poets. How much of a story or a dialog can you compress into one tweet? How can you use the time-based element of a twitter stream to effect the pacing of a poem? Rita Raley points to Teju Cole's "Seven short stories about drones" as an excellent example of how writers could use the Twitter medium effectively to compress narratives such that could actually be effective as a single-line tweet, as in the first of Cole's tweets: "1. Mrs Dalloway said she would buy the flowers herself. Pity. A signature strike leveled the florist's" (Cole, 2013). In each tweet, a classic work of Western literature is cut short by a deadly drone strike. There is a darkly comic tone to this gesture, but a serious intent to communicate to Western readers the sense of arbitrary horror of living under the threat of the drones.

Online writing communities

Although we tend to think of electronic literature as characterized by works that self-consciously engage with the specific capacities of the networked computer, writing platforms and communities have emerged that are more focused on producing fiction which could be intended for print but that are developed within writing communities that are particular to the Internet.

Platforms such as Wattpad are dedicated to novel writing, writing that takes place openly within a support structure. Fellow Wattpadders read along, giving feedback and encouragement to the authors as they are writing. The platform skews toward younger writers whom mainly produce genre fiction and fan fiction – fictions that expand upon, mash up, and provide alternative versions of both print fictions and other popular narratives. Steve Tomasula references the example of *The Kissing Booth* by Beth Reeks, read by nineteen million readers on Wattpad before Random House picked it up for a three-book series (Tomasula, 2018, p. 48). Fan fiction has also spawned huge online writing communities. Fan fiction authors rewrite or spin off elements of their favorite novels, TV shows, films, comic books, etc., often in playfully subversive ways – there is a whole subgenre of "slash" fictions that imagine sexual relationships between characters who are not directly portrayed in that way in the source work, e.g. Kirk/Spock retellings of *Star Trek* in which the captain is in love with the Vulcan. These works are not engaged with computation as explicitly as most forms of electronic literature, but the communities surrounding them are network-based and their rise in popularity maps to the rise of the Web.

Collective narrative

Social media platforms such as Facebook and most significantly Twitter have provided not only platforms for individual writing but also for collective writing projects that take the form of networked writing performances among large groups, collective narratives.

Before Rob Wittig experimented with email novels and fictional homepages, he was involved in a large-scale collective narrative project that strongly anticipated collective writing on the Internet. In 1983, a group of writers and artists known as the Invisibles gathered in Seattle and settled up an audacious project: to use the occasion of the Bumbershoot Arts Festival to produce a novel about Seattle written by the city itself. Literary workers put on white overalls with words stenciled on them and wore construction hats bearing question marks and fanned out on the streets, bars, and coffee shops of Seattle with clipboards, stopping passers-by and asking them: "Excuse me, we're building a novel, could we borrow some of your words?" Those who were willing answered questions such as "Where could a stranger go to get killed around here?" or "Could you describe a car? Could you describe the body of your real or imagined lover?" (Wittig, 2012). Through mad-lib-style fill-in-the-blank questionnaires; clip-out-and-return coupons encouraging readers to contribute photos along with descriptions of settings and major plot developments; descriptions of quotidian life gathered via a call-in radio show and other stunts, the Invisibles developed a large database of writing. The text-gathering culminated with a performance installation at the Bumbershoot, in the form of a writing booth sculpted into something that looked a bit like a spaceship or some kind of Jules Verne personal submarine, a "cyberno-ziggurat" named Scheherazade II with a word processor in the place of a dashboard in front of the pilot's seat. The mayor of Seattle showed up to throw out the first word, and literary workers ushered festivalgoers into booths throughout the festival. Ken Kesey even dropped in to contribute a few phrases. After the festival, the Invisibles sorted through the mass of texts the city had written together and published one (of several) edited arrangements of material. Harry Mathews commented on the book that emerged from the project: "In this 'novel of Seattle by Seattle' they have completed an exhilarating task, providing, in addition to 200 pages of engaging text, a vast and discrete critique of many of our cultural and political assumptions – about authorship, for instance, the uses of the computer, and the way communities function." (Seattle, 1983) Like the Collective Observers, the Invisibles attempted to assemble the observations and the anecdotes of the masses into a collective story that no one human would have individually composed. "We saw that the encyclopedic goal of modernist lit – one author doing many voices – " writes Wittig, "was better accomplished by many writers." (Wittig, 2012)

In his *Invisible Rendezvous: Connection and Collaboration in the New Landscape of Electronic Writing* (1994) Wittig recounts both the adventure of the creation of *Invisible Seattle* and the early writing community that sprang out of it IN.S.OMNIA. Given access to an early BBS, the Invisibles explored practices of live collective writing, developing writing games that involved shared writing spaces and simultaneity. Invisibles would log in anonymously or with assumed identities, writing into each other's texts on a real-time basis. More than a decade before the World Wide Web, the Invisibles were discovering the strangeness of writing together in time-based social media.

In "All Together Now: Hypertext, Collective Narratives, and Online Collective Knowledge Communities" (Rettberg, 2011) I considered the architectures of participation in a number of works and identified three different types of participation in collective narrative projects:

• Conscious participation: Contributors are fully conscious of explicit constraints, of the nature of the project, and of how their contribution to it might be utilized.
• Contributory participation: Contributors may not be aware of how their

contribution fits into the overall architecture of the project, or even of the nature of the project itself, but they do take conscious steps to make their contribution available to the project.

- Unwitting participation: Texts utilized in the collective narrative are gathered by the text-machine itself, and contributors have no conscious involvement in the process of gathering the material.

An early web project organized for the trAce online writing community by Sue Thomas and Teri Hoskins, *Noon Quilt* (1998), is a simple example of conscious participation. *Noon Quilt* and several successive quilt collections were composed of short pieces written by writers in forty different countries who looked out of their windows at noon and wrote in one hundred words what they could see. The main interest of the quilt project was not narrative cohesion, but the creation of a kind of international panorama told in many voices, bound together by the fact that they all were looking out a window as the clock struck twelve. Each of these short narratives became a patch in the quilt that grew larger and large as many contributors sent in their observation.

The Impermanence Agent (1999) by Noah Wardrip-Fruin was a work that demonstrated all three types of participation. The *Agent* functioned as a storytelling plugin for a web browser. It customized its story for each user. The story took a week to tell, in the corner of the screen, as the user browses other sites on the Web. The core story, which centered on themes of loss and memory based on Wardrip-Fruin's experience of his grandmother's death and memory, was gradually modified over time by the user's browsing of websites. Text and phrases would be pulled into a narrative, scraped by the agent from the pages the user visited over the course of the week. In this case, Wardrip-Fruin and his direct collaborators were conscious participants, having written the core story and the software. Users who signed on to the *Agent* were contributory participants, as their behaviors and browsing habits were used to modify the story. The authors of the web pages scraped were unwitting participants, as the *Agent* simply harvested language from their sites.

A Million Penguins (2007) was an attempt to produce a novel written by hundreds of contributors in a wiki platform. Organized by the De Montfort University Institute of Creative Technologies and Penguin Books and led by Sue Thomas and Kate Pullinger, the experiment took place over a five-week period. Although the project itself is no longer online, a research report by Bruce Mason and Sue Thomas (2008) provides documentation of its outcome. The project used MediaWiki, the same platform as Wikipedia, in a wide-open, largely unstructured writing experiment. The organizers seeded the text with one line from *Jane Eyre*, "There was no possibility of taking a walk that day," and then stepped back to watch the sparks fly. The project was well publicized, and one of the first things that happened out of the gate was a server crash, as the site was overwhelmed with visitors. Once the project was moved to a more robust server and the initial fascination wore off, a somewhat smaller but nevertheless large group of people continued to write the wikinovel in a chaotic, carnivalesque fashion. Over the course of the period that the project was open for submissions "1,476 people had registered as users and had between them made over 11,000 edits to its 1,000 plus pages" (Mason and Thomas, 2008, p. 4). The result, everyone involved in organizing the project agreed, was not a good novel, but a compelling social experiment in collective writing. While many people made small edits to the project, a relatively small group of them became deeply engaged in the writing experiment and did the bulk of the writing and editing. One contributor alone made 1,780 edits to the wiki. The process described in *A Million Penguins Research Report* reads more like the story of a failed utopia than a successful collaboration, a struggle between structuralists and anarchists. Even as some contributors tried to create a narrative architecture, coherent characters, and plot, others came in with the intent of vandalizing the text. The organizers described several different types of participants in the project: vandals, performers, and gardeners: "'gardeners' intent on nurturing the novel; 'vandals' determined to ruin it, and 'performers' hoping to make it a showcase for their talents." The gardeners spent most of their efforts trying to clean up spelling and grammar and remove edits that were clearly intended to disrupt cohesion, the performers did the bulk of the actual writing toward a kind of novel, and the vandals were there to romp and ridicule, splattering graffiti on the walls.

One wonders if the experiment of *A Million Penguins* would have been more successful if writing and editorial roles were designed more carefully or, as in the experiments of the Mass-Observer moment or *Invisible Seattle*, if the input the readers provided had been more granular, or the final product more directly filtered by an editor.

One strategy for including contributions while maintaining literary control chosen in *Flight Paths: A Networked* by Kate Pullinger and Andy Campbell (2007) was to engage the user in the story development process through online discussion and submission of creative content. The story, developed as a fiction in the Flash platform, was released episodically. Readers were invited to discuss the development of the project with Pullinger and Campbell at each stage of the project's release, to contribute personal stories and images that could be woven into the story, remaining in contact with the authors throughout the process. In addition, beyond the multimedia work, Pullinger developed the novel *Landing Gear* (2014) based on the story she built with the contributory participation of *Flight Paths* readers.

In other cases, the very act of relinquishing control is part of the artistic project. The *exquisite_code* (2010) project by Brendan Howell et al. is "an algorithmic performance system for heterogeneous groups of writers and live performance," that has been performed on several occasions. A performance of *exquisite_code* involves a time-based writing session by a group of writers sitting at a table. It is both a combinatory and constrained writing project, inspired by the cut-up method and Oulipian constraints, and a collective narrative system that results in a linear work. The participating writers are fed writing prompts at short intervals. They then write individually in response to the prompts. At the conclusion of the period, their text is fed into "worm software" which redacts the text, cutting and pasting, removing and replacing words and merging texts from the various writers' streams into one. The redacted texts are sometimes sent back to their writers in modified form for them to edit and feed back into the system. At the end of the daylong writing performance, the system outputs a final text, which is then made into a print-on-demand book, a "life-novel." The book *Exquisite_code* (2010) was derived from a London performance of the work. In comparison to *A Million Penguins* this project does not rely on humans responding to texts produced by other humans but instead on human responses to algorithmically modified text. The writers are "heterogeneous" in the sense that they are not in direct collaboration with each other at the level of writing a joint text. The software makes decisions about how their writing fits together. In the construction of the collective narrative, the software is the control and editorial layer.

Netprov

Rob Wittig and Mark Marino explore "network styles" of writing and experiment with ways that social media can function as an environment and stage for new kinds of participatory performance writing with "Netprov." Netprovs use some of the same strategies as the collective narrative projects discussed above, but have a stronger focus on group improvisation based on a prompt or set of constraints. Wittig identifies three moves from earlier literary forms that background his approach to netprov in new media:

1. The first is the travesty of *facsimile graphic design* (satirically donning the attire of power) and the pleasure of technologically self-aware art.

2. The second is the fundamental gesture of *mimicry and impersonation* and what it implies currently for notions of *identity*, particularly in the era of what I'll call the "consumer ego."
3. The third is the post-romantic art of creating and maintaining *generative collaborations* – ways of inviting and modeling public participation. (Wittig, 2018, p. 114)

Netprovs are structured collective writing performances that unfold on various social media platforms. Wittig writes that their aim is to "invite people into new forms for new adventures" through mimicry of everyday language and recognizable tropes of writing on the Internet, writing of a kind that is more accessible than avant-garde forms that he describes as "one step too far" (Wittig, 2018, p. 119). Wittig highlights the value of the pure novelty to be found in noticing changes that accompany a shift to new writing media, such as changes in orthography that can be found in instant messages, emails, and tweets. Feeding archetypal plots, hoaxes, and other shenanigans through these emergent conventions heightens their comic effects.

Marino and Wittig both wrote fiction that played with emerging conventions and social practices of network communication platforms before they met in 2011 and launched their netprov collaborations. In addition to the aforementioned projects, Wittig produced a fiction, *Friday's Big Meeting* (2000), a romantic comedy that unfolded over time on what was purportedly a corporate intranet forum. Marino had produced works such as *The Loss Wikiless Timespedia* (2009), a parodic collaborative writing project based on the premise that the *Los Angeles Times* had switched to a wiki-only publishing model, with all articles written by unpaid contributors, and *The Ballad of Work Study Seth* (2009), based on the premise that Marino's Twitter stream had been hijacked by a work-study student Marino had hired to tweet for him. Wittig was preparing his Master's project at the time, the netprov *Grace, Wit & Charm*. The two identified a number of common elements in their network-writing projects, eventually loosely codified into a provisional definition of Netprov as: "Netprov = networked improv literature. Netprov uses everyday social technology plus the ol' tricks of literature, graphic design, and theater to create stories that unfold in realtime within public mediascapes" (Marino, 2011b). Wittig and Marino identified common elements that bound most of these experiments together and would be the seed of netprov: they all took the form of prose fiction, unfolded in real time, adhered to temporal unity between the reader's real world and the characters' fictional worlds, they used vernacular media, were collaborative works produced by multiple writers, interactive in the sense that readers could comment or join in the writing of the work, designed to be "read at work" in a tertiary and modular way, they were partially scripted and partially improvised, they included current events, they were satirical, and they were designed for incomplete reading.

Wittig's University of Bergen thesis *Networked Improv Narrative (Netprov) and the Story of Grace, Wit & Charm* (Wittig, 2011) served as a manifesto of sorts for netprov, identifying sources for the new form in networked games, improv theatre, mass media, literature, and the Internet and pulling lessons from each of those forms on how to best plan and execute a netprov. *Grace, Wit & Charm* was an attempt to pull those principles together. In this case, the improvisation mixed an online component and a live theatrical element. The premise of the work was that people could hire workers from the Grace, Wit, and Charm company to help them through difficult social situations by serving as their avatars, whether through social media interaction or through remote motion-capture performance in arenas such virtual worlds, online games, or even ultimately, remote surgical theatres. The drama unfolded first on Twitter and then migrated for its culmination into live theatrical performance.

Among many netprovs produced by Marino, Wittig, and collaborators in the years since, common themes have included a parodic treatment of contemporary social behaviors on the Web, an interest in testing and exploring a variety of platforms as storytelling environments, and a subversive streak that uses satire as a mode of critique. The form and intent of the projects has varied. Many of them emerge out of Marino and Wittig's writing and design courses, and student writers as well as a group of "featured players." Among the most notable of the Netprovs is *Occupy MLA* (2011) – a performance that involved fictional adjunct faculty forming a group on Twitter, complaining to each other about institutional subjugation, and then proposing a protest movement that would culminate in an Occupy-style protest at the Modern Language Association conference. Not everyone was pleased when the project was revealed to be a fiction and a hoax. Michael Bérubé, then president of the MLA, weighed in against the project in a posting on an article in the *Prof. Hacker* blog in *The Chronicle of Higher Education* (Marino and Wittig, 2013). Some readers of the performance also felt disappointed that it was a fiction playing with the systemically flawed circumstances involved in the treatment of non-tenure-track faculty in the American university system – which increasingly relies on low-paid adjunct faculty with little or no job security in place of full-time positions. They would have preferred activism that was working toward a material outcome rather than a parody of such a protest movement. But as Kathi Inman Berens notes, "Just because OMLA did not prompt immediate structural transformation in higher ed doesn't mean, however, that it did no work. Speaking truth to power in the guise of fiction; making access to such speech open, participatory, collective and persistently visible: this is important cultural work" (Berens, 2015).

Some netprovs are essentially prompts for comparatively simple writing games. A recent netprov, *One Star Reviews* (2017) challenged participants to write effusive and elaborate reviews, in the style of Yelp or Amazon, for fictional places or items that they were nevertheless rating with only one star. Other netprovs are based on only marginally more complex prompts. *Monstrous Weather* (2016) proposed that the Internet went down for a week amid strange weather, during which people sat around marveling at the weather and telling stories. From this simple prompt an accumulation of stories of monstrous weather unfolded. The writers began to respond to each other's stories, developing different sets of themes and plotlines over the course of the month, resulting in a cross between an anthology of flash fictions and an interwoven serial. The netprov took place during the 2016 US presidential election campaign season, and was contemporaneous with the Republican National Convention, which cast an orange shadow that also inevitably worked its way into the fiction.

A number of netprovs address the absurdities of common behaviors on social media. *I Work for the Web* (2015) treated the fact that the majority of contemporary web content is produced by users in social media (your likes, your posts, your comments, your photos) for the financial benefit of large international corporations. *I Work for the Web* was a comic fiction that considered this situation in terms of labor and labor disputes. *#1WkNoTech* (2015a) parodied a situation that often occurs on social media when a Facebook or Twitter user loudly declares that they have had enough of the information overload and is therefore going offline for a while to recuperate. *#1WkNoTech* challenged its participants to assiduously document their experience of going without technology through posts and photographs on social media. In their comic, but nevertheless, pointed critique of human foibles as represented in contemporary social media, netprovs share characteristics with a strand of work in electronic literature that expressly critiques the contemporary distribution of power reflected on the network.

Although it is neither collaborative nor directly published on a social network, Alan Bigelow's *How to Rob a Bank* (2017), winner of the 2017 Robert Coover Award, is a work very much in the spirit of netprov. It offers a superb comic reflection of how Google searches, online shopping sites, instant messaging, Google maps, Instagram, and other online interactions have changed the way we conduct our lives. Bigelow tells a hilarious story of love and crime exclusively through the activities that take place on the screen of a bank robber's iPhone before, during, and after a heist.

Network critique

One strand of practice that has manifested recently is the use of the digital artifact as a mode of critique of the contemporary network itself, drawing attention to the ways that corporate actors are using the network to harvest language and manipulate consumers. Works by authors and artists such as John Cayley, Daniel Howe, Jason Huff, Mimi Cabell, and Ben Grosser function as critiques of particular practices of Google and Amazon. These entities are impacting language, not only in a sense of how it is styled and communicated, but also how it is commoditized. Google has amassed the largest archive of human language ever assembled and treats it as a proprietary corpus. Facebook has gathered the largest collection of "people data" ever harvested and retains the rights to use it as they see fit. Amazon has mapped the buying habits of everyone who uses its service and put its listening devices into our homes. Some feel that all of this tracking, profiling, and harvesting calls for artistic responses that either directly challenge these practices or at least raise awareness that they are taking place.

How It Is in Common Tongues (2012) by John Cayley and Daniel Howe is one such project. It is a complex multi-layered artwork built on top of *The Readers Project*. The "readers" of *The Readers Project* are essentially bots based on particular ways of procedurally reading a text. They are like web crawlers in a sense, but they are more closely related to reading as an embodied human activity in the sense that they "see" the text by following different patterns and behaviors. These agents include a simple reader, perigram reader, spawning reader, mesostic reader, and grammatical reader. Their behaviors are visualized in a series of installations that feature the system reading through texts in a "typographically structured literary environment" (Cayley and Howe, 2013). The readers also write, in the sense that as they move through texts in particular ways, they generate new combinations of text. *How It Is in Common Tongues* is a book that demonstrates some of the potential text (re)writing capabilities of *The Readers Project* while simultaneously demonstrating some problems with conceptions of copyright and the ownership of language. *How It Is* is a novel by Samuel Beckett. The Beckett estate is notorious for their strict enforcement of copyright on the dead author's work. The text of *How It Is in Common Tongues* includes the same text as *How It Is* with one difference: Cayley and Howe developed a program to conduct procedural searches on Google for the longest strings of any given phrase used in the book from a source other than Beckett. The resulting book includes the text of *How It Is*, with each phrase in the book citing a source webpage where it was written. Cayley and

Howe thus assembled a text that reads the same as Beckett's work, but did so along with computationally verifiable proof that their source texts were not the Beckett work. By also showing new work generated by *The Readers Project*'s readings as writing based on the same text, the authors further demonstrate that nothing about language is intrinsically fixed or propri-etary. This has particular relevance in relationship to Google's proprietary enclosure of all of the language that all of its users have contributed to its constantly updated database of human language (which the contributor/users cannot themselves access).

American Psycho (2012) by Mimi Cabell and Jason Huff similarly explored the poetics of citation in the networked society. They published a version of Bret Easton Ellis' novel *American Psycho* that did not include any of the text of the novel but instead a series of headlines and annotations for web-based ads on each page, which is otherwise blank. These were harvested by feeding Ellis' novel through Gmail one page at a time and then pulling out the text of the ads that Google placed with the text when it displayed in the Gmail browser. The project is not about Ellis' novel but about how Gmail reads the mail we send to it and responds with relational advertising. The authors report that the ads sometimes seem irrelevant to the content of the page, while in some cases the relevance was frankly disturbing: "In one scene, where first a dog and then a man are brutally murdered with a knife, Google supplied ample ads regarding knives and knife sharpeners" (Cabell & Huff, 2012).

Another sort of compelling response to the challenges of corporate control of the Internet are artistic responses that actually have a degree of efficacy in combating what they critique. Daniel Howe and Helen Nissenbaum's *TrackMeNot* (2012) is both a software artwork and a practical tool for network browsers who wish to intervene in violations of their privacy. *TrackMeNot* is a web browser plugin. When users installed it, every time they sent a search query, the plugin would also send a number of other queries that were linguistically but not semantically related to the actual search. This had the effect of making the search query useless to Google in terms of tracking a user's individual search behavior. *AdLiPo* (Howe, 2014) is a selective ad blocker that replaces selected ads with short generated critical language about the nature of advertising, in a process that is in part based on a machine reading of the contents of a page. *AdNauseam* by Howe et al. (2015) is another ad blocker that on the surface seems to work like any other. In addition to blocking the ads, however, the program simultane-ously registers a click on every single ad on the page, both disrupting the economic system and trust relations between advertisers and their clients and obfuscating any user profiling on the basis of what ads are clicked. The plugin also harvests images from all of the ads that are blocked and clicked. This generates a collage of images that together represent a profile of the type of consumer that the advertisers on the websites you visit believe you to be.

ScareMail (2011) by Ben Grosser is a Gmail extension that is designed to protest and disrupt NSA surveillance of email communications. The program produces "scary mail" by attaching short nonsense stories to every message sent, making use of words from a large list of terms that NSA crawlers use to trigger investigation, flooding it with useless nonsense information. The stories created are syntactically close enough to normal language to be interesting as texts, interventionist spam that is nearly but not quite coherent narrative writing.

Bots can similarly be used for critical interventions. Mark Sample's @NSA_PRISMbot (2013) for example was produced in the wake of Edward Snowden's revelations about the NSA surveillance program PRISM. The bot generates tweets that illustrate the sort of useless information that the NSA might harvest by automatically flagging phrases in data-mining social media and other online communications. The bot is a kind of speculative activism, both demonstrating that the majority of these invasions of privacy are pointless, and, by its unremitting production of new tweets, representing the aggregate scale of a program that is purported to scan the majority of Internet communications passing through American networks for keywords to identify potential threats.

John Cayley's *The Listeners* (2015) questions the implications of the new mode of aural communication between humans and a network interface represented by devices such as the Amazon Echo and the Google Home Assistant. These network devices sit in our homes, continuously recording and interpreting what we say, in spoken and heard language. Cayley proposes that "aurature" is linguistic work that is produced out of performative spoken dialogue with one of these devices. The media of aurality are distinguished from oral literature because aurature is "heard and interpreted," not only produced, in spoken language. Cayley proposes that "digital audio recording, automatic speech recognition and automatic speech synthesis technologies fundamentally reconfigure – in their cumulative amalgamation – the relationship between linguistic objects in aurality and the archive of cultural practice" (Cayley, 2018, p. 73).

The Listeners is an Alexa skill for the Amazon Echo. In interacting with *The Listeners* the user can ask Alexa to "go on" and "continue" but can also interact by expressing emotions such as "I am filled with worry" and by asking Alexa how she is feeling. It recognizes nine affects and shapes an emergent narrative which varies every time it runs but always centers on the anxious relationship of the human to the device, the cognizing and inter-locuting device, as for the first time significant relationships form between humans and robot listeners they have invited into their own homes.

The function of network writing

The forms of network writing discussed here all share one thing in common – through their self-reflexive nature they encourage audiences to recon-sider the situation of the human in the contemporary network apparatus. Whether through forms of writing that via code/language hybrids reflect increasingly complex relationships between humans and machines, through fictional forms that express themselves and are structured by network-based communication technologies, through collaborative writing projects that foreground aspects of networked collectivity, or through projects that parody the practices of multinational corporations that increasingly mediate our online experience, these works all provide us with opportunities to defamiliarize and rethink the ways that we engage with the network. This is perhaps one of the most important functions electronic literature can fulfill – digital literary art can serve as a critical mirror to help us better understand the networked society that we co-create, that we are subject to, and that we together inhabit.

7   Divergent Streams

In preceding chapters, we have considered five core genres of electronic literature: combinatory poetics, hypertext fiction, interactive fiction and other gamelike forms, kinetic and interactive poetry, and network writing. As discussed in the introduction, naming these as genres is not to suggest that they are completely distinct from one another – in fact they are most often intermingled. We have identified particular characteristics, specific technological contexts, and historical influences that have shaped each strand of practice. This set of five genres also does not exhaust the categories of practice that could have been extensively detailed in this book. Indeed, some of the most interesting current practices in digital writing have not yet been discussed. In this concluding chapter I will briefly describe some other genres that deserve fuller treatment than the space of this volume will allow. Locative narrative, digital literary installations, virtual and augmented reality narrative, and interactive and combinatory cinema are each areas of electronic literature that have been substantially developed, if not yet in the same sustained way as the core genres detailed here. Each in some way builds upon those other genres while expanding them into new spaces and environments, as well as into other disciplines. Extensions of electronic literature into the physical world, into virtual reality, into performance, gallery arts, and cinema environments could in fact be the subject of a successor volume to this book. In this concluding chapter I will also provide the reader with some information on the research infrastructure of the field and where to find work, and finally consider the present situation and potential future of electronic literature as a discipline.

Locative narratives

Other than the Internet, the most significant change in our relationship to computational technology in recent years is the increasing ubiquity of mobile devices and locative technologies. Contemporary smartphones are also GPS devices able to pinpoint a user's specific location. Even without GPS, the IP address of a given user (who has not gone to specific effort to mask it) supplies information about his or her location in the physical world. This locative dimension has changed the nature of our interactions with both the physical world and the Internet. We are never completely lost; we can always find our way with Google Maps and a mobile phone. We can not only map directions from wherever we are to any other address: we can also zoom into much of the world, and look at the surroundings in 360 degrees with Google Earth and Street View. Our interactions with contemporary social networks and online shopping sites are not only based on who we are and what we do, but also where we are and the situation of the world around us. This has both positive and negative effects. It is very useful to know the weather or traffic conditions immediately in front of us. It is even arguably useful that an advertiser suggests we buy snow tires as a severe winter storm approaches. On the other hand, the fact that we allow tracking not only of our behavior online but also our physical location represents a surrender of privacy of Orwellian scale. Location tracking also limits our experience of the global network, as our access to the Internet can be controlled on the basis of our physical location. For the most part, our desires for the conveniences of location-aware technology have trumped fears of the abuse of that information by the entities we surrender it to. At the same time as we confront practical questions of how we should conduct our lives in a geolocated world, various locative technologies now available to writers and artists have opened up exciting opportunities for storytelling and for performative interaction that is based on our location.

Electronic literature authors have begun to explore how locative technologies can enable us to layer narrative and poetic experiences on the world around us. In addition to GPS, technologies such as radio frequency identification (RFID) and QR codes have allowed us to tag stories on locations. The possibilities of locative narrative are broad and varied. We could investigate a murder mystery by retracing the steps of the killer at the scene of the crime. We could situate historical fiction set in a different era on the streets of the contemporary city. We could write poems, layered in augmented reality in the sky above the mountains they describe, as we sweep across the landscape and watch the live video on the screens of our phones. Digital language artists have only begun to exploit the potential of locative narrative, though a number of compelling works have already been produced.

Art practices designed to reformulate our understanding of and relationship to our physical environment are not entirely new. Consider the work of the Situationist International during the 1950s and 60s and the practice of the *dérive*, a practice of consciously breaking habits of movement and interaction with the city, for example by walking in as close to a straight line as possible through a given city, regardless of the arrangement of streets, or tearing apart and reassembling a map of given city in random arrangement, and then trying to go from place to place in as close as possible a journey to the reconfigured map. The idea was to expose and better understand the "pyschogeography" of a place by navigating it in a constrained way that is different from the mundane patterns of usual life. As Guy Debord described it, the participants in a *dérive* "drop their relations, their work and leisure activities, and all their other usual motives for movement and action, and let themselves be drawn by the attractions of the terrain and the encounters they find there" (Debord, 1956). The essential feature of the Situationist *dérive* is breaking apart our preconceived notions of the world around us, reframing our experience of the lived environment. This idea of reframing reality is important for a number of digital locative narrative projects, which use technology to layer narratives onto the mundane world of everyday existence.

The majority of locative narrative projects share a common interest in the relationship of physical space and geographic location to the narrative and poetic dimensions of literature. They reflect on and relate to the migration of the contemporary computer user's experience from the desktop computer with keyboard and mouse user interface to an always-connected situation of ubiquitous computing in mobile environments. Some characteristics of these works include an interest in how experience can be mapped, and cartography personalized, a shift in "setting" from a narrated quality of story to a physically embodied situation in the world, an engagement with the reader as interactive performer of the work, and an interest in the interactor's embodiment within the narrative architecture.

The nature of technological approaches to locative narrative and the uses of different multimedia elements have varied a great deal from quite simple to extremely complex. In the previous chapter I referenced the sticker novel *Implementation*, a distributed novel that could also be considered a locative project. In this case the core technology was as simple as adhesive labels. The locative element was in the choice of the participant readers on where to physically place the stickers and thus frame the narrative segments. A number of mapped narrative projects published on the Internet have taken advantage of interactive maps and open APIs of mapping services like Google Maps to provide narratives that are tied to specific locations. *Mr. Beller's Neighborhood* (1998), edited by Thomas Beller, is a simple example of this approach. The website includes stories situated in New York City, submitted by authors and selected by the editors of the site. Each story is tagged with a physical location and with themes. The stories are then located on a map of the city, so that one can navigate the city via this ongoing, collectively written online anthology of short stories. The

German novel *Senghor on the Rocks* by Christoph Benda (2008) also uses the Google Maps API in a relatively simple way. Presented in a booklike interface, each scene of the novel includes an image from Google Maps on the facing page, tracking characters' movements from a bird's eye satellite view. María Mencía's *Gateway to the World* (2014) uses information from a maritime database to visualize on a map the routes of the vessels arriving and leaving the Port of Hamburg (and subsequently other cities). To each vessel a string of text associated with the name of the vessel is attached, resulting in a calligramatic kinetic poem. Two works in Roderick Coover's *Unknown Territories* series are also based on using maps as interfaces for narrative explorations of the American West. Produced in Flash, *Voyage into the Unknown* (2007) and *Canyonlands: Edward Abbey and the Great American Desert* (2009) use custom maps as interfaces for a narrativization of John Welsey Powell's 1869 exploration of the Colorado River and for an interactive documentary (a "cinemascape") about Edward Abbey's work and environmental activism.

A number of locative narrative projects are not preconfigured narratives produced by their developers but architectures of participation in collective narratives. The *Yellow Arrow Project* by Christopher Allen, Brian House, and Jesse Shapins (2004) was a locative project that made use of SMS and an interactive database, as well as physical markers in the world. People interested in participating in the project could order stickers from the project's website. The stickers were in the shape of a yellow arrow and each included a unique numeric identifier. After placing the stickers in a public place, participants would send a text message to the project's phone number, including the identifier and a short message, observation, or poetic fragment about whatever the sticker was pointing to. When others encountered the stickers, they could then call the same number to retrieve the text that the participant had posted. The nature of the contributions was not determined by the developers of the project except through the constraint that the message had to fit within the confines of a short text message. *Yellow Arrow* was thus a street art project and a project of collective metatagging, an ephemeral form of locative social media. A number of other locative projects, such as Anders Sundnes Løvlie's 2008 *Flâneur* project (Løvlie, 2015) have also been built around gathering stories from collective contributors.

34 North 118 West by Jeremy Hight, Jeff Knowlton, and Naomi Spellman (2002) is a locative narrative developed well before smartphones became ubiquitous. Described by its authors as the first "site specific, location aware, GPS driven narrative," (Hight et al., 2015) the work is set in a specific industrial neighborhood in Los Angeles. The interactor is outfitted with a backpack including a GPS unit and a tablet computer. Walking to specific hotspots in the area triggered audio files, spoken audio narratives set within those locations. The work is a historical narrative in the sense that the narratives were primarily set in the late nineteenth century around a rail yard. The short narratives are fragments from the lives of characters like a railroad worker describing finding a body on the tracks, or a rubber tire plant worker describing an explosion at the factory. Hight describes the project as a kind of "narrative archeology" in which the interactor, wandering streets where century-old buildings that are still mostly intact, would encounter layers of history and ghost voices that may have once occupied them (Hight, 2010).

The audio walk format has been a popular mode of locative narrative, perhaps because it only demands that the participant dedicate one sense to the narrative input, using the ears to free the eyes to take in the details of the embodied present. A number of Teri Rueb's projects have used this format to engage participants in soundscapes that range from fictional narrative, to contributory collective work, to ecological narrative. Her *Itinerant* (2005), situated in central Boston, juxtaposed segments of Mary Shelley's *Frankenstein* with a narrative written by Rueb centered on a mysterious uncle who would occasionally appear in his family's life, disrupting their lives and tantalizing them with tales of adventures before vanishing again. Rueb reimagined areas of Boston including Commonwealth Avenue, the Public Garden, and Boston Commons as narrative spaces of paradise and purgatory. The project functioned like a hypertext in the sense that Rueb described participants experiencing the work "as a patchwork narrative that may or may not be navigated in its entirety" (Rueb, 2008) depending on what parts of the work they wandered into and in what order. In more recent work, Rueb has developed apps that simplify locative narrative from a technological standpoint. Early projects of this kind required that participants lug around heavy equipment to enable the delivery of location-based narrative, but now all that is required to realize them is a smartphone and a pair of headphones.

The L.A. Flood Project (2011) by Mark Marino and the LAinundacion collective was a locative project that spread across a number of different platforms. The project was based on narratives of disaster collected by University of Southern California students, which were then adapted to fit within an overall narrative frame of a disastrous deluge in Los Angeles. Project participants could access the narrative in a number of different ways: through an annotated Google Map interface, through a mobile phone interface in which parts of the narrative were delivered as voice monologues, and through Netprov-style Twitter performances which also included written contributions from the general public. Kathi Inman Berens and Davin Heckman describe the Twitter participatory performance component of the project, which resulted in more than 70,000 tweets, as "an opportunity to explore the social geography of a multi-nodal city," (Berens and Heckman, 2013) as Angelinos tweeted about the effects of the fictional disaster in their specific neighborhoods. The project brought together elements of locative narrative and collective narrative around a frame tale that could be reiterated and experienced in a number of different ways. Just as a major disaster unfolds in a scattered, uncertain, and decentered manner, it makes sense for a narrative about a large fictional disaster to be spread across diffuse media.

Michelle Teran's projects often make innovative use of the locative features of social media in the production of experiential performances and narratives. Several of her projects harness locative information from publicly accessible social media postings in order to develop projects that lead to real-life interactions and performances. Teran's *Buscando Al Sr. Goodbar (Looking for Mr. Goodbar)* (2009) was a performance project based on the use of the geographic coordinates published with some YouTube videos. YouTube videos published with this information also automatically appear as points of interest on Google Earth maps. Teran spent time on Google Earth virtually visiting Murcia, a city in Southeastern Spain, getting to know some of its inhabitants by watching the videos they had posted on YouTube, doing things such as performing billiard tricks, singing a favored song drunkenly, or playing a piano solo. For the performance work, Teran hired a tour bus in Murcia. The audience on the tour bus watched some of the selected videos as the bus moved through the city, and then stopped at various locations to meet the YouTube performers and to ask them to reiterate their tricks in real life. The overall gesture of the performance was thus to retrieve personal embodied human connection from the stream of public imagery on the Internet, reasserting the material grounding of human-built networks.

Folgen (2012) used a similar approach to a different end. In this case, Teran found geolocated videos from a number of people in Berlin who were using YouTube as a kind of personal archive, building narratives of their own lives. The people she chose to track each had distinctive qualities as characters. They included among others a house painter involved in the neo-Nazi movement, a bodybuilder, and an elderly man tracking his last days of life. Teran then attempted to retrace their movements through the city, searching out the places her protagonists had been. Finally, she wrote a book in which she addressed each of her characters individually, both imagining dialogues with them and imagining aspects of their interior lives as projected through their video traces. As in the previous project, Teran used locative information to de-anonymize network content, and then used it as the basis for a narrative of imagined intimacy.

Locative technologies open up new dimensions to our experience of storytelling by blurring or modifying the diegetic distinction between imagined setting and the physical world. Writers and artists are still experimenting with understanding the constraints and affordances of this new narrative access to the physical and geographic aspects of the reader/interactor's situation in the world. The locative specificity of many of these locative narratives can be a double-edged sword – at the same time as it enhances the narrative experience of a particular place, narratives that are tied to a specific place are not easily transferable and are thus inherently limited in reach. If the promise of works published on the Internet was that they could be read everywhere, many locative narratives are very precisely site-specific and can be experienced only in one location. For some projects this site-specificity is necessary: Teran's works, tied as they are to traces of individual lives in specific locations, could not be relocated. But one can imagine locative narratives that could be accessible to wider audiences by reconfiguring their relationship to the specificities of place. A locative narrative set in a city environment could pull in location information specific to a given city at the time the application is loaded rather than in advance. A scene set in front of a police station or in the parking lot of an Irish bar could happen in many different cities. The location elements can also be tied to the movements of an application's user rather than to the specific place in the world – the popular fitness app *Zombies, Run!* by Naomi Alderman (2015) for example delivers a narrative of a zombie apocalypse based on the user's movements, but not on the specific place in which she flees the brain-devouring undead. As technologies complicate the distinction between the map and the territory, and as we increasingly live in a reality in which our movements are virtually mapped and monitored, these locative works provide us with tools to reflect on the meaning of mapping in our everyday lives.

Interactive Installations

Interactive installations, which may feature kinetic text, narrative storytelling, or network inputs, are another genre of practice that extends techniques from electronic literature into arts and performance environments. Interactive literary installations bring elements of spectacle and meaning into tension with each other. Language is treated as a signifier but often more significantly as a material in the same sense as paint is a material on an abstract expressionist's canvas. When our embodied interaction with a large-scale work that is providing direct sensory feedback in response to the physical movement of our bodies, as is the case with many new media art installations, the distinction between text and image may become less important: sensation may be foregrounded in place of reading. Roberto Simanowski argues "ornament and spectacle, one may conclude, obviate the need for interpretation, while the focus on formal aesthetic experiments tends to make us aware of the material" (Simanowski, 2011, p. 82). In the works of new media installation (language) artist Simon Biggs, for example, meaning can often be found more directly in our interaction with text in a generalized sense than in the particular selection of the (often appropriated) text itself.

Text Rain by Romy Achituv and Camille Utterback (1999) is a classic interactive kinetic text installation. In *Text Rain*, the interactor stands before a projection. The mirrored image of her own body appears before her. Letters begin to fall from the top to the bottom of the screen. As the letters touch the mirrored image of the body, they move in response, as if the projected body were a solid object. As the interactor moves her body, then, play with the letters becomes possible: the letters can be scooped up in cupped hands or brushed aside. By carefully interacting with the text, the reader can occasionally gather a word or a phrase, but the interaction generally frustrates linear reading, emphasizing play. There is a fixed coherent text in *Text Rain*, the poem "Talk, You" by Evan Zimroth (1993, p. 40), but in museum installation situations it is unlikely that most users will actually read the whole text. The poem in some sense mirrors the activity of the installation itself, as the poem is about conversation, imagined as a physical act, including lines such as "At your turning, each part/ of my body turns to verb." and "We are synonyms/ for limbs' loosening/ of syntax," but the focus of the user experience is more on virtual physics than it is on parsing the lines of the poem. The conversation that takes place in the work is between the human body interacting with a technological apparatus more than it is a representation of communication between two humans. Interestingly, the text of the original poem is a bit longer than the excerpted version used in the installation. The excised lines of the original poem make a clear correlation between a sexual relationship between the speaker and another person. The deletion of these lines changes the nature of the poem's central metaphor, to some degree desexualizing it and allowing the reader to imagine it differently, as a reiteration of the interface rather than as a representation of physical and linguistic intimacy between two people. The technical innovation of *Text Rain* has been reiterated more often in museum installations that are presented without language content than it has in other literary works. When Vilvite, our local children's science museum in Bergen, opened, the first thing museum-goers encountered when they entered was an interactive installation very much like *Text Rain*, but the interactive objects were not texts. I have seen versions of the installation mechanic with colorful spheres, snowflakes, or raindrops, rather than letters, and they have always been mobbed with kids fascinated with the interactive aspect of the work, not with any text, but with the way they could gather and play with the rain.

Still Standing by Bruno Nadeau and Jason Lewis (2005) presents a kind of inversion of *Text Rain* within a very similar interface. While the user of *Text Rain* needed to move and gather text to gradually develop a sense of what the poem was about, the more that one moves in *Still Standing*, the more frustrating reading it becomes. In *Still Standing*, when the interactor approaches the projection, text is jumbled about in a heap as if piled on the floor. When the interactor approaches the text, it reacts as if kicked or pushed, and the more she moves, the more the text is scattered about. When the interactor pauses and remains still, however, the text is attracted and flows into a form that is the shape of the interactor's body, and at this point the text of the poem becomes legible. In their introduction to the work in the *Electronic Literature Collection, Volume 2*, the authors describe the work as a "response to the 'collapse of the interval'; a phenomenon of fast pace culture that rarely allows us a moment to stop and observe; a habit that weakens the fragile approach toward design with dynamic typography" (Nadeau and Nelson, 2011) The text of the poem in *Still Standing*, once made accessible by the reader's stillness, valorizes pausing for contemplation, reading in part "I order my personal commotion and bring my brain to a stop. The inception of a sedation is needed for the waves to break and the spin to reduce." In both *Text Rain* and *Still Standing* we see how the movement of not only the text but of the interactor's body in space functions as gestural metaphor in correlation with the semantic intent of the works' texts.

Simon Biggs, one of the most prolific artists working in new media arts installations, has produced a number of works involving interactive language from the 1990s through to the present. Biggs has taken a variety of approaches to using language as a material for interactive installations. *The Great Wall of China* (1999) is a combinatory work which moved through instantiations as a website, CD-ROM, and installation. Using all of the words from the Kafka story with the same title, Biggs' project generated texts on the fly, described in project documentation as "based on pattern recognition, redundancy algorithms and Chomskian Formal Grammars." Biggs often explores the interface between the human body, space, spoken language, written language, and machine interpretation of language. Several of his works are produced in collaboration with dancers, such as *Crosstalk*

(2013), a work Biggs co-produced with composer Garth Paine, dancer Sue Hawksley, and software developer Hadi Mehrpouya. *Crosstalk* makes use of 3D motion tracking, voice recognition from multiple speakers, an interpretative language system, projected 3D visualization, and audio synthesis. Speech and language is acquired from the dancers or performers, which is then interpreted by the system and visualized. The movement of the dancers causes the visualized language to interact and recombine, and also modifies sound synthesis. The work generates a complex ecosystem of transcoded inputs and outputs, with human input interpreted and reprocessed in different ways by the system. Like many of Biggs' works, there is no fixed "text" in the work. The language and the other elements of the experience produced by the system are specific to the given performance. As such it calls into question the nature of "reading." While the use of language in the work is not trivial (it does not merely serve as background to the movement of the dancers) it is also not predetermined or authored in any conventional sense. Although the majority of Biggs' later works operate independently of a given corpus of language (they are systems, bespoke software that will work with whatever texts that are fed to them) in some cases the selected corpus does have an explicit authorial intent. In *Dark Matter* (2016) a field of language floats in 3D space. The movement of people in the installation space determines the movement of fragments of language, and the rendering of language shifts from first-, to second-, and third-person based on the number of people present in the space. The corpus of language in this case included fragments of interviews with prisoners held indefinitely in the Guantanamo Bay detention camp. Through interaction with the piece, the audience gradually realizes the cultural context to which it refers. The shifts in perspective from "I" to "you" to "we" call to mind questions of objectification, othering, and complicity.

As we can see from Biggs' works, many digital language art installations build upon elements of the core genres of electronic literature discussed in this book, such as hypertext, combinatory poetics, and kinetic and interactive poetry, in the development of works that work within multiple sensory and semantic registers. Language is often only one element, and sometimes not the predominant one. Yet letters, reading, and literary interpretation remain core aspects of the experiences they produce.

Expanded Cinema, Virtual Reality, and Augmented Reality

In 1970, Gene Youngblood wrote a volume title *Expanded Cinema* that projected a future in which computers and alternative cinema environments would play an important part in filmmaking. Youngblood detailed experiments in the late 1960s with films produced using early computer animations, as well as video artworks from the likes of Nam June Paik and Otto Peine. This future has already come to pass, in the sense that the commercial filmmaking process is now almost entirely digitized from the cameras, to the editing studio, to the CGI animation, to the technologies that project the image on the screen. 3D or even "4D" cinema experiences are now commonplace. In a somewhat humbler way, expanded cinema has also crossed over into electronic literature, as a number of writers and artists have produced works that apply techniques and approaches common in electronic literature in the construction of cinematic experiences. These range from combinatory cinema works that are structured and work much like poetry generators to films that are hypertextual and interactive or in which user responses have an effect on the narrative outcome. Electronic literature authors have also developed projects that involve interactive kinetic poetry or narratives in virtual reality and augmented reality environments and performance projects that merge digital literature, video, and live performance.

A number of filmmakers, including some prominent directors, were interested in the possibilities of using hypertextual database logic to produce interactive cinema experiences in CD-ROM and web-based projects. *Wax or the Discovery of Television Among the Bees* by David Blair (1991) is a film project that merged experimental techniques and an embrace of the Web. The film was a kind of psychedelic fable that was shot in part from an imagined perspective of a bee and touched on themes involving the military-industrial complex. The film mixed digital animations, found footage, and live action. A review in *The New York Times* described it as "a fantastic story of time travel, reincarnation and communion with the dead that conflates science fiction, biblical myth and entomology into a convoluted fable. The tale, among other things, is a multi-generational family saga as it might be imagined by a cyberpunk novelist" (Holden, 1992). After its theatrical release, Blair decided to release it on the Web in 1993; it is in fact described as the first film to be streamed on the Internet. *Waxweb* (1993), a hypermedia version of the film that the viewer could navigate nonlinearly, was also released at this point on the Web. In 1995, recording and performance artist Laurie Anderson produced a CD-ROM *Puppet Motel*, which included spoken-word poetry, virtual environments, and interactive elements. In 1997 experimental filmmaker Chris Marker released *Immemory* on CD-ROM. The project mixed documentary and fiction, and was multimedial, including images, texts and film clips. In a sense, the project was a nonlinear exploration of Marker's own memory as well as a meditation on what becomes of memory in a digital era. *Immemory* considered matters including war, the histories of cinema and photography, and literature. It was a highly intertextual work, for example frequently referencing Proust and Hitchcock. Peter Greenaway's *Tulse Luper Suitcases* (2003–2005) was an expansive multimedia project that involved four feature-length films, two books, a participatory contest for designers who produced interactive "suitcases," and an online game. The central character of all of the projects, Luper, was a "professional prisoner" born in 1911 whose travels spanned a number of hotspots from World War II to the end of the Cold War.

Steve Tomasula's *TOC: a New-Media Novel* (2009, 2013) and Danny Cannizzaro and Samantha Gorman's *Pry* (2014) are works that could also be described as expanded cinema; though they both more clearly emerge from an electronic literature context and were produced by artists who are first and foremost writers.

Tomasula worked with a number of different collaborators on *TOC,* including design and creative direction by Stephen Farrell, animations by Matt Lavoy and Christian Jara, and surrealist imagery by Maria Tomasula, as well as music by a number of contributors. The work was first published on DVD and subsequently in an iPad version. The novel as a whole is framed by an epic battle between Chronos and Logos, the two sons of Ephemera, as well as the concepts after which they are named. The twins are inheritors of an island, over which they will battle for eternity. Where Chronos frames and drives the progression of experience, Logos makes possible some articulation of it. This frame tale is told via a cinematic animation. After experiencing this cinematic frame tale, the reader then has an opportunity to choose between Chronos and Logos. Chronos is a time-based story appropriately told within another fairly lengthy cinematic animation, while Logos delivers an anthology of written stories that can be read on a collection of "scrolls." The Chronos narrative is a parable about time and agency, focused on a woman from the nation of X, a *Vogue* model who is confronting a couple of awful choices as she has to decide whether or not to disconnect the life support system of her husband, who has been left in a vegetative state after a terrible accident, or to continue in suspended state of diminishing hope. Although *TOC* has many cinematic elements, it is clearly a writerly work that merges philosophy, storytelling, and design.

Cannizzaro and Gorman's *Pry*, winner of the 2015 Robert Coover Award, is an iPad application, a hybrid novella that borrows elements from electronic literature, cinema, and games in developing a narrative that engages with the specific materialities of the touch screen interface. *Pry* is a story about a soldier, demolitions expert James, returned home from Iraq with PTSD and failing sight. The interactor's play with *Pry* is primarily about reaching into the protagonist's mind to uncover his thoughts and emotions. The story is presented through live action video, animations, and texts. In *Pry*, gesture functions as a powerful metaphor as well as an interface element. The interactor accesses the narrative through touch, by for example prying open James' eyes, or pulling apart lines of text to read between the lines. It is both a novella that we read and a work of expanded cinema that responds intimately to our touch.

Combinatory poetics have also been explored in a number of narrative cinema projects. *Terminal Time* (1998) by video producer Steffi Domike, computer scientist Michael Mateas, and digital artist Paul Vanouse is a project that integrated story generation, audience response, and a database of audio-visual elements in the production of a believable 30-minute combinatory historical documentary. The project presented the audience first with an expository prologue of a history that moved from far past (1000 AD) to recent present. At several different points in the story, the cinema audience was presented with multiple choice questions and asked to clap for the options they preferred. The questions were designed in such a way that they reflected certain ideological biases. The subsequent sections of the documentary were then shaped by an audience ideology profile that became more and more refined over the course of a session.

In *Three Rails Live* (2012) by Roderick Coover, Nick Montfort, and Scott Rettberg and *Toxi•City: a Climate Change Narrative* (2016) by Roderick Coover and Scott Rettberg, combinatory systems produce different versions of database films algorithmically, but independent of audience interaction. *Three Rails Live* is a system that produces short narrative videos, stories with a moral to them. The three collaborators put the system together at some remove from each other. Coover sent a selection of short video clips and images to Montfort and me. After viewing the clips, I sorted them into themes such as "Landscape and Fate" or "Death by Snake," and then wrote three short narratives for each theme, and recorded readings of each of these narratives. Montfort selected particular images, and, borrowing a technique from Harry Mathews, wrote "perverbs" – remixes of two different proverbs that subvert the original – and paired each of these texts to an image. Montfort also produced a title generator that arbitrarily creates a title for each run of the work. The system selects two videos and two of the narrative voice tracks from a constrained randomized selection. The juxtaposition of image and text are not predetermined but made by the system on the fly. A perverb with a moral to the story is then assigned and the process begins anew. The system thus results in short narrative videos with new juxtapositions of images, voice-over texts, and perverbs each time it runs.

The system does not repeat a voice track for 45 minutes, so a holistic first-person narrative develops as the individual short films aggregate. The films produced will always be different, but over time a coherent story dealing with environmental degradation, memory, mortality, alienation, and regret takes shape.

Toxi•City: a Climate Change Narrative works in a similar way, building a new version of the film each time it runs, but in this case the segments that are joined together have the same juxtaposition of voice and image; only the appearance and ordering of the clips vary on an algorithmic basis. *Toxi•City* takes place in one of the most polluted industrial environments in North America, the Delaware River Estuary, during a time of hurricanes, flooding, and the release of toxic waste. The narrative includes two layers, one that posits a (slightly alternate) near future in which multiple hurricanes have hit the East Coast of the United States in rapid succession, and another based on factual accounts of people who died in 2012 during Hurricane Sandy. The fictional narrative follows six characters whose lives are changed in different ways by the environmental catastrophe, while the elegiac layer tells the story of dozens of individual deaths. The algorithm changes the ordering and character focus in the fictional layer (on a given run, different characters' stories will receive more or less focus) as well as the death stories that will be encountered. In this way, the algorithmic recombination of the film helps to establish a panoramic narrative approach. Neither the ordering of the events as experienced by characters nor the stories of individual deaths are presented to the viewer in the same arrangement on any given run.

Virtual and augmented reality have also provided new tools and approaches for the presentation of narrative and poetic works of electronic literature in immersive environments. Well before the recent surge of interest in head-mounted display (HMD) virtual reality (VR) systems such as the Oculus Rift, HTC Vive, Google Daydream, and Samsung Gear, literary artists were exploring potential of VR in CAVE (Cave automatic virtual environment) systems. HMD VR systems provide individual experiences, in which the user is literally wearing a stereoscopic screen mounted on their face. This produces a strange sensation of being removed from one's body and environment. While an HMD user can move around in 360 degrees of the virtual space, they cannot see their own body. Movement within the virtual environment and control of interactive elements can be achieved both through this embodied movement and through handheld devices. CAVE environments on the other hand take place in physical spaces, making use of multiple projectors or LCD screens for the 3D visualization of the virtual environment. Many literary experiments have been produced in CAVE environments since the early 2000s, largely because of the fact that Brown University has made Cave writing (now Writing3D) courses a regular offering in its Literary Arts program since 2001 in courses led first by Robert Coover and subsequently by John Cayley (Cayley, 2014). *Screen* (2002) by Noah Wardrip-Fruin with Josh Carroll, Robert Coover, Shawn Greenlee, Andrew McClain, and Ben Shine was one of the first and is likely still the most often cited literary work produced for a CAVE environment. In *Screen*, words are projected on three walls and on the floor. The user's position is tracked, so that the visualization responds to her movement and perspective, and a glove allows her to trigger interactive elements.

As *Screen* begins, words appear and cover the three screens in the Cave and are read aloud. On each wall a different text describes a double moment in time, a woman or a man remembering and feeling the memory slip away, hidden by the present. The texts describe intimate memories, "She uncurls her arm,/ reaches back to lay her hand across/ his thigh, to welcome him home,/ but touches only a ridge of sheet,/ sun warmed, empty." The reading of these texts concludes with the spoken line, "We hold ourselves in place by memories," before the state of the work changes. The memories at this point refuse to stay still and begin to peel off the walls. The interactor can try to catch them, and might succeed in forcing them back where they belong, but before too long the words collide and fracture as the interactor loses control. This experience in virtual reality is very different from the Holodeck vision of total immersion in a mimetic representation of the world. *Screen* instead immerses the user in a reflexive literary representation, one in which words and narratives remain predominant.

In part because of the nature of the custom software developed at Brown, which privileges writing in the sense of material texts made of letters, many of the most notable works produced in Brown's CAVE, such as *Word Museum* (2004) by William Gillespie, *Lens* (2007) by John Cayley, and *Canticle* (2010) by Samantha Gorman feature text prominently and can be understood as expanding on the genre of kinetic poetry by carrying it into immersive 3D VR environments. The winner of the 2016 Robert Coover Award, *Hearts and Minds: The Interrogations Project* (2015) produced by Roderick Coover, Arthur Nishimoto, Scott Rettberg, and Daria Tsoupikova, is on the contrary a CAVE work driven by modeled environments and voice-over narratives rather than by letters moving in space. *Hearts and Minds* merges elements of documentary, hypertext, gamelike environments, and visual art in a project that is focused on the cycles of institutionalized violence surrounding the American abuse of detainees during the Iraq War in the early 2000s. This project about human rights foregrounds veterans' testimonies of US military enhanced interrogation practices and human rights abuses during the Iraq War, often by young and ill-trained soldiers who never entered the military to become torturers and still find themselves struggling to reconcile the activities they were asked to do. The work was first developed at the Electronic Visualization Lab (EVL) at the University of Illinois Chicago in the CAVE2™, a large-scale 320-degree panoramic virtual reality environment. It has subsequently been shown in other versions including a version that can be shown in conventional cinema environments.

Hearts and Minds is based on research by social scientist John Tsukayama for his dissertation *By Any Means Necessary: An Interpretive Phenomenological Analysis Study of Post 9/11 American Abusive Violence in Iraq* (2014). Tsukayama interviewed a number of soldiers who had either tortured prisoners themselves or witnessed such acts in the battlefield. *Hearts and Minds* is a VR performance artwork intended to communicate some of the very difficult stories these soldiers told Tsukayama and to promote reasoned consideration of the problems generated by using torture as an interrogation tactic. *Hearts and Minds* is intended for collective viewing. The CAVE2™ is a quite large facility in comparison to most CAVEs. About 20 people can fit comfortably into the space. A single performer navigates the work through his movement and by his selection of trigger objects with a handheld controller. The first part of the work takes place in a 3D modeled temple-like space, a reflective environment. As the performer moves through the modeled environment, the audience hears the voices of four soldier characters describing their motivations for joining the military. Four doors lead out of the temple into spaces of a different character, each based on an American domestic environment (a boy's bedroom, a living room, a backyard with a shed, a kitchen). In these rooms, certain objects present themselves with targets and sound cues. When the performer triggers the given object, the walls of the space fall away and the audience members find themselves in a surreal desert landscape, as they listen to one of the soldiers telling a story of torture or its aftermath. The stories themselves were directly excerpted from Tsukayama's interviews then interpreted by voice actors. *Hearts and Minds* in some sense models an experience of post-traumatic stress and is intended to put the audience in the challenging position of identifying with the difficult subject position of soldiers who never set out to become torturers, but who now have to confront what they have done in the name of their country.

Literary works have also been developed for HMD virtual reality systems and for augmented reality (AR) environments. In chapter 5 we considered *Between Page and Screen*, an AR kinetic poetry book. In Aaron Reed and Jacob Garbe's *The Ice-Bound Compendium* (2015b) and *The Ice-Bound Concordance* (2015a), the authors use an AR book as one layer of a narrative project that also brings elements of generated text and interactive fiction to a sprawling narrative about an "author simulacrum." A number of Caitlin Fisher's projects have used AR for storytelling. Fisher has augmented both books and other types of physical installations not only with virtual texts but also voice-overs, images, video, and animations. Fisher's poem *Andromeda* (2008), winner of the Ciutat de Vinaròs Digital Literature Award, builds upon the concept of the pop-up children's book. Fisher overlaid a found pop-up book with AR markers. The interactor activated the work by holding the pop-up book in front of the computer camera. A MAX/MSP program recognized multiple markers simultaneously and launched multiple video and audio tracks as they were recognized by the system. Fisher compared the system to "the diegetic scene of a mother reading to a child." Fisher also uses AR in other ways, as the markers need not be restricted to placement in a book. In the installation *Mother/Home/Heaven* (Fisher & Viere, 2013) the interactor uses an iPad to look at photographs and objects. When seen through the AR lens, the images and objects spring to life to tell stories of everyday life in a Canadian pioneer village.

Judd Morrissey has also used AR in a number of different projects, often as one element in a complex live performance situation that involves live vocal performance and other elements, such as scripted text mixed in with text pulled live from Twitter streams, video, and animations. In *The Operature* (2014) members of the audience are invited to use smartphones and iPads to scan tattoos on the bodies of the dancers performing the work, revealing texts and media layers. In some presentations of *Kjell Theøry*, AR texts are located both on bodies of performers and in specific geolocated environments. Morrissey blends AR elements, texts layered on top of our view of the surrounding world, with locative narrative.

These divergent forms of interactive installations and expanded cinema projects have shared roots in electronic literature and other artistic disciplines and serve as excellent examples of how – even as genres of electronic literature are being created – traditional boundaries between artistic media and disciplines are breaking down. These forms represent experiments in the future of narrative and poetics which, while retaining aspects of traditional literary form, use new conceptions of narrative structure, multiple sensory registers, visual, aural, and haptic sensation, fully embodied interaction, and new modes of affect in creating experiences that flow between media art and literature. These examples are also indicative of how a "project" in electronic literature can extend across a variety of iterations and cultural venues. Some of these examples, such as *Pry*, are among the more commercially successful examples in the field and may point both to new audiences and venues for interactive literary experiences.

Finding and Keeping Electronic Literature: Collections, Databases, and Archives

Digital objects present special challenges for libraries, archives, and other cultural institutions. The challenge of distributing, documenting, and preserving works of electronic literature has largely fallen to writers and researchers active in the field. Because works of electronic literature tend toward technological obsolescence, the task of creating an archive is more pressing for electronic literature than many other fields of literary practice. Collections, databases, and archives are essential to the sustainability of the field, both in terms of providing access to available work in the field and in providing documentation to works that are no longer accessible.

The *Electronic Literature Collection, Volume One* (Montfort et al., 2006) provided a new publishing model situated between prior models of commercial publishing and completely independent publishing on the Web with an open-access, Creative Commons-licensed anthology representing many different practices in electronic literature. In gathering together a collection of sixty diverse works of electronic literature, and publishing them both on physical media in a case suitable for library distribution and on the Web, the *Collection* addressed both issues related to the difficulty of locating works in transient media and to some extent, problems of preservation. The ELO published subsequent volumes of the *Collection*, including *Volume 2* in 2011 (Borrás et al., 2011), and *Volume 3* in 2016 (Boluk et al., 2016). The ELMCIP project also published the multilingual *ELMCIP Anthology of European Electronic Literature* (Engberg et al., 2012). Together these projects provide a durable selection of works selected by editorial collectives on the basis of submissions via an open call.

While electronic literature is not yet systematically catalogued in library catalogs, there are a number of active databases that document and provide information about works of electronic literature. Interested readers can find concise critical descriptions of works in the ELO's *Electronic Literature Directory*. NT2 is a major ongoing research project based in Quebec and focused on providing a similar resource for the francophone world. Leonardo Flores' *I Love E-Poetry* site offers hundreds of records of short-form scholarship that describe individual works of digital poetry. The distinctive aspect of the *ELMCIP Electronic Literature Knowledge Base*, established in 2010, is that it provides information architecture for documenting works of electronic literature in a critical ecology that also includes extensive documentation of critical writing, authors, publishers, organizations, events, databases, archives, and teaching resources.

Archives and media archeology labs are another essential aspect of electronic literature research infrastructure that has become increasingly well developed in recent years. Important archival projects are taking a number of forms. There are single-author special collections, such as the Deena Larsen collection at the University of Maryland, the Stephanie Strickland collection at Duke University, and the Michael Joyce Collection at the Ransom Center. The PO.EX archive bridges between database functions and archival functions, documenting and publishing an extensive online archive of Portuguese electronic literature and experimental writing. Finally there are a number of projects that gather and document physical media and technology, ranging from a collection of posters, documents, and ephemera from electronic literature events housed at the University of Bergen, to the collections of works of early electronic literature and vintage computers required to run them put together by Dene Grigar at the Washington State University Electronic Literature Lab, to an extensive collection of interactive fiction, games, computers and early gaming systems at Nick Montfort's Trope Tank lab at MIT, to the Media Archeology Lab curated by Lori Emerson at the University of Colorado.

The Future of Electronic Literature: Endings, Experiments, or Transitions?

In spite of the short life span of many individual works of electronic literature, *genres* of electronic literature don't die, nor do they fade away. It is more appropriate to consider how genres of electronic literature are absorbed into new genres and forms, how they serve as building blocks for other forms that follow them. Because experiments in electronic literature have moved at the speed of technology, it is also the case that many interesting projects have opened avenues of technical innovation and literary expression that were not close to exhausted, or even developed into mature forms, before their authors moved on to the next platform, the next innovation. This does not necessarily mean that those techniques or genres should be declared dead. We should not make the mistake of assuming that there is a clear linear progression from genre to genre, or from one technological advance to the next. When people ask me what became of the hypertext novel, I ask them in turn what became of the haiku? Perhaps there are not as many poets writing haiku now as there were in Tokugawa Japan, but a number of Twitter bots are now churning them out by the thousands, and those haiku are still read. The example of the Twine community, suddenly producing hundreds of hypertext fictions long after most of the electronic literature community had left hypertext for dead, is also instructive.

The speed with which hardware platforms, software, and even storage media are developed and abandoned clearly poses some problems for the field of electronic literature. In order for electronic literature to be teachable and in order for future artists to learn from work of past artists, the works themselves need to be documented, preserved, and kept available. The scale of the challenge is sometimes daunting: even in the time since I wrote the outline for this book in 2016 and that I am finishing the manuscript in early 2018, dozens of works, particularly those made using Flash and Director, are becoming more and more difficult to access. Yet I am hopeful this problem of technological obsolescence will be surmountable. The examples of *First Screening* (discussed in chapter 5) or the *Renderings* project (Montfort, 2014b) offer models of how works that slip into obsolescence can be migrated and translated across both human and machine languages, sometimes decades after they first go "out of print." Provided that code and documentation of works are preserved somewhere, they can be resuscitated at a later date. The emulation of early personal computer hardware and software platforms is increasingly becoming a focus of cultural heritage institutions. These projects will once again make it possible for us to read files, and read works of electronic literature, that we might now only be able to access in facilities that maintain old computers. Some important lessons have also been learned as we have watched works become inaccessible. Among these, perhaps the most important is that free and open-source platforms tend to survive longer than proprietary formats. The more dependencies, more different media formats, in a sense the more bells and whistles that a work has, the shorter its accessible life span is likely to be.

The rhetoric of innovation can sometimes be overblown. Those who in the 1990s believed or feared that hypertext would spell the "end of books" have not seen any such conclusion come to pass, and they won't see that any time soon. Certainly e-books have taken up an increasing percentage of market-share, but printed books have their own specific affordances, which have been supplanted neither by e-books nor electronic literature. It seems to me that this is exactly as it should be: electronic literature should not be understood as an attempt to "replace" the book, but instead as an effort to open up new genres and venues of literary arts practice. If anything, it should drive us to awareness of the material and aesthetic affordances of many different types of reading and writing experiences. The book is not the only game in town, not the only writing platform on which contemporary writers should expend their energies, not the only cultural site in which compelling literary experiences can occur.

In his essay on aurature, John Cayley speculates that "the contemporary and evolving cultural practices of reading – what reading is and will become – will be determined not by the innovators of electronic literature; they will be determined by those cultural power brokers who build and control the Big Software architecture of reading" (Cayley, 2018, p. 87). I agree that Amazon and Google will likely have a greater impact on the future of reading platforms than the experiments and the genres of electronic literature detailed in this book, but I would not be so quick to dismiss the importance or the potential aesthetic impact of electronic literature on the plural *futures* of reading. I have always thought of electronic literature as a network of loosely affiliated movements more than I have as any kind of monolithic tectonic shift in literary culture. As far as movements go, electronic literature has done very well, spanning more than two decades, becoming established as an academic field, developing its own research infrastructure, linking communities of creative practice across Europe and the Americas, and continuing to grow, year after year. Consider the fact that Dada, probably the most influential art movement of the twentieth century, existed as a specific affiliated movement for only about a decade, and was comparatively marginal during the period it was most active. But as more artists learned about Dada, as it was absorbed into the culture at large, as its ideas and techniques were taken up and reinvented by subsequent movements, its influence became more profound over time.

Writers and artists will always be drawn to new tools, venues, and opportunities within a changing culture and a changing technological apparatus. Those waiting for the first "#1 bestseller" of electronic literature are largely missing the point: electronic literature is not about replacing print literary culture, it is instead about extending storytelling and poetics to the contemporary digital environment and creating literary experiences specific to this cultural moment. Electronic literature is experimental literature that generates productive tests of particular admixtures of literature and technology, but it is also fundamentally about a sense of play and a sense of wonder. What kind of stories can our digital tools help us to tell? What will we think of next?

In parting, I want to come back to what brought me to electronic literature to begin with, and what has kept me reading and writing it for the past twenty years. In 1999, after *The Unknown* won the trAce/AltX award, Robert Coover invited me and my coauthors to Brown University for the Technology Platforms for 21ˢᵗ Century Literature conference. After a rousing interactive reading of the hypertext novel, we gathered in the Brown Graduate Center bar, where Coover bought us a round of beers. I was talking with Coover about how fascinating it had been to write hypertext, writing fiction together with friends, exploring new ways of developing and connecting stories, publishing them instantaneously on the network, and in short discovering how just how much fun electronic writing can be. Coover raised his glass and said, "Never forget that. Always remember the fun."

References

Creative Works Referenced

Achituv, R. & Utterback, C. (1999) *Text Rain* [online]. Available from: http://camilleutterback.com/projects/text-rain/ (Accessed 20 December 2017).

Acker, K. (1988) *Empire of the Senseless*. New York: Grove / Atlantic.

Activision. (1991) *The Lost Treasures of Infocom*.

Adams, D. & Meretzsy, S. (1984) *The Hitchhiker's Guide to the Galaxy*. Infocom.

Adams, T. & Adams, Z. (2002) "*Dwarf Fortress*," in *Electronic Literature Collection, Volume 3*. [online]. Available from: http://collection.eliterature.org/3/work.html?work=dwarf-fortress (Accessed 18 December 2017).

Alderman, N. (2015) *Zombies, Run!* [online]. Available from: https://zombiesrungame.com/ (Accessed 5 February 2018).

Allen, C. et al. (1998) *The Yellow Arrow Project* [online]. Available from: https://brianhouse.net/works/yellow_arrow/ (Accessed 26 February 2018).

Amerika, M. (1997) *Grammatron* [online]. Available from: http://grammatron.com (Accessed 5 December 2017).

Annapura Interactive. (2017) *What Remains of Edith Finch*. Los Angeles.

Andersen, T. et al. (1978) *Zork*.

Anderson, L. (1995) *Puppet Motel*. [online]. Available from: https://archive.org/details/puppet-motel-1998 (Accessed 26 February 2018).

Andrews, J. (1999) 'Stir Fry Texts', in *Electronic Literature Collection, Volume One*. [online]. Available from: http://collection.eliterature.org/1/works/andrews__stir_fry_texts.html (Accessed 26 February 2018).

Andrews, J. (2001) *Nio* [online]. Available from: http://www.vispo.com/nio/ (Accessed 19 December 2017).

Andrews, J. (2002) *Arteroids* [online]. Available from: http://vispo.com/arteroids/indexenglish.htm (Accessed 18 December 2017).

Anthropy, A. (2013) *The Hunt for a Gay Planet* [online]. Available from: http://ifdb.tads.org/viewgame?id=boeof1y11dr27wod (Accessed 18 December 2017).

Archangel, C. (2002) *Super Mario Clouds* [online]. Available from: http://www.coryarcangel.com/things-i-made/2002-001-super-mario-clouds (Accessed 17 December 2017).

Arellano, R. (1996) *Sunshine '69* [online]. Available from: http://www.sunshine69.com/noflash.html (Accessed 16 December 2017).

Baldwin, S. (2003) 'New Word Order: Basra', in *Electronic Literature Collection, Volume 2*. [online]. Available from: http://collection.eliterature.org/2/works/baldwin_basra.html (Accessed 18 December 2017).

Balpe, J. P. (2003) *Babel poésie*.

Balpe, J. P. (1993) *La Mort dans l'âme*.

Balpe, J. P. (2015.) Textbots. *Hyperrhiz: New Media Cultures*. [Online] (11 (Spring 2015)). [online]. Available from: http://dx.doi.org/10.20415/hyp/011. g01 (Accessed 5 December 2017).

Barth, J. (1968) 'Frame Tale', in *Lost in the Funhouse*. New York: Doubleday. pp. 1–2.

Barthelme, D. (1969) Sentence. *The New Yorker* (Jan 18) p.31.

Bates, B. (1987) *Witness*. Infocom.

Baum, L. F. (1913) *Patchwork Girl of Oz*. Chicago: Reilly & Britton.

Beckett, M. et al. (2006) *Lonelygirl15* [online]. Available from: https://www.youtube.com/channel/UCVEfyEuLJpgw_y4jSgV8Rtg (Accessed 10 December 2017).

Beiguelman, G. (2004) 'Code Movie 1', in *Electronic Literature Collection, Volume One*. [online]. Available from: http://collection.eliterature.org/1/works/beiguelman__code_movie_1.html (Accessed 6 December 2017).

Beller, T. (1998) *Mr. Beller's Neighborhood* [online]. Available from: https://mrbellersneighborhood.com/ (Accessed 31 January 2018).

Benda, C. (2008) 'Senghor on the Rocks', in *Electronic Literature Collection, Volume 2*. [online]. Available from: http://collection.eliterature.org/2/works/benda_senghor_on_the_rocks.html (Accessed 31 January 2018).

Berlyn, M. (1983) *Suspended*. Infocom.

Bevan, B. & Wright, T. (2001) *Online Caroline* [online]. Available from: http://www.onlinecaroline.com/ (Accessed 11 December 2017).

Bhatnagar, R. (n.d.) *Pentametron* [online]. Available from: https://twitter.com/pentametron?lang=en (Accessed 14 December 2017).

Bigelow, A. (2017) *How to Rob a Bank* [online]. Available from: http://webyarns.com/howto/howto.html (Accessed 23 February 2018).

Biggs, S. (2013) *Crosstalk* [online]. Available from: http://littlepig.org.uk/installations/crosstalk/index.htm (Accessed 5 February 2018).

Biggs, S. (2016) *Dark Matter* [online]. Available from: http://littlepig.org.uk/installations/darkmatter/index.htm (Accessed 5 February 2018).

Biggs, S. (1999) *The Great Wall of China* [online]. Available from: http://littlepig.org.uk/wall/greatwall.htm (Accessed 5 February 2018).

Blair, D. (1991) *Wax, or the Discovery of Television Among the Bees*.

Blair, D. (1993) *Waxweb* [online]. Available from: http://www.waxweb.org/ (Accessed 7 February 2018).

Blank, M. (1982) *Deadline*. Infocom.

Blank, M. & Lebling, D. (1986) *Zork I: The Great Underground Empire*. Infocom.

Bogost, I. (2007) *Bloomsday on Twitter* [online]. Available from: http://bogost.com/writing/blog/bloomsday_on_twitter/ (Accessed 8 December 2017).

Bök, C. (2001) *Eunoia*. Toronto: Coach House Books.

Boluk, S. et al. (eds) (2016) *Electronic Literature Collection, Volume 3*. Cambridge, MA: Electronic Literature Organization. [online]. Available from: http://collection.eliterature.org/3/ (Accessed 19 March 2017).

Bookchin, N. (1999) *The Intruder* [online]. Available from: https://bookchin.net/projects/the-intruder/ (Accessed 18 December 2017).

Bootz, P. (2012) *Small Uncomfortable Reading Poems*.

Borges, J. L. (1962) 'The Garden of Forking Paths', in *Ficciones*. New York: Grove Press. pp. 89–101.

Borrás, L. et al. (2011) *Electronic Literature Collection, Volume 2*. Cambridge, MA: Electronic Literature Organization. [online]. Available from: http://collection.eliterature.org/2/ (Accessed 19 March 2016).

Borsuk, A. et al. (2017) *ABRA*. iPad application. Available from: http://www.a-b-r-a.com/ (Accessed 22 March 2018).

Borsuk, A. & Bouse, B. (2012) *Between Page and Screen*. New York: Siglio.

Bouchardon, S. (2011) *Loss of Grasp / Déprise* [online]. Available from: http://www.lossofgrasp.com/ (Accessed 16 December 2017).

bpNichol (1970) *Cosmic Chef: An Evening of Concrete*. Ottawa: Oberon Press.

bpNichol (2007) 'First Screening', in *Electronic Literature Collection, Volume 3*. [online]. Available from: http://collection.eliterature.org/3/work.html?work=first-screening.

bpNichol (1984) *First Screening: Computer Poems*. Toronto: Underwhich Editions.

Breeze, M. (2011) '_cross.ova.ing 4rm.blog.2.log 07/08 XXtracts_', in *Electronic Literature Collection, Volume 2*. [online]. Available from: http://collection.eliterature.org/2/works/mez_crossovaing.html.

Camp Santo. (2016) *Firewatch*. San Francisco.

Cabell, M. & Huff, J. (2012) *American Psycho*. Vienna: Traumawien.

Cadre, A. (1999) *Varicella*. [online]. Available from: http://adamcadre.ac/if/varicella.html (Accessed 17 December 2017).

Cannizzaro, D. & Gorman, S. (2014) *Pry*. iPad application. Available from: http://prynovella.com/ (Accessed 26 February 2018).

Carpenter, J. (2004) *Erica T. Carter: The Collected Works | ELMCIP* [online]. Available from: http://elmcip.net/creative-work/erica-t-carter-collected-works (Accessed 22 March 2016).

Carpenter, J. R. (2006) *Entre Ville* [online]. Available from: http://luckysoap.com/entreville/index.html (Accessed 16 December 2017).

Carpenter, J. R. (2008) *in absentia* [online]. Available from: http://luckysoap.com/inabsentia/index.html (Accessed 16 December 2017).

Carpenter, J. R. (2009) *Gorge* [online]. Available from: http://luckysoap.com/generations/gorge.html (Accessed 14 December 2017).

Carpenter, J. R. (2011) *Generation[s]*. Vienna: Traumawien.

Carpenter, J. R. (2016) *The Gathering Cloud* [online]. Available from: http://luckysoap.com/thegatheringcloud/ (Accessed 16 December 2017).

Carr, J. (2002) Breathing /Secret of Roe. *Poems That Go*. [online]. Available from: https://web.archive.org/web/20131028204904/http://www.poemsthatgo.com/gallery/winter2002/secret.htm (Accessed 26 February 2018).

Carter, E. T. (2008) *Issue 1: Fall 2008*. Jim Carpenter & Stephen McLaughlin (eds).

[online]. Available from: https://www.goodreads.com/book/show/4932117-issue-one (Accessed 26 February 2018).

Cayley, J. (2007) *Lens*. [online]. Available from: http://programmatology.shadoof. net/?lens (Accessed 8 February 2007).

Cayley, J. (1995) *Speaking Clock*. [online]. Available from: http://programmatol ogy.shadoof.net/?clocks (Accessed 18 December 2017).

Cayley, J. (2015) *The Listeners* [online]. Available from: http://programmatology. shadoof.net/?thelisteners (Accessed 11 December 2017).

Cayley, J. (1999) 'Windsound', in *Electronic Literature Collection, Volume One*. [online]. Available from: http://collection.eliterature.org/1/works/cayley__wind sound.html (Accessed 19 December 2017).

Cayley, J. (2005) *Wotclock*. [online]. Available from: http://programmatology.sha doof.net/?wotclock (Accessed 18 December 2017).

Cayley, J. & Howe, D. C. (2012) *How It Is in Common Tongues*. NLLF Press.

Chamberlain, W. & Etter, T. (1983) *Racter*.

Chamberlain, W. & Racter (1984) *The Policeman's Beard Is Half-Constructed*. New York: Warner Software/Warner Books. [online]. Available from: http://www. ubu.com/historical/racter/ (Accessed 26 February 2018).

Chang, Y. -H. & Voge, M. (2002) *DAKOTA* [online]. Available from: http:// www.yhchang.com/DAKOTA.html (Accessed 19 December 2017).

Charity Heartscape, P. (2012) *Howling Dogs* [online]. Available from: http://slime daughter.com/games/twine/howlingdogs/ (Accessed 17 December 2017).

Charity Heartscape, P. (2014) *With Those We Love Alive* [online]. Available from: http://slimedaughter.com/games/twine/wtwla/ (Accessed 17 December 2017).

Cho, P. (2002) 'Wordscapes & Letterscapes', in *Electronic Literature Collection, Volume 2*. [online]. Available from: http://collection.eliterature.org/2/works/ cho__letterscapes_and_wordscapes.html (Accessed 19 December 2017).

Clark, D. (2009) *88 Constellations for Wittgenstein* [online]. Available from: http:// www.88constellations.net (Accessed 16 April 2018).

Cole, T. (2013) *Seven stories about drones* [online]. Available from: https:// storify.com/joshbegley/teju-cole-seven-short-stories-about-drones (Accessed 8 December 2017).

Compton, K. (2015) *Tracery* [online]. Available from: http://tracery.io (Accessed 14 December 2017).

Coover, R. (1992) *A Night at the Movies, or, You Must Remember This*. 3rd edn. Normal, IL: Dalkey Archive Press.

Coover, R. (2009) *Canyonlands, Edward Abbey in the Great American Desert* [online]. Available from: https://unknownterritories.org/UnknownTerritories/ Canyonlands/index.html (Accessed 31 January 2018).

Coover, R. et al. (2015) *Hearts and Minds: The Interrogations Project*. [online]. Available from: http://www.crchange.net/hearts-and-minds/ (Accessed 26 February 2018).

Coover, R. (1969) *Pricksongs and Descants*. New York: Dutton.

Coover, R. et al. (2012) *Three Rails Live*. [online]. Available from: http://crchange. net/threerails (Accessed 26 February 2018).

Coover, R. (2008) 'Voyage Into the Unknown', in *Electronic Literature Collection, Volume 2*. [online]. Available from: http://collection.eliterature.org/2/works/ benda_senghor_on_the_rocks.html (Accessed 31 January 2018).

Coover, R. & Rettberg, S. (2016) *Toxi•City: A Climate Change Narrative*. [online]. Available from: http://www.crchange.net/toxicity/ (Accessed 7 February 2018).

Cortazar, J. (1963) *Rayuela*. Buenos Aires: Editorial Sudamericana.

Cortazar, J. (1987) *Hopscotch: A Novel*. 1st Pantheon pbk edn. New York: Pantheon.

Coverley, M. D. (2000) *Califia*. Watertown: Eastgate Systems.

Coverley, M. D. (2006) *Egypt: The Book of Going Forth by Day*. Newport Beach: Horizon Insight.

Cramer, F. (1996) *Permutations* [online]. Available from: http://permutations. pleintekst.nl/index.cgi#gysin/cut-up.cgi (Accessed 14 May 2016).

Crowther, W. & Woods, D. (1976) *Colossal Cave Adventure*. Cambridge, MA and Stanford, CA.

Cummings, E. E. (1958) *95 Poems*. New York: Liveright.

Danielewski, M. Z. (2000) *House of Leaves*. 2nd edn. New York: Pantheon.

Daniels, D. (2000) *The Gates of Paradise*. [online]. Available from: http://www. thegatesofparadise.com/ (Accessed 19 December 2017).

Davis, L. (2010) *The Collected Stories of Lydia Davis*. 7th edn. New York, NY: Picador.

Döhl, R. (1965) *Apfel mit wurm* [online]. Available from: https://www.reinhard-doehl.de/ (Accessed 18 December 2017).

Domike, S. et al. (1998) *Terminal Time*. [online]. Available from: http://studiofor creativeinquiry.org/projects/terminal-time (Accessed 7 February 2018).

Duchamp, M. (1926) *Anemic Cinema*. [online]. Available from: https://www.you tube.com/watch?v=dXINTf8kXCc (Accessed 12 December 2017).

Edit-Software In Python (ed.) (2010) *Exquisite_code*. London: Mute Publishing, Ltd.

Eliot, T. S. (1922) *The Waste Land*. New York: Horace LIveright.

Engberg, M. et al. (2012) (eds) (n.d.) *ELMCIP Anthology of European Electronic Literature*. Bergen, Norway: ELMCIP. [online]. Available from: http://anthol ogy.elmcip.net/.

Evens, A. (2018) 'Combination and Copulation: Making Lots of Little Poems', in *The Bloomsbury Handbook of Electronic Literature*. pp. 217–236.

Fisher, C. (2008) 'Andromeda', in *Electronic Literature Collection, Volume 2*. [online]. Available from: http://collection.eliterature.org/2/works/fisher_ andromeda.html (Accessed 13 February 2018).

Fisher, C. (2001) *These Waves of Girls* [online]. Available from: http://www.yorku. ca/caitlin/waves/ (Accessed 16 December 2017).

Fisher, C. & Viere, T. (2013) *Mother/Home/Heaven*. [online]. Available from:

http://hyperrhiz.io/hyperrhiz14/featured-works/07-fisher-mother-home.html (Accessed 13 February 2017).

Fletcher, J. (2012) *Pentimento* [online]. Available from: http://www.poetrybeyond text.org/fletcher.html (Accessed 19 December 2017).

Fulbright Company, The. (2013) *Gone Home*. Portland, OR.

Funkhouser, C. (2012) *New Directions in Digital Poetry*. 1st edn. New York: Bloomsbury Academic.

Garbe, J. & Reed, A. (2015a) *The Ice-Bound Compendium*. Santa Cruz: Simulacrum Liberation Press.

Garbe, J. & Reed, A. (2015b) *The Ice-Bound Compendium*. [online]. Available from: http://www.ice-bound.com (Accessed 13 February 2018).

Gibson, W. (1984) *Neuromancer*. New York: Ace.

Gillespie, W. et al. (1998) *The Unknown* [online]. Available from: http://unknown hypertext.com/ (Accessed 26 February 2018).

Gillespie, W. et al. (2002) *The Unknown: An Anthology*. Urbana: Spineless Books.

Gillespie, W. (2004) *Word Museum*. [online]. Available from: http://spineless books.com/wordmuseum/ (Accessed 7 February 2018).

Goldsmith, K. (2003) *Day*. Great Barrington, MA: Figures.

Gomringer, E. (1953) 'Silencio', in *Konstellationen*. Berne: Spiral Press.

Gorman, S. (2010) *Canticle*. [online]. Available from: http://samanthagorman.net/ Canticle (Accessed 8 February 2018).

Greenaway, P. (2003) *Tulse Luper Suitcases* [online]. Available from: http://peter greenaway.org.uk/tulse.htm (Accessed 7 February 2018).

Gysin, B. & Sommerville, I. (1965) *Permutation Poems*.

Gysin, B. et al. (2014) *Permutation Poems (Reimplmentation)* [online]. Available from: https://nickm.com/memslam/permutation_poems.html (Accessed 26 February 2017).

Hall, J. (1994) *links.net* [online]. Available from: http://links.net/ (Accessed 11 December 2017).

Harris, J. (2013) *Times Haiku: Serendipitous Poetry from The New York Times* [online]. Available from: http://haiku.nytimes.com (Accessed 14 December 2017).

Hatcher, I. (2015a) *[][Total Runout]*. [online]. Available from: https://elmcip.net/ creative-work/total-runout (Accessed 20 December 2017). [online].

Hatcher, I. (2015b) *Drone Pilot*. [online]. Available from: https://vimeo. com/145887878 (Accessed 20 December 2017). [online].

Hatcher, I. (2013) *Prosthesis*. [online]. Available from: https://vimeo.com/86922462 (Accessed 26 February 2018).

Hayles, N. K. et al. (eds) (2006) *Electronic Literature Collection, Volume One*. College Park, Maryland: Electronic Literature Organization. [online]. Available from: http://collection.eliterature.org/1/ (Accessed 19 March 2016).

Heemskerk, J. and Paesmans, D. (2001) *www.jodi.org* [online]. Available from: http://www.jodi.org (Accessed 4 December 2017).

Heldén, J. & Jonson, H. (2013) *Evolution* [online]. Available from: http://www.johanneshelden.com/evolution/ (Accessed 22 March 2016).

Herbert, G. (1633) *The Temple*. Cambridge, UK: University of Cambridge.

Hight, J. et al. (2002) '34 North 118 West: Mining the Urban Landscape', in *Electronic Literature Collection, Volume 3*. [online]. Available from: http://collection.eliterature.org/3/work.html?work=34-north-118-west (Accessed 31 January 2018).

Howe, D. C. (2014) *AdLiPo* [online]. Available from: https://rednoise.org/adlipo/ (Accessed 4 March 2018).

Howe, D. C. et al. (2015) *AdNauseam* [online]. Available from: https://adnauseam.io/ (Accessed 11 December 2017).

Howe, D. C. & Karpinska, A. (2004) 'open.ended', in *Electronic Literature Collection, Volume One*. [online]. Available from: http://collection.eliterature.org/1/works/howe_kaprinska__open_ended.html (Accessed 22 March 2016).

Howe, D. C. & Nissenbaum, H. (n.d.) *TrackMeNot* [online]. Available from: https://rednoise.org/daniel/detail.html#trackmenot (Accessed 11 December 2017).

Howell, B. (2010) *exquisite_code* [online]. Available from: http://www.wintermute.org/brendan/?p=exquisite-code (Accessed 22 March 2016).

Ingold, J. (2001) *All Roads*. [online]. Available from: http://ifdb.tads.org/viewgame?id=4s7uohdncurgqb0h (Accessed 17 December 2017).

Jackson, S. (1997) *My Body & A Wunderkammer* [online]. Available from: http://www.altx.com/thebody/.(Accessed 17 December 2017).

Jackson, S. (1995) *Patchwork Girl*. Watertown: Eastgate Systems.

Jackson, S. (2003) *Skin*. [online]. Available from: https://ineradicablestain.com/skindex.html. (Accessed 16 April 2018).

Jennings, H. & Madge, C. (eds) (1987) *May the Twelfth: Mass Observation Day Surveys 1937 by Over Two Hundred Observers*. London: Faber & Faber.

Johnson, B. S. (1969) *The Unfortunates*. London: Panther Books.

Johnston, D. J. (2016) *BDP (Big Data Poetry)* [online]. Available from: http://bdp.glia.ca/ (Accessed 14 December 2017).

Johnston, D. J. (2005) *Sooth* [online]. Available from: http://www.glia.ca/SAIC/ (Accessed 19 December 2017).

Joyce, J. (1939) *Finnegan's Wake*. London: Faber & Faber.

Joyce, J. (1922) *Ulysses*. Paris: Sylvia Beach.

Joyce, M. (1987) *afternoon, a story*. Watertown: Eastgate Systems.

Knowles, A. et al. (2014) *A House of Dust (Reimplementation)* [online]. Available from: https://nickm.com/memslam/a_house_of_dust.html.

Knowles, A. & Tenney, J. (1967) *The House of Dust*.

Knowlton, K. and Vanderbeek, S. (1966) *Visualizing Poetry with 1960s Computer Graphics -- PoemField No. 2 (1966). AT&T Tech Channel*. [online]. Available from: https://www.youtube.com/watch?v=V4agEv3Nkcs (Accessed 19 December 2017).

Lialina, O. (1996) *My Boyfriend Came Back from the War* [online]. Available from: http://myboyfriendcamebackfromth.ewar.ru/ (Accessed 16 December 2017).

Lutz, T. (1959a) Stochastic Textes (Stochastische Texte). *augenblick.* (4), 3–9. [online]. Available from: https://web.archive.org/web/20130616173633/http://tracearchive.ntu.ac.uk/frame6/talan_fr.htm (Accessed 30 June 2016).

Lutz, T. (2014) *Stochastic Texts (Reimplementation)* [online]. Available from: http://nickm.com/memslam/stochastic_texts.html (Accessed 19 March 2016).

Lye, L. (1937) *Trade Tattoo.* [online]. Available from: https://www.youtube.com/watch?v=WNSiqCazkic (Accessed 19 December 2017).

Maciunas, G. (1962) *12 Piano Compositions for Nam June Paik.* [online]. Available from: https://www.moma.org/collection/works/127428 (Accessed 11 December 2017).

Malarmé, S. (1879) Un coup de dés Jamais N'Abolira Le Hasard. Cosmpolis.

Malloy, J. (1986) *Uncle Roger* [online]. Available from: https://people.well.com/user/jmalloy/uncleroger/partytop.html (Accessed 15 December 2017).

Marinetti, F. T. (1914) *Zang Tumb Tumb.* Milan.

Marino, M. C. (2009) *The Loss Wikiless Timespedia* [online]. Available from: https://web.archive.org/web/20121110190808/http://bunkmagazine.com/mediawiki/index.php?title=Newy_new_new_shiny_wiki_wow_Main_Page (Accessed 26 February 2018).

Marino, M. C. & LAinundacion collective (2011) *LA Flood Project (Google Map)* [online]. Available from: https://www.google.com/maps/d/viewer?mid=1A8gPFywpHzewvWVpeZ95xvpwV1M (Accessed 4 February 2018).

Marino, M. C. & Wittig, R. (2015a) *#1WkNoTech* [online]. Available from: http://1wknotech.org/ (Accessed 11 December 2017).

Marino, M. C. & Wittig, R. (2015b) *I Work for the Web* [online]. Available from: http://robwit.net/iwfw/ (Accessed 4 December 2017).

Marino, M. C. & Wittig, R. (2016) *Monstrous Weather* [online]. Available from: http://meanwhilenetprov.com/index.php/project/monstrous-weather/ (Accessed 11 December 2017).

Marino, M. C. & Wittig, R. (2017) *One-Star Reviews* [online]. Available from: https://www.reddit.com/r/onestarreviewsnetprov/ (Accessed 11 December 2017).

Marker, C. (1997) *Immemory.* [online]. Available from: https://chrismarker.org/?s=immemory (Accessed 7 February 2018).

Markson, D. (2001) *This Is Not a Novel by Markson, David.* Berkeley: Counterpoint.

Markson, D. (1988) *Wittgenstein's Mistress.* Normal, IL: Dalkey Archive Press.

Maso, C. (1993) *Ava.* Normal, IL: Dalkey Archive Press.

Mass-Observation (1937) *Britain.* London: Penguin.

Mass-Observation (1987) *May the Twelfth: Mass Observation Day Surveys 1937 by Over Two Hundred Observers.* Charles Madge & Humphrey Jennings (eds). London: Faber & Faber.

Mass-Observation (1943) *The Pub and the People: A Worktown Study.* London: Victor Gollancz.

McCaffery, S. (1973a) *Carnival: The First Panel, 1967–1970*. Toronto: Coach House Books.

McCaffery, S. (1973b) *Carnival: The Second Panel 1970–75*. Toronto: Coach House Books.

McDaid, J. (1993) *Uncle Buddy's Phantom Funhouse*. Watertown: Eastgate Systems.

de Melo e Castro, E. M. (1968) *Roda Lume*. [online]. Available from: http://po-ex. net/taxonomia/materialidades/videograficas/e-m-de-melo-castro-roda-lume (Accessed 19 December 2017).

Memmot, T. (2000) 'Lexia to Perplexia', in *Electronic Literature Collection, Volume One*. [online]. Available from: http://collection.eliterature.org/1/works/mem mott__lexia_to_perplexia.html (Accessed 4 December 2017).

Memmot, T. (2006) The Hugo Ball. *Drunken Boat*. (8). [online]. Available from: http://www.drunkenboat.com/db8/panlitjudges/memmott/hugo_db/thehu goball.html (Accessed 19 December 2017).

Memmot, T. (2011b) 'Toy Garbage', in *Electronic Literature Collection, Volume 3*. [online]. Available from: http://collection.eliterature.org/3/work.html?work= toy-garbage (Accessed 14 December 2017).

Memmott, T. (2003) 'Self Portrait(s) [as Other(s)]', in *The Electronic Literature Collection, Volume One*. [online]. Available from: http://collection.eliterature. org/1/works/memmott__self_portraits_as_others.html (Accessed 26 February 2017).

Memmott, T. (2001) Translucidity. *Frame: Online Journal of Art and Technology*. (6). [online]. Available from: https://web.archive.org/web/20130704144027/ http://tracearchive.ntu.ac.uk/frame6/talan_fr.htm (Accessed 26 February 2018).

Mencía, M. (2001) 'Birds Singing Other Birds' Songs', in *Electronic Literature Collection, Volume One*. [online]. Available from: http://collection.eliterature. org/1/works/mencia__birds_singing_other_birds_songs.html (Accessed 19 December 2017).

Mencía, M. (2014) *Gateway to the World* [online]. Available from: http://www. mariamencia.com/pages/gatewaytotheworld.html (Accessed 4 March 2018).

Meretzsy, S. (1986) *Leather Goddesses of Phobos*. Infocom.

Meretzsy, S. (1983) *Planetfall*. Infocom.

Michel, K. & Vis, D. (2002) 'Ah', in *Electronic Literature Collection, Volume 2*. [online]. Available from: http://collection.eliterature.org/2/works/michel_ ah.html (Accessed 19 December 2017).

Mohammad, K. S. (2009) Poems About Trees. *Poetry*. (July /August). [online]. Available from: https://www.poetryfoundation.org/poetrymagazine/ poems/52687/poems-about-trees (Accessed 4 December 2017).

Montfort, N. (2014a) *#!*. Denver: Counterpath.

Montfort, N. (2000) *Ad Verbum*. [online]. Available from: https://nickm.com/if/ adverbum.html (Accessed 17 December 2017).

Montfort, N. (2012) *ppg256 (Perl Poetry Generators in 256 characters)* [online]. Available from: http://nickm.com/poems/ppg256.html (Accessed 21 March 2016).

Montfort, N. (ed.) (2014b) *Renderings*. The Trope Tank. [online]. Available from: http://nickm.com/trope_tank/renderings/ (Accessed 22 March 2016).

Montfort, N. (2009) *Taroko Gorge* [online]. Available from: http://nickm.com/taroko_gorge/ (Accessed 21 March 2016).

Montfort, N. & Rettberg, S. (2004) *Implementation* [online]. Available from: http://nickm.com/montfort_rettberg/implementation/ (Accessed 26 February 2018).

Montfort, N. & Rettberg, S. (2012) *Implementation*. Bergen, Norway: Blurb. [online]. Available from: http://www.blurb.com/b/3442475-implementation (Accessed 26 February 2018).

Montfort, N. & Strickland, S. (2012) *Sea and Spar Between* [online]. Available from: http://nickm.com/montfort_strickland/sea_and_spar_between/ (Accessed 22 March 2016).

Moriarty, B. (1986) *Trinity*. Infocom.

Moriarty, B. (1985) *Wishbringer*. Infocom.

Morrissey, J. (2015) *Kjell Theøry*. [online]. Available from: http://hyperrhiz.io/hyperrhiz14/featured-works/04-morrissey-kjell-theory.html (Accessed 13 February 2018).

Morrissey, J. (2000) 'The Jew's Daughter', in *Electronic Literature Collection, Volume One*. [online]. Available from: http://collection.eliterature.org/1/works/morrissey__the_jews_daughter.html (Accessed 13 December 2017).

Morrissey, J. (2007) *The Last Performance* [online]. Available from: http://thelastperformance.org/title.php (Accessed 7 December 2017).

Morrissey, J. & Jeffery, M. (2014) *The Operature*. [online]. Available from: http://www.judisdaid.com/theoperature.php (Accessed 13 February 2017).

Moulthrop, S. (1987) *forking paths*.

Moulthrop, S. (1997) Hegirascope. *The New River*. [online]. Available from: http://www.cddc.vt.edu/journals/newriver/moulthrop/HGS2/Hegirascope.html (Accessed 16 December 2017).

Moulthrop, S. (2003) *Pax: An Instrument*. [online]. Available from: http://www.smoulthrop.com/lit/pax/ (Accessed 26 February 2017).

Moulthrop, S. (1999) 'Reagan Library', in *Electronic Literature Collection, Volume One*. [online]. Available from: http://collection.eliterature.org/1/works/moulthrop__reagan_library.html (Accessed 16 December 2017).

Moulthrop, S. (1991) *Victory Garden*. Watertown: Eastgate Systems.

Nadeau, B. & Nelson, J. (2005) 'Still Standing', in *Electronic Literature Collection, Volume 2*. [online]. Available from: http://collection.eliterature.org/2/works/nadeau_stillstanding.html (Accessed 5 February 2018).

Needham, Martine. (1996) 'To Be or Not Be Mouchette', in *ELMCIP Anthology of European Electronic Literature*. Bergen: ELMCIP. [online]. Available from: https://anthology.elmcip.net/works/to-be-or-not-to-be-mouchette.html (Accessed 26 February 2018).

Nelson, J. (2007) *Game, game, game, and again game* [online]. Available from: http://www.secrettechnology.com/gamegame/gamegamebegin.html (Accessed 17 December 2017).

Nelson, J. (2013) Nothing You Have Done Deserves Such Praise. *Turbulence.* [online]. Available from: http://turbulence.org/project/nothing-you-have-done-deserves-such-praise/ (Accessed 26 February 2018).

Nelson, J. (2011) *Textual Skyline* [online]. Available from: http://www.secrettech nology.com/textsky/textsky.html (Accessed 4 December 2017).

Nelson, J. (2005) 'This is how you will die', in *Electronic Literature Collection, Volume 2.* [online]. Available from: http://collection.eliterature.org/2/works/nelson_thisishowyouwilldie.html (Accessed 13 December 2017).

Nelson, J. & Nadeau, B. (2014) *Poetry for Excitable [Mobile] Media* [online]. Available from: http://www.poemm.net/ (Accessed 20 December 2017).

Ness, M. & Deed, M. (n.d.) 'Oulipoems', in *Electronic Literature Collection, Volume One.* [online]. Available from: http://collection.eliterature.org/1/works/niss__oulipoems.html (Accessed 22 March 2016).

Nichols, M. (2009) I Google Myself. *Poetry.* (July/August). [online]. Available from: https://www.poetryfoundation.org/poetrymagazine/poems/52685/i-google-myself (Accessed 4 December 2017).

O'Neill, J. (1987) *Nord and Bert Couldn't Make Head or Tail of It.* Infocom.

Ormstad, O. (2015) *Long Rong Song.* [online]. Available from: https://vimeo.com/143451232 (Accessed 19 December 2017).

Ormstad, O. (2009) *Lyms.* [online]. Available from: https://vimeo.com/74233796 (Accessed 19 December 2017).

Ormstad, O. (2016) *Navn Nome Name.* [online]. Available from: https://vimeo.com/157416894 (Accessed 19 December 2017).

Parrish, A. (2007) *@everyword* [online]. Available from: https://twitter.com/everyword?lang=en (Accessed 14 December 2017).

Pavić, M. (1984) *Хазарски речник, Hazarski rečnik.* Belgrade: Prosveta.

Pavić, M. (1989) *Dictionary of the Khazars: A Lexicon Novel in 100,000 Words.* Vintage International Edition (Male edn). New York: Vintage.

Perec, G. (2008) *A Void.* New York: Vintage Classics.

Perec, G. (1969) *La Disparition.* Paris: Éditions Gallimard.

Philips, T. (1966) *A Humument.* Sixth. London: Thames & Hudson. [online]. Available from: http://www.tomphillips.co.uk/humument (Accessed 14 December 2017).

Pinsky, R. et al. (1984) *Mindwheel.* Synapse.

Pipkin, K. R. (2014) **tiny star field** [online]. Available from: https://twitter.com/tiny_star_field (Accessed 14 December 2017).

Piringer, J. (2002) [soundpoems]. *Poems That Go.* [online]. Available from: http://joerg.piringer.net/index.php?href=soundpoems/soundpoems.xml (Accessed 26 February 2019).

Plotkin, A. (1998) *Photopia.* [online]. Available from: http://ifdb.tads.org/viewgame?id=2xyccw3pe0uovfad (Accessed 26 February 2018).

Pound, E. (1934) *The Cantos of Ezra Pound.* New York: New Directions.

Pullinger, K. (2014) *Landing Gear.* New York: Touchstone Books.

Pullinger, K. & Campbell, A. (2007) *Flight Paths* [online]. Available from: http://www.flightpaths.net/ (Accessed 10 December 2017).

Pullinger, K. & Joseph, C. (2005) *Inanimate Alice* [online]. Available from: https://inanimatealice.com. (Accessed 10 December 2017).

Queneau, R. (1961) *Cent mille milliards de poèmes*. Paris: Gallimard.

Queneau, R. (1981) *Exercises in Style*. 2nd edn. New York: New Directions.

Quinn, Z. (2013) *Depression Quest*. [online]. Available from: http://www.depressionquest.com/ (Accessed 24 February 2018).

Reed, A. A. (2009) *Blue Lacuna*. [online]. Available from: http://blue-lacuna.textories.com (Accessed 17 December 2017).

Reed, A. A. (2005) *Whom the Telling Changed*. [online]. Available from: http://www.aaronareed.net/telling.html (Accessed 17 December 2017).

Reed, A. A. & Garbe, J. (2015) *Ice-Bound Compendium*. Down to the Wire.

Rengetsu, O. & Ankerson, I. (2002) Murmuring Insects. *Poems That Go*. [online]. Available from: https://rhizome.org/art/artbase/artwork/murmuring-insects/ (Accessed 26 February 2018).

Rettberg, S. (2009a) 'Frequency', in *Electronic Literature Collection, Volume 3*. [online]. Available from: http://collection.eliterature.org/3/work.html?work=frequency (Accessed 22 March 2016).

Rettberg, S. (2009b) 'Tokyo Garage', in *Electronic Literature Collection, Volume 3*. [online]. Available from: http://collection.eliterature.org/3/work.html?work=tokyo-garage (Accessed 14 December 2017).

Rettberg, S. (2002) *Kind of Blue* [online]. Available from: http://retts.net/kindofblue/ (Accessed 11 December 2017).

Sample, M. (2009) 'Takei, George', in *Electronic Literature Collection, Volume 3*. [online]. Available from: http://collection.eliterature.org/3/work.html?work=takei-george (Accessed 14 December 2017).

Sample, M. (2013) *@NSA_PRISMbot* [online]. Available from: https://twitter.com/NSA_PRISMbot (Accessed 28 February 2018).

Saporta, M. (1961) *Composition No. 1*. Paris: Seuil.

Saporta, M. (1963) *Composition No. 1*. New York: Simon and Schuster.

Saporta, M. (2011) *Composition No. 1*. iPad application. London: Visual Editions.

Seattle (1983) *Invisible Seattle: The Novel of Seattle*. Seattle: Function Industries Press.

Shelley, M. W. (1818) *Frankenstein*. London: Lackington, Hughes, Harding, Mavor & Jones.

Short, E. (2012) *Counterfit Monkey*. [online]. Available from: http://ifdb.tads.org/viewgame?id=aearuuxv83plclpl (Accessed 17 December 2017).

Short, E. (2000) *Galatea*. [online]. Available from: http://ifdb.tads.org/viewgame?id=urxrv27t7qtu52lb (Accessed 17 December 2017).

Snodgrass, E. (2011) 'Yoko Engorged', in *Electronic Literature Collection, Volume 3*. [online]. Available from: https://nickm.com/taroko_gorge/yoko_engorged/ (Accessed 14 December 2017).

Sondheim, A. (1994) *Internet Text* [online]. Available from: http://collection.eliter ature.org/1/works/sondheim__internet_text.html (Accessed 9 December 2017).

Sondheim, A. (2012) *Writing Under*. Computing Literature. Morgantown: Center for Literary Computing.

Spiegelman, A. (1994) CD-ROM. *The Complete Maus, a Survivor's Tale (Macintosh CD-ROM Version)*. Voyager.

Stefans, B. K. (2000) 'The Dreamlife of Letters', in *The Electronic Literature Collection, Volume One*. [online]. Available from: http://collection.eliterature. org/1/works/stefans__the_dreamlife_of_letters.html (Accessed 18 December 2017).

Sterne, L. (1761) *The Life and Opinions of Tristam Shandy, Gentleman*. London: Ann Ward (vol. 1–2), Dodsley (vol. 3–4), Becket & DeHondt (5–9).

Strachey, C. (1952) *Love Letters*.

Strachey, C. & Montfort, N. (2014) *Love Letters (Reimplementation)*. [online]. Available from: http://nickm.com/memslam/love_letters.html (Accessed 26 February 2018).

Strickland, S. & Hatcher, I. (2015) *House of Trust* [online]. Available from: http:// www.house-of-trust.org/ (Accessed 15 December 2017).

Strickland, S. & Jaramillo, C. L. (2007) *Slippingglimpse* [online]. Available from: http://www.slippingglimpse.org (Accessed 19 December 2017).

Strickland, S. & Jaramillo, C. L. (2002) *V: Vniverse* [online]. Available from: http://vniverse.com (Accessed 18 December 2017).

Sutherland, W. M. (2012) 'Negative Thoughts', in Craig Hill & Nico Vassilakis (eds) *The Last Vispo Anthology*. Seattle: Fantagraphics. p. 50.

Swenson, D. (2001) *Kaycee Nicole*.

Swift, J. (1726) *Gulliver's Travels*. London: Benjamin Motte.

Szilak, I. (2012) *Queerskins* [online]. Available from: http://online.queerskins.com/ (Accessed 18 December 2017).

Teran, M. (2009) *Buscando Al Sr. Goodbar (Looking for Mr. Goodbar)* [online]. Available from: http://www.ubermatic.lftk.org/blog/?p=225 (Accessed 26 February 2018).

Teran, M. (2012) *Folgen* [online]. Available from: http://www.ubermatic.org/?p= 1607 (Accessed 5 February 2018).

Thomas, S. & Hoskins, T. (1998) *Noon Quilt*. Nottingham: trAce. [online]. Available from: http://web.archive.org/web/20131130140859/http:// tracearchive.ntu.ac.uk/quilt/info.htm (Accessed 26 February 2018).

Tiselli, E. (2005a) *degenerative* [online]. Available from: http://www.motorhueso. net/degenerative/ (Accessed 8 December 2017).

Tiselli, E. (2005b) *regenerative* [online]. Available from: http://www.motorhueso. net/regenerative/regenerative.php (Accessed 8 December 2017).

Tomasula, S. (2009a) *TOC: a New-Media Novel*. DVD. Available from: http:// www.tocthenovel.com/index.html (Accessed 7 February 2018).

Tomasula, S. (2013) *TOC: a New-Media Novel*. iPad application. Available from: http://www.tocthenovel.com/index.html (Accessed 7 February 2018).

United States Army (2002). *America's Army*. online]. Available from: https://www.americasarmy.com (Accessed 20 December 2017).

Valve. (2011) *Portal 2*. Bellevue, WA.

Vonnegut, K. (1973) *Breakfast of Champions*. New York: Delacorte Press.

Wallace, D. F. (1996) *Infinite Jest*. New York: Little, Brown.

Wardrip-Fruin, N. et al. (2002) 'Screen', in *Electronic Literature Collection, Volume 2*. [online]. Available from: http://collection.eliterature.org/2/works/wardrip-fruin_screen.html (Accessed 20 December 2017).

Wardrip-Fruin, N. et al. (1999) *The Impermanence Agent*. [online]. Available from: http://www.impermanenceagent.org/agent/ (Accessed 26 February 2018).

Weizenbaum, J. (1966) *ELIZA*.

Weizenbaum, J. & Landsteiner, N. (2005) *ELIZA javascript emulator*. [online]. Available from: http://www.masswerk.at/elizabot/ (Accessed 20 March 2016).

White, C. (1998) *Memories of My Father Watching TV*. Normal, IL: Dalkey Archive Press.

Wilks, C. (2008) *Tailspin* [online]. Available from: http://crissxross.net/elit/Tailspin.html.

Wilks, C. (2010) *Underbelly* [online]. Available from: http://crissxross.net/elit/underbelly.html.

Winterson, J. (1989) *Sexing the Cherry*. London: Bloomsbury.

Wittig, R. (2002) *Blue Company* [online]. Available from: http://www.robwit.net/bluecompany2002/ (Accessed 11 December 2017).

Wittig, R. (2000) *Friday's Big Meeting* [online]. Available from: http://robwit.net/fbm/ (Accessed 10 December 2017).

Wittig, R. (1999) 'The Fall of the Site of Marsha', in *Electronic Literature Collection, Volume One*. [online]. Available from: http://collection.eliterature.org/1/works/wittig__the_fall_of_the_site_of_marsha.html (Accessed 4 December 2017).

Woolf, V. (1925) *Mrs Dalloway*. Richmond: Hogarth Press.

Woolf, V. (2014) *To the Lighthouse*. London: CRW Publishing Limited.

Worthy, R. M. (1962) Auto-Beatnik. *Horizon*. 4 (5). p. 405–419.

Wylde, N. (2002) 'Storyland', in *Electronic Literature Collection, Volume One*. [online]. Available from: http://collection.eliterature.org/1/works/wylde__storyland.html (Accessed 12 December 2017).

Zimroth, E. (1993) 'Talk, You', in *Dead, Dinner or Naked: Poems*. TriQuarterly Books. Evanston, IL: Northwestern University Press. p. 40.

Critical Writing Referenced

Aarseth, E. J. (1997) *Cybertext: Perspectives on Ergodic Literature*. Baltimore, MD: Johns Hopkins University Press.

Andersen, C. U. & Pold, S. B. (2014) Manifesto for a Post-Digital Interface Criticism. *The New Everyday: A Mediacommons Project*. [online]. Available from: http://mediacommons.futureofthebook.org/tne/pieces/manifesto-post-digital-interface-criticism (Accessed 3 March 2018).

Andrews, J. et al. (2007) *bpNichol's 'First Screening' -- Introduction* [online].

Available from: http://vispo.com/bp/introduction.htm (Accessed 19 December 2017).

Anon (2016) *Rhizome Net Art Anthology: Mezangelle* [online]. Available from: https://anthology.rhizome.org/mez-breeze (Accessed 29 November 2017).

Apted, M. (1997) *David Bowie – the Verbasizer*. [online]. Available from: https://www.youtube.com/watch?v=x3IKLMgFaDA.

Aristotle (1997) *Poetics*. London: Penguin Classics.

Aspley, K. (2010) *Historical Dictionary of Surrealism*. Lanham, MD: Scarecrow Press.

Baldwin, S. (2015) *The Internet Unconscious: On the Subject of Electronic Literature*. New York: Bloomsbury Academic.

Ball, H. (1916) *Dada Manifesto* [online]. Available from: http://391.org/manifestos/1916-dada-manifesto-hugo-ball.html (Accessed 19 December 2017).

Barbosa, P. (1977) *A Literatura Cibernética 1: Autopoemas Gerados por Computador*. Porto: Edições Árvore.

Barbosa, P. (1980) *A Literatura Cibernética 2: Um Sintetizador de Narrativas*. Porto: Edições Árvore.

Barnet, B. (2010) Crafting the User-Centered Document Interface: The Hypertext Editing System (HES) and the File Retrieval and Editing System (FRESS). *Digital Humanities Quarterly*. 4 (1). [online]. Available from: http://www.digitalhumanities.org/dhq/vol/4/1/000081/000081.html (Accessed 15 December 2017).

Barnet, B. (2013) *Memory Machines: The Evolution of Hypertext*. Anthem Press.

Barthes, R. (1977) 'The Death of the Author', in Roland Barthes (ed.) *Image, Music, Text*. New York: Hill and Wang. pp. 142–148.

Beaulieu, D. (2012) 'Concrete & "What Looks Like Poetry"', in Craig Hill & Nico Vassilakis (eds) *The Last Vispo Anthology*. Seattle: Fantagraphics. p. 50.

Beebee, T. O. (2004) *The Ideology of Genre: A Comparative Study of Generic Instability*. Penn State Press.

Bell, A. et al. (eds.) (2014) *Analyzing Digital Fiction*. Routledge Studies in Rhetoric and Stylistics. New York: Routledge.

Belles, S. et al. (1960) *Minutes to Go*. Paris: Two Cities Editions.

Berens, K. I. (2014) Judy Malloy's Seat at the (Database) Table: a Feminist Reception History of Early Hypertext Literature. *Literary and Linguistic Computing*. 29 (3), 340–348. [online]. Available from: https://academic.oup.com/dsh/article/29/3/340/986452 (Accessed 7 December 2017).

Berens, K. I. (2015) Live/Archive: Occupy MLA. *Hyperrhiz*. (11). [online]. Available from: http://hyperrhiz.io/hyperrhiz11/essays/live-archive-occupy-mla.html (Accessed 11 December 2017).

Berens, K. I. & Heckman, D. (2013) "Use the # & Tweet yr escape": LA Flood as Mobile Dystopic Fiction. *Los Angeles Review of Books* [online]. Available from: https://lareviewofbooks.org/article/use-the-tweet-yr-escape-la-flood-as-mobile-dystopic-fiction (Accessed 4 February 2018).

Berners-Lee, T. (1989) *Information Management: A Proposal* [online]. Available from: https://www.w3.org/History/1989/proposal.html (Accessed 27 June 2018).

Bogost, I. & Montfort, N. (2009) *Platform Studies: Frequently Questioned Answers.* [online]. Available from: http://bogost.com/downloads/bogost_montfort_dac_2009.pdf (Accessed 27 February 2018).

Bohn, W. (2011) *Reading Visual Poetry.* Lanham, MD: Fairleigh Dickinson Press.

Bolter, J. D. et al. (1999) *Getting Started with Storyspace for Macintosh.* Watertown, MA: Eastgate Systems.

Bolter, J. D. (2001) *Writing Space: Computers, Hypertext, and the Remediation of Print.* 2nd edn. Mahwah, NJ: Routledge.

Bolter, J. D. & Grusin, R. (1999) *Remediation: Understanding New Media.* Cambridge, MA: The MIT Press.

Boluk, S. & LeMieux, P. (2013) 'Dwarven Epitaphs: Procedural Histories in Dwarf Fortress', in *Comparative Textual Media: Transforming the Humanities in the Postprint Era.* University of Minnesota Press. pp. 125–154.

Borràs, L. et al. (2011) *Electronic Literature Collection, Volume 2.* Cambridge, MA: Electronic Literature Organization. [online]. Available from: http://collection.eliterature.org/2/ (Accessed 19 March 2016).

Bouchardon, S. & López-Varela, A. (2011) Making Sense of the Digital as Embodied Experience. *CLCWeb: Comparative Literature and Culture.* 13 (3). [online]. Available from: http://docs.lib.purdue.edu/clcweb/vol13/iss3/7/ (Accessed 16 December 2017).

Braffort, P. (2002) *ALAMO, Une expérience de douze ans* [online]. Available from: http://www.paulbraffort.net/litterature/alamo/alamo_experience.html (Accessed 10 May 2016).

Breton, A. (1972) 'Manifesto of Surrealism', in *Manifestos of Surrealism.* Ann Arbor: University of Michigan Press. pp. 1–39.

Briceno, H. et al. (2000) *Down From the Top of Its Game The Story of Infocom, Inc.* [online]. Available from: http://web.mit.edu/6.933/www/Fall2000/infocom/infocom-paper.pdf (Accessed 17 December 2017).

Buckles, M. A. (1985) *Interactive Fiction: The Computer Storygame "Adventure."* University of California, San Diego.

Burroughs, W. S. (2003) 'The Cut-Up Method of Brion Gysin', in *The New Media Reader.* pp. 89–92.

Bush, V. (1945) As We May Think. *The Atlantic* [online]. Available from: https://www.theatlantic.com/magazine/archive/1945/07/as-we-may-think/303881/ (Accessed 15 December 2017).

Campbell, J. (2012) Ian Hamilton Finlay: the concrete poet as avant gardener. *The Guardian.* 16 November. [online]. Available from: https://www.theguardian.com/books/2012/nov/16/ian-hamilton-finlay-concrete-poetry (Accessed 18 December 2017).

de Campos, A. & de Campos, H. (1956) Poesia concreta. *Diário Popular.* 22 December 1956.

de Campos, A. et al. (1958.) Pilot Pan for Concrete Poetry. *Noigrandes* (4).

Carey, B. (2015) The reader-assembled narrative: Representing the random in print fiction. *Text*. 19 (2). [online]. Available from: http://textjournal.com.au/oct15/carey.htm (Accessed 16 December 2017).

Cayley, J. (2018) 'The Advent of Aurature and the End of (Electronic) Literature', in *The Bloomsbury Handbook of Electronic Literature*. pp. 73–83.

Cayley, J. (2002) The Code is not the Text (unless it is the Text). *electronic book review*. [online]. Available from: http://www.electronicbookreview.com/thread/electropoetics/literal (Accessed 29 November 2017).

Cayley, J. (2005) Bass Resonance. *electronic book review*. [online]. Available from: http://www.electronicbookreview.com/thread/electropoetics/dynamic (Accessed 19 December 2017).

Cayley, J. (2014) 'Cave', in *The Johns Hopkins Guide to Digital Media*. Johns Hopkins University Press. pp. 49–52.

Cayley, J. (2009) 'Time Code Language: New Media Poetics and Programmed Signification', in *New Media Poetics: Contexts, Technotexts, and Theories*. pp. 307–333.

Cayley, J. & Howe, D. C. (2013) Reading, Writing, Resisting: Literary Appropriation in the Readers Project. *Proceedings of the 19th International Symposium of Electronic Art, ISEA 2013*. [online]. Available from: http://theread ersproject.org/ (Accessed 11 December 2017).

Charity Heartscape, P. & Chan, D. (2017) Porpentine Charity Heartscape. *Artforum* [online]. Available from: https://www.artforum.com/words/id=67067 (Accessed 17 December 2017).

Charity Heartscape, P. & Short, E. (2012) Interview with Porpentine, author of howling dogs. Emily Short's Interactive Storytelling [online]. Available from: https://emshort.blog/2012/11/23/interview-with-porpentine-author-of-howl ing-dogs/ (Accessed 17 December 2017).

Ciccoricco, D. D. (2007) *Reading Network Fiction*. Tuscaloosa: University Alabama Press.

Connor, M. (2016) *Speaking in Net Language: My Boyfriend Came Back from the War* [online]. Available from: https://rhizome.org/editorial/2016/nov/10/my-boyfriend-came-back-from-the-war/.

Cooper, S. (2012) Introduction to Isodore Isou. *E.R.O.S.: A Journal of Desire*. [online]. Available from: http://www.drsamcooper.com/situationist-research/introduction-to-isidore-isou/ (Accessed 19 December 2017).

Corneliussen, H. G. & Rettberg, J. W. (eds) (2011) *Digital Culture, Play, and Identity: A World of Warcraft® Reader*. Cambridge, MA: The MIT Press.

Crain, C. (2006) Surveillance Society: The Mass-Observation Movement and the Meaning of Everyday Life. *The New Yorker* [online]. Available from: https://www.newyorker.com/magazine/2006/09/11/surveillance-society (Accessed 4 December 2017).

Cramer, F. (2014) What is 'Post-Digital'? *APRA: A Peer-Reviewed Journal About Post-Digital Research*. 3 (1). [online]. Available from: http://www.aprja.net/what-is-post-digital/ (Accessed 16 December 2017).

Cramer, F. (2001) *Digital Code and Literary Text* [online]. Available from: https://www.netzliteratur.net/cramer/digital_code_and_literary_text.html (Accessed 29 November 2017).

Daniels, D. et al. (2004) *Interview David Daniels* [online]. Available from: http://arteonline.arq.br/museu/interviews/david.htm (Accessed 19 December 2017).

Debord, G. (1956) Theory of the Dérive. *Les Lèvres Nues #9*. [online]. Available from: http://www.cddc.vt.edu/sionline/si/theory.html (Accessed 28 December 2017).

Dena, C. (2009) *Transmedia Practice: Theorising the Practice of Expressing a Fictional World across Distinct Media and Environments*. Sydney: University of Sydney. [online]. Available from: https://ciret-transdisciplinarity.org/biblio/biblio_pdf/Christy_DeanTransm.pdf (Accessed 27 February 2018).

Derrida, J. (1980) The Law of Genre. *Critical Inquiry*. 7 (1), 55–81.

Dickey, W. & Landow, G. P. (1991) 'Poem Descending a Staircase: Hypertext and the Simultaneity of Experience', in Paul Delaney (ed.) *Hypermedia and Literary Studies*. Cambridge, MA: The MIT Press. pp. 143–152.

Douglas, J. Y. (2000) *The End of Books – or Books Without End?: Reading Interactive Narratives*. Ann Arbor: University of Michigan Press.

Douglass, J. et al. (2015) *Reading Project: A Collaborative Analysis of William Poundstone's Project for Tachistoscope {Bottomless Pit}*. Iowa City: University of Iowa Press.

Drucker, J. (1994) *The Visible Word: Experimental Typography and Modern Art, 1909–1923*. Chicago: University of Chicago Press.

Drucker, J. (1989) *The Word Made Flesh*. Cambridge, MA: Druckwerk.

Emerson, L. (2012) Activist Media Poetics: Electronic Literature Against the Interface-free. [online]. Available from: https://loriemerson.net/2012/01/12/activist-media-poetics-electronic-literature-against-the-interface-free-mla-2012/ (Accessed 14 February 2017).

Emerson, L. (2014) *Reading Writing Interfaces: From the Digital to the Bookbound*. Minneapolis: University of Minnesota Press.

Emerson, L. (2008) *The Rematerialization of Poetry: From the Bookbound to the Digital*. Buffalo: State University of New York, Buffalo.

Engberg, M. et al. (2012) *Anthology of European Electronic Literature*. Bergen: ELMCIP. [online]. Available from: http://anthology.elmcip.net/ (Accessed 21 March 2016).

Eskelinen, M. (2012) *Cybertext Poetics: The Critical Landscape of New Media Literary Theory*. Continuum: International Texts in Critical Media Aesthetics. New York: Bloomsbury.

Eno, B. (1996) *Generative Music: Evolving metaphors, in my opinion, is what artists do*. [online]. Available from: http://www.inmotionmagazine.com/eno1.html (Accessed 26 February 2018).

Ensslin, A. (2014) *Literary Gaming*. Cambridge, MA: The MIT Press.

Evenson, B. K. (2003) *Understanding Robert Coover*. Columbia: University of South Carolina Press.

Fedorova, N. (2017) 'Digital Letterisms: Alternumeric Orders', in Maria Mencia (ed.) *#WomenTechLit*. Morgantown: West Virginia University Press. pp. 131–152.

Finlay, I. H. (2012) 'Detached Sentences on Gardening', in Alec Finlay (ed.) *Ian Hamilton Finlay: Selections*. Poets for the Millennium. University of California Press. pp. 179–185.

Flores, L. (2013) Genre: Bot. *I Love E-poetry* [online]. Available from: http://iloveepoetry.com/?p=5427 (Accessed 14 December 2017).

Foucault, M. (1988) 'What Is an Author?', in David Lodge (ed.) *Modern Criticism and Theory: A Reader*. London: Longman. pp. 196–210.

Frow, J. (2006) *Genre: The New Critical Idiom*. Abingdon and New York: Routledge.

Frye, N. (2000) *Anatomy of criticism: four essays*. 15. pr. Princeton, NJ: Princeton Univ. Press.

Funkhouser, C. (2007) *Prehistoric Digital Poetry: An Archaeology of Forms, 1959–1995*. 1st edn. Tuscaloosa: University Alabama Press.

Funkhouser, C. (2008) 'Digital Poetry: A Look at Generative, Visual, and Interconnected Possibilities in its First Four Decades', in Ray Seimens & Susan Schreibman (eds) *A Companion to Digital Literary Studies*. Chicester, West Sussex: John Wiley and Scons. pp. 318–335.

Funkhouser, C. (2012) *New Directions in Digital Poetry*. New York: Bloomsbury Academic.

Gendolla, P. & Schäfer, J. (eds) (2007) *The Aesthetics of Net Literature: Writing, Reading and Playing in Programmable Media*. Bielefeld: Transcript-Verlag.

Gijsbers, V. (2015) Interactive Fiction Top 50 of all time (2015 edn). Interactive Fiction Database [online]. Available from: http://ifdb.tads.org/viewcomp?id=p6s9uem6td8rfihv (Accessed 17 December 2017).

Gillespie, W. et al. (2011) 'The Unknown (Authors' introduction)', in *Electronic Literature Collection, Volume 2*. [online]. Available from: http://collection.eliterature.org/2/works/rettberg_theunknown.html (Accessed 16 December 2017).

Glazier, L. P. (2001) *Digital Poetics: The Making of E-Poetries*. Tuscaloosa: University Alabama Press.

Goldsmith, K. (2008) 3,785 Page Pirated Poetry Anthology. *Poetry Foundation* [online]. Available from: https://www.poetryfoundation.org/harriet/2008/10/3785-page-pirated-poetry-anthology (Accessed 12 December 2017).

Goldsmith, K. (2009) Flarf is Dionysus. Conceptual Writing is Apollo. *Poetry* [online]. Available from: https://www.poetryfoundation.org/poetrymagazine/articles/69328/flarf-is-dionysus-conceptual-writing-is-apollo (Accessed 4 December 2017).

Grigar, D. & Moulthrop, S. (2016) Judy Malloy's *Uncle Roger*. *Pathfinders* [online]. Available from: http://scalar.usc.edu/works/pathfinders/judy-malloy (Accessed 15 December 2017).

Grigar, D. & Moulthrop, S. (2017) *Traversals: The Use of Preservation for Early Electronic Writing*. Cambridge, MA: The MIT Press.

Gysin, B. (n.d.) *Ubuweb: Sound Brion Gysin.* [online]. Available from: http://www. ubu.com/sound/gysin.html (Accessed 27 February 2018).

Hall, J. (2015) *overshare: The links.net story.* [online]. Available from: https:// archive.org/details/overshare-the_links.net_story (Accessed 10 December 2017).

Haraway, D. J. (1991) 'A Cyborg Manifesto: Science, Technology, and Socialist Feminism in the Late 20th Century', in *Simians, Cyborgs, and Women: The Reinvention of Nature.* New: Routledge. pp. 149–182.

Hartman, O. C. (1996) *Virtual Muse: Experiments in Computer Poetry.* Hanover, NH: University Press of New England.

Harrigan, P. & Wardrip-Fruin, N. (eds) (2007) *Third Person: Authoring and Exploring Vast Narratives.* Cambridge, MA: The MIT Press.

Harrigan, P. & Wardrip-Fruin, N. (eds) (2009) *Second Person: Role-Playing and Story in Games and Playable Media.* Cambridge, MA: The MIT Press.

Hayles, N. K. (1999) *How We Became Posthuman: Virtual Bodies in Cybernetics, Literature, and Informatics.* Chicago: University of Chicago Press.

Hayles, N. K. (2000) Open-work: Dining at the Interstices. *Riding the Meridian.* [online]. Available from: http://www.heelstone.com/meridian/templates/ Dinner/haylesfr.htm (Accessed 18 December 2017).

Hayles, N. K. (2002) *Writing Machines.* Cambridge, MA: The MIT Press.

Hayles, N. K. (2004) Print Is Flat, Code Is Deep: The Importance of Media-Specific Analysis. *Poetics Today.* 25 (1), 67–90.

Hayles, N. K. (2005) *My Mother Was a Computer: Digital Subjects and Literary Texts.* Chicago: The University of Chicago Press.

Hayles, N. K. (2008a) Distributed Cognition at/in Work: Strickland, Lawson Jaramillo, and Ryan's *slippingglimpse. Frame: Journal of Literary Studies.* 21 (1), 15–29.

Hayles, N. K. (2008b) *Electronic Literature: New Horizons for the Literary.* Notre Dame: University of Notre Dame Press.

Hayles, N. K. (2009) 'The Time of Digital Poetry: From Object to Event', in *New Media Poetics: Contexts, Technotexts, and Theories.* pp. 181–209.

Hayles, N. K. (2012) *How We Think: Digital Media and Contemporary Technogenesis.* Chicago: University of Chicago Press.

Heckman, D. (2010) Individual Work: *Hugo Ball. The Electronic Literature Directory* [online]. Available from: http://directory.eliterature.org/individual-work/825 (Accessed 19 December 2017).

Heldén, J. & Jonson, H. (2013) *Evolution.* Stockholm: OEI Editör.

Higgins, D. (1980) *A Taxonomy of Sound Poetry* [online]. Available from: http:// www.ubu.com/papers/higgins_sound.html (Accessed 19 December 2017).

Higgins, D. (1987) *Pattern Poetry: Guide to an Unknown Literature.* Albany: State University of New York Press.

Hight, J. (2010) 'Locative Narrative, Literature, and Form', in *Beyond the Screen: Transformations of Literary Structures, Interfaces and Genres.* pp. 315–331.

Holden, S. (1992) Review/Film: Atoms to Bees in Alternative Realities. *The New York Times.* 21 August. [online]. Available from: http://www.nytimes.com/

movie/review?res=9E0CE6DB1739F932A1575BC0A964958260 (Accessed 27 February 2018).

Iadarola, A. (2017) Interview with Porpentine Charity Heartscape. *Mask* [online]. Available from: http://maskmagazine.com/the-carnal-issue/work/porpentine-charity-heartscape (Accessed 17 December 2017). (40). [online]. Available from: http://maskmagazine.com/the-carnal-issue/work/porpentine-charity-heartscape (Accessed 17 December 2017).

Jerz, D. (2007) Somewhere Nearby is Collasal Cave: Examining Will Crowther's Original 'Adventure' in Code and in Kentucky. *Digital Humanities Quarterly*. 1 (2). [online]. Available from: http://www.digitalhumanities.org/dhq/vol/1/2/000009/000009.html (Accessed 17 December 2017).

Johnson, R. (2017) *Mail Art and Ephemera* [online]. Available from: http://www.rayjohnsonestate.com/art/mail-art-and-ephemera/ (Accessed 4 December 2017).

Johnston, D. J. (2011) David Clark's *88 Constellations for Wittgenstein*. Digital Poetry Overview: a chronology of digital poetry's anscestors and contemporaries [online]. Available from: http://glia.ca/conu/digitalPoetics/prehistoric-blog/2011/04/15/2009-david-clarks-88-constellations-for-wittgenstein/ (Accessed 16 December 2017).

Johnston, D. J. (2016) *Aesthetic Animism: Digital Poetry's Ontological Implications*. Cambridge, MA: The MIT Press.

Johnston, D. J. (2008) Theo Lutz, Stochastic Text. Digital Poetry Overview: a chronology of digital poetry's anscestors and contemporaries [online]. Available from: http://glia.ca/conu/digitalPoetics/prehistoric-blog/2008/07/16/1959-theo-lutz-stochastic-text/ (Accessed 12 December 2017).

Joyce, M. (1987b) Nonce Upon Some Times: Rereading Hypertext Fiction. *Modern Fiction Studies*. 43 (3), pp. 579–597.

Joyce, M. (1996) *Of Two Minds: Hypertext Pedagogy and Poetics*. Ann Arbor: University of Michigan Press.

Kac, E. (2007) 'Holopoetry', in Eduardo Kac (ed.) *Media Poetry: An International Anthology*. Bristol: Intellect Books. pp. 129–156.

Kenner, H. & O'Rourke, J. (1984) A Travesty Generator for Micros. BYTE 9 (12) pp.129–131, 449–469.

Kern, A. M. (2009) *The Exquisite Corpse: Chance and Collaboration in Surrealism's Parlor Game*. Kanta Kochhar-Lindgren et al. (eds). Lincoln: University of Nebraska Press.

Kirschenbaum, M. G. (2012) *Mechanisms: New Media and the Forensic Imagination*. Cambridge, MA.: The MIT Press.

Kirschenbaum, M. G. (2016) *The Poetics of Macintosh: Recovering the Digital Poetry of Kamau Brathwaite and William Dickey*. [online]. Available from: https://www.youtube.com/watch?v=XX4KstPpFa4.

Kittler, F. A. (1999) *Gramophone, Film, Typewriter*. Stanford: Stanford University Press.

Koenitz, H. et al. (eds) (2015) *Interactive Digital Narrative: History, Theory and Practice*. New York: Routledge.

Koskimaa, R. (2000) *Digital Literature: From Text to Hypertext and Beyond*. PhD thesis. Jyväskylä: University of Jyväskylä. [online]. Available from: http://users. jyu.fi/~koskimaa/thesis/thesis.shtml (Accessed 16 December 2017).

Kress, G. (2010) *Multimodality: A Social Semiotic Approach to Contemporary Communication*. New York: Routledge.

Landow, G. P. (1997) *Hypertext 2.0*. Baltimore: Johns Hopkins University Press.

Landow, G. P. (2006) *Hypertext 3.0: Critical Theory and New Media in an Era of Globalization*. Baltimore: Johns Hopkins University Press.

Landow, G. P. (1992) *Hypertext: The Convergence of Contemporary Critical Theory and Technology*. Baltimore: Johns Hopkins University Press.

Landow, G. P. (ed.) (1994) *Hyper/Text/Theory*. Baltimore: Johns Hopkins University Press.

Leclair, T. (2000) False Pretenses, Parasites, and Monsters. *electronic book review*. [online]. Available from: http://www.electronicbookreview.com/thread/webarts/ noisy (Accessed 21 December 2017).

Lee, S. (2005) How Do I Cool Down the Overheated Medium? Reading Stuart Moulthrop's *Hegirascope 2*, 'the most typical hypernovel'. *Dichtung Digital* (2005: 2). [online]. Available from: http://www.dichtung-digital.de/2005/2/ Lee/index.htm (Accessed 16 December 2017).

Lehto, L. (2006) Plurifying the Languages Of the Trite: In Dialogue With Régis Bonvicino and Alcir Pécora, Sibila, 2006. *nypoesi*. 2 (6). [online]. Available from: http://www.nypoesi.net/tidsskrift/206/?tekst=27 (Accessed 19 December 2017).

Leishman, D. (2012) The Flash Community Implications for Post-Conceptualism. *Dichtung Digital*. (41). [online]. Available from: http://www.dichtung-digital. org/2012/41/leishman/leishman.htm (Accessed 19 December 2017).

Lessig, L. (1999) *Code and Other Laws of Cyberspace*. New York: Basic Books.

Løvlie, A. S. (2015) 'Flâneur, a Walkthrough: Locative Literature as Participation and Play', in *Electronic Literature Communities*. pp. 151–168. [online]. Available from: https://elmcip.net/sites/default/files/media/critical_writing/attachments/ lovlie_flaneur.pdf.

Magnuson, J. (2009) *Photopia*: Not a Mediocre Short Story. Necessary Games [online]. Available from: http://www.necessarygames.com/reviews/photopia- game-free-download-independent-glulx-z-machine-interactive-fiction-fictional (Accessed 17 December 2017).

Malloy, J. (2015) *Notes on Uncle Roger*. [online]. Available from: https://people. well.com/user/jmalloy/uncleroger/uncle.html (Accessed 18 December 2017).

Malloy, J. & Moulthrop, S. (2011) Interview with Stuart Moulthrop. Authoring Electronic Literature [online]. Available from: http://www.narrabase.net/stuart- moulthrop.html (Accessed 16 December 2017).

Manovich, L. (2002a) *Generation Flash*. [online]. Available from: http://manovich. net/index.php/projects/generation-flash (Accessed 19 December 2017).

Manovich, L. (2001) *The Language of New Media*. Cambridge, MA: The MIT Press.

Marinetti, F. T. (2002) 'The Founding and Manifesto of Futurism', in Michael

Huxley & Noel Witts (eds) *The Twentieth Century Performance Reader*. London: Psychology Press. pp. 289–294.

Mass-Observation. (2017) *Mass Observation: Recording Everyday Life in Britain* [online]. Available from: http://www.massobs.org.uk/ (Accessed 9 December 2017).

Marino, M. C. (2011b) Netprov – Networked Improv Literature. WRT: Writer Response Theory [online]. Available from: http://writerresponsetheory.org/wordpress/2011/05/12/netprov-networked-improv-literature/ (Accessed 10 December 2017).

Mathews, H. (1997) Translation and the Oulipo: The Case of the Persevering Maltese. *electronic book review*. [online]. Available from: http://www.electronic bookreview.com/thread/electropoetics/ethno-linguist (Accessed 10 May 2016).

McCaffery, S. (1978) *Sound Poetry: A Catalogue for the Eleventh International Sound Poetry Festival*. bpNichol & Steve McCaffery (eds). Underwhich Editions. [online]. Available from: http://www.ubu.com/papers/mccaffery.html (Accessed 19 December 2017).

McHugh, H. (2001) *(2001 Electronic Literature Award) Comments by Heather McHugh, Poetry Judge* [online]. Available from: http://eliterature.org/Awards2001/comments-poetry.php (Accessed 22 February 2018).

McLuhan, M. (1964) *Understanding Media: The Extensions of Man*. New York: McGraw-Hill.

Memmott, T. (2011) *Digital Rhetoric and Poetics: Signifying Strategies in Electronic Literature*. Malmö: Malmö University. [online]. Available from: http://dspace.mah.se/handle/2043/12547 (Accessed 4 December 2017).

Montfort, N. et al. (eds) (2006) *Electronic Literature Collection, Volume One*. College Park, MD: Electronic Literature Organization. [online]. Available from: http://collection.eliterature.org/1/ (Accessed 19 March 2016).

Montfort, N. (2003) *Twisty Little Passages: An Approach to Interactive Fiction*. Cambridge, MA: The MIT Press.

Montfort, N. & Short, E. (2015) 'Interactive Fiction Communities: From Preservation Through Promotion and Beyond', in *Electronic Literature Communities*. pp. 113–129.

Morris, A. & Swiss, T. (eds) (2009) *New Media Poetics: Contexts, Technotexts, and Theories*. Cambridge, MA: The MIT Press.

Moulthrop, S. (2018) 'Lift This End: Electronic Literature in a Blue Light', in *The Bloomsbury Handbook of Electronic Literature*. pp. 59–72.

Murray, J. H. (1997) *Hamlet on the Holodeck: The Future of Narrative in Cyberspace*. Cambridge, MA: The MIT Press.

Nelson, G. (2001) *The Inform User's Manual*. 4th edn. St Charles, IL: The Interactive Fiction Library.

Nelson, T. H. (1965) 'Complex information processing: a file structure for the complex, the changing and the indeterminate', in *ACM '65 Proceedings of the 1965 20th national conference*. Cleveland: ACM. pp. 84–100. [online]. Available from: https://dl.acm.org/citation.cfm?id=806036 (Accessed 15 December 2017).

Nelson, T. H. (2003) 'Computer Lib / Dream Machines', in *The New Media Reader*. pp. 301–339.

Nietzsche, F. W. (1956) *The Birth of Tragedy and The Genealogy of Morals*. New York: Doubleday.

Norman, D. (1999) Affordance, conventions, and design. *Interactions*. 6 (3), pp. 38–43.

Oliphant, R. (1961) The Auto-Beatnik, the Auto-Critic, and the Justification of Nonsense. *The Antioch Review*. 21 (4), 405–491.

Parkin, S. (2014) Zoe Quinn's Depression Quest. *The New Yorker* [online]. Available from: https://www.newyorker.com/tech/elements/zoe-quinns-depression-quest (Accessed 23 February 2018).

Perloff, M. (2004) *Differentials: Poetry, Poetics, Pedagogy*. Tuscaloosa: University of Alabama Press.

Perloff, M. (1998) *Inner Tension / In Attention": Steve Mccaffery's Book Art* [online]. Available from: http://epc.buffalo.edu/authors/perloff/mccaf.html (Accessed 18 December 2017).

Portela, M. (2010) *DigLitWeb: Digital Literature Web* [online]. Available from: http://www.ci.uc.pt/diglit/DigLitWebEdeEdicaoElectronicaEnsaio36.html (Accessed 19 December 2017).

Portela, M. (2013) *Scripting Reading Motions: The Codex and the Computer as Self-Reflexive Machines*. Cambridge, MA: The MIT Press.

Pound, E. (1934) *Make It New: Essays*. London: Faber & Faber.

Pressman, J. (2014) *Digital Modernism: Making It New in New Media*. New York: Oxford University Press.

Pressman, J. (2008) The Strategy of Digital Modernism: Young-Hae Chang Heavy Industries' Dakota. *Modern Fiction Studies*. 54 (299–326).

Raley, R. (2002) Interferences: [Net.Writing] and the Practice of Codework. *electronic book review*. [online]. Available from: http://www.electronicbookreview.com/thread/electropoetics/net.writing (Accessed 9 December 2017).

Raley, R. (2011) Living Letterforms: The Ecological Turn in Contemporary Digital Poetics. *Contemporary Literature*. 52 (4), 883–913.

Raley, R. (2009) *Tactical Media*. Minneapolis: University of Minnesota Press.

Rau, A. (2001) Wreader's Digest – How To Appreciate Hyperfiction. *Journal of Digital Information*. 1 (7). [online]. Available from: https://journals.tdl.org/jodi/index.php/jodi/article/view/28/29 (Accessed 15 December 2017).

Rettberg, J. W. (2012) Electronic Literature Seen from a Distance: The Beginnings of a Field. *Dichtung Digital*. (41). [online]. Available from: http://www.dichtung-digital.org/2012/41/walker-rettberg/walker-rettberg.htm (Accessed 18 December 2017).

Rettberg, J. W. (2014) *Blogging*. 2nd edn. Cambridge, UK: Polity.

Rettberg, S. (2002) The Pleasure (and Pain) of Link Poetics. *electronic book review*. [online]. Available from: http://www.electronicbookreview.com/thread/electropoetics/pragmatic (Accessed 16 December 2017).

Rettberg, S. (2008) Dada Redux: Elements of Dadaist Practice in Contemporary

Electronic Literature. *Fibreculture*. (11). [online]. Available from: http://eleven.fibreculturejournal.org/fcj-071-dada-redux-elements-of-dadaist-practice-incon-temporary-electronic-literature/ (Accessed 19 March 2018).

Rettberg, S. (2010) Performative Reading: Attending The Last Performance [dot org]. *Dichtung Digital*. (40). [online]. Available from: http://dichtung-digital.de/2010/rettberg/rettberg.htm (Accessed 21 December 2017).

Rettberg, S. (2011) 'All Together Now: Hypertext, Collective Narratives, and Online Collective Knowledge Communities', in Ruth Page & Browen Thomas (eds) *New Narratives: Stories and Storytelling in the Digital Age*. University of Nebraska Press. pp. 187–204.

Rettberg, S. (2014) 'Electronic Literature', in Lori Emerson et al. (eds) *The Johns Hopkins Guide to Digital Media*. Baltimore: Johns Hopkins University Press. pp. 169–173.

Rettberg, S. & Baldwin, S. (eds.) (2014) *Electronic Literature as a Model of Creativity and Innovation in Practice: A Report from the HERA Joint Research Project*. Computing Literature. Morgantown: Center for Literary Computing, ELMCIP. [online]. Available from: https://elmcip.net/sites/default/files/media/critical_writing/attachments/rettberg_baldwin_ elmcip.pdf. (Accessed 19 March 2018).

Rettberg, S. et al. (eds.) (2015) *Electronic Literature Communities*. Computing Literature. Morgantown: The Center for Literary Computing, ELMCIP. [online]. Available from: https://elmcip.net/sites/default/files/media/critical_writing/attachments/elmcip_2_electronicliteraturecommunities.pdf. (Accessed 19 March 2018).

Richter, H. (1995) *Art and Anti-Art*. London: Thames & Hudson.

Rueb, T. (2008) On Itinerant. *electronic book review*. [online]. Available from: http://www.electronicbookreview.com/thread/firstperson/located (Accessed 31 January 2018).

Ryan, M. L. (2006) *Avatars of Story*. Minneapolis: University of Minnesota Press.

Ryan, M. L. (2001) *Narrative as Virtual Reality: Immersion and Interactivity in Literature and Electronic Media*. Baltimore: John Benjamins Publishing.

Ryan, M. L. et al. (eds) (2014) *The Johns Hopkins Guide to Digital Media*. Baltimore: Johns Hopkins University Press.

Saemmer, A. (2010) 'Digital Literature – A Question of Style', in Roberto Simanowski et al. (eds) *Reading Moving Letters: Digital Literature in Research and Teaching: a Handbook*. pp. 163–182.

Salter, A. & Murray, J. (2014) *Flash: Building the Interactive Web*. Cambridge MA: The MIT Press.

Schäfer, J. & Gendolla, P. (eds.) (2010) *Beyond the Screen: Transformations of Literary Structures, Interfaces and Genres*. Media Upheavals. Bielefeld: Transcript-Verlag.

Schwitters, K. (n.d.) *Kurt Schwitters (1887–1948)* [online]. Available from: http://www.ubu.com/sound/schwitters.html (Accessed 19 December 2017).

Seiça, Á. (2018a) 'The Freedom Adventure of Portuguese Experimentalism and Kinetic Poetry', in *The Bloomsbury Handbook of Electronic Literature*. pp. 165–177.

Seiça, Á. (2018b) *setInterval(): Time-Based Readings of Kinetic Poetry*. Bergen: University of Bergen. [online]. Available from: http://bora.uib.no/handle/1956/17267 (Accessed 27 February 2018).

Simanowski, R. (2004) Concrete Poetry in Digital Media Its Predecessors, its Presence and its Future. *Dichtung Digital*. 2004 (3). [online]. Available from: http://www.dichtung-digital.org/2004/3/simanowski/index.htm (Accessed 18 December 2017).

Simanowski, R. (2011) *Digital Art and Meaning: Reading Kinetic Poetry, Text Machines, Mapping Art, and Interactive Installations*. Minneapolis: Univ Of Minnesota Press.

Simanowski, R. et al. (eds.) (2010) *Reading Moving Letters: Digital Literature in Research and Teaching: a Handbook*. Bielefeld: Transcript-Verlag.

Solt, M. A. (1968) 'Introduction', in *Concrete Poetry, A Worldview*. Bloomington: Indiana University Press. [online]. Available from: http://www.ubu.com/papers/solt/intro.html (Accessed 18 December 2017).

Sondheim, A. (2001) Introduction: Codework. *American Book Review*. 22 (6). [online]. Available from: http://litline.org/ABR/issues/Volume22/Issue6/sondheim.pdf (Accessed 29 November 2017).

Stafford, B. M. (1991) *Body Criticism: Imagining the Unseen in Enlightenment Art and Medicine*. Cambridge, MA: The MIT Press.

Stefans, B. K. (2017) *Word Toys*. Tuscaloosa: University Alabama Press.

Stefans, B. K. (2003) *Fashionable Noise on Digital Poetics*. Berkeley: Atelos.

Stiegler, B. (2010) 'Memory', in W. J. T. Mitchell & Mark B. N. Hansen (eds) *Critical Terms for Media Studies*. Chicago: University of Chicago Press. pp. 64–87.

Strachey, C. (1954) The 'Thinking' Machine. *Encounter*. 25–31. [online]. Available from: http://www.unz.org/Pub/Encounter-1954oct-00025 (Accessed 27 February 2018).

Strickland, S. (2009) Born Digital. Poetry Foundation [online]. Available from: https://www.poetryfoundation.org/articles/69224/born-digital (Accessed 7 December 2017).

Sullivan, G. (2006) Jacket Flarf feature: Introduction. *Jacket*. (30). [online]. Available from: http://jacketmagazine.com/30/fl-intro.html (Accessed 11 December 2017).

Szilak, I. (2013) A Book Itself Is a Little Machine: Emily Short's Interactive Fiction. Huffington Post [online]. Available from: https://www.huffingtonpost.com/illya-szilak/a-book-itself-is-a-little_b_4168309.html (Accessed 17 December 2017).

Tabbi, J. (2009) On Reading 300 Works of Electronic Literature: Preliminary Reflections. On the Human: a Project of the National Humanities Center [online]. Available from https://nationalhumanitiescenter.org/on-the-human/2009/07/on-reading-300-works-of-electronic-literature-preliminary-reflections/.

Tabbi, J. (2010) Electronic Literature as World Literature, or: The Universality of Writing Under Constraint. *Poetics Today*. 31 (1), 17–50.

Tabbi, J. (2018) *The Bloomsbury Handbook of Electronic Literature*. London: Bloomsbury Academic.

Taylor, S. (2009) *Alison Knowles, James Tenney and the House of Dust at CalArts*. [online]. Available from: http://blog.calarts.edu/2009/09/10/alison-knowles-james-tenney-and-the-house-of-dust-at-calarts/ (Accessed 1 July 2016).

Todorov, T. (1976) The Origin of Genres. *New Literary History*. [Online] 8 (1), 159–170. [online]. Available from: http://www.jstor.org/stable/468619 (Accessed 15 March 2016).

Tomasula, S. (2018) 'Our Tools Make Us (and Our Literature) Post', in *The Bloomsbury Handbook of Electronic Literature*. pp. 39–58.

Tsukayama, J. (2014) *By Any Means Necessary: An Interpretive Phenomenological Analysis Study of Post 9/11 American Abusive Violence in Iraq*. Ph.D. dissertation thesis. Saint Andrews: Saint Andrews University. [online]. Available from: https://research-repository.st-andrews.ac.uk/handle/10023/4510 (Accessed 19 March 2018).

Turing, A. (1950) Computing Machinery and Intelligence. *Mind*. LIX (236), 433–460.

Tristan Tzara (2006) 'Dada Manifesto 1918', in Dawn Ades (ed.) *The Dada Reader: A Critical Anthology*. Chicago: University of Chicago Press. pp. 36–42.

Vassilakis, N. (2012) 'The Last Vispo: Toward Vispoetics', in Craig Hill & Nico Vassilakis (eds) *The Last Vispo Anthology*. Seattle: Fantagraphics. pp. 8–10.

Walker, J. (1999) 'Piecing together and tearing apart: finding the story in *afternoon*', in *Proceedings of ACM Hypertext 1999*. [Online]. 1999 ACM Press. pp. 111–117. [online]. Available from: http://portal.acm.org/citation.cfm?doid=294469.294496 (Accessed 19 March 2016).

Walker, J. (2005) 'Distributed Narrative: Telling Stories Across Networks', in Mia Consalvo et al. (eds) *The 2005 Association of Internet Researchers Annual*. New York: Peter Lang. pp. 91–102. [online]. Available from: http://jilltxt.net/txt/Walker-AoIR-3500words.pdf (Accessed 19 March 2018).

Walker, J. (2005b) 'Weblog', in David Herman et al. (eds) *Routledge Encyclopedia of Narrative Theory*. Abingdon-on-Thames: Routledge. [online]. Available from: http://jilltxt.net/?p=227 (Accessed 11 December 2017).

Wardrip-Fruin, N. (2011) 'Digital Media Archeology: Interpreting Computational Processes', in Erkki Huhtamo and Jussi Parikka (eds) *Media Archaeology: Approaches, Applications, and Implications*. Berkeley: University of California Press. pp. 302–322.

Wardrip-Fruin, N. (2009) *Expressive Processing: Digital Fictions, Computer Games, and Software Studies*. Cambridge, MA: The MIT Press.

Wardrip-Fruin, N. (2005) Playable Media and Textual Instruments.

Dichtung Digital (2005: 1). [online]. Available from: http://www.dichtung-digital.de/2005/1/Wardrip-Fruin/index.htm (Accessed 16 December 2017).

Wardrip-Fruin, N. & Harrigan, P. (eds) (2004) *First Person: New Media as Story, Performance, and Game.* Cambridge, MA: The MIT Press.

Wardrip-Fruin, N. & Montfort, N. (eds) (2003) *The New Media Reader.* Cambridge, MA: The MIT Press.

Wardrip-Fruin, N. (2004) 'What Hypertexst Is', in *Hypertext '04: Proceedings of the Fifteenth ACM Conference on Hypertext and Hypermedia.* 2004 ACM. pp. 126–127. [online]. Available from: https://dl.acm.org/citation.cfm?id=1012844. (Accessed 19 March 2018).

Weizenbaum, J. (1966) ELIZA – a computer program for the study of natural language communication between man and machine. *Communications of the ACM.* 9 (1), 36–45. [online]. Available from: http://portal.acm.org/citation.cfm?doid=365153.365168 (Accessed 19 March 2016).

Weizenbaum, J. (1976) *Computer Power and Human Reason: From Judgement to Calculation.* San Francisco: W. H. Freeman & Co.

Wittig, R. (1994) *Invisible Rendezvous: Connection and Collaboration in the New Landscape of Electronic Writing.* Hanover, NH: Wesleyan University Press.

Wittig, R. (2018) 'Literature and Narrative in Social Media: A Travesty, or, in Defense of Pretension', in *The Bloomsbury Handbook of Electronic Literature.* pp. 113–132.

Wittig, R. (2011) *Networked Improv Narrative (Netprov) and the Story of Grace, Wit & Charm.* Bergen: University of Bergen. [online]. Available from: http://bora.uib.no/bitstream/handle/1956/6305/89114012.pdf?sequence=1 (Accessed 10 December 2017).

Woods, N. L. (2012) Object/Poems: Alison Knowles' Feminist Archite(x)ture. *X-tra.* 15 (1). [online]. Available from: http://x-traonline.org/article/object poems-alison-knowless-feminist-architexure/ (Accessed 1 July 2016).

Youngblood, G. (1970) *Expanded Cinema.* New York: P. Dutton & Co.

Other Resources Referenced

Arquivo Digital Da Po.Ex (Po.Ex Digital Archive) [online]. Available from: https://po-ex.net (Accessed 28 February 2018).

electronic book review [online]. Tabbi, J. (ed.) Available from: http://electronic bookreview.com/about (Accessed 1 March 2018).

Electronic Literature – posters and other historical documents [online]. Available from: http://marcus.uib.no/instance/collection/ubb-ela (Accessed 8 December 2017).

Electronic Literature Directory [online]. Available from: http://directory.eliterature. org (Accessed 7 December 2017).

Electronic Literature Lab (ELL): For Advanced Inquiry into Born Digital Media [online]. Available from: http://dtc-wsuv.org/wp/ell/ (Accessed 8 December 2017).

ELMCIP Electronic Literature Knowledge Base [online]. Available from: http://elmcip.net/knowledgebase (Accessed 21 March 2016).

Guide to the Stephanie Strickland Papers, 1955–2016 [online]. Available from: https://library.duke.edu/rubenstein/findingaids/stricklandstephanie/ (Accessed 8 December 2017).

Hyperrhiz: New Media Cultures. Burgess, H. (ed.) [online]. Available from: http://hyperrhiz.io (Accessed 1 March 2018).

Media Archeology Lab [online]. Available from: https://mediaarchaeologylab.com/ (Accessed 8 December 2017).

Michael Joyce: An Inventory of His Papers at the Harry Ransom Center [online]. Available from: http://norman.hrc.utexas.edu/fasearch/findingAid.cfm?eadid=00743 (Accessed 8 December 2017).

Recherche Répertoire [online]. Available from: http://nt2.uqam.ca/ (Accessed 17 December 2017).

The Deena Larsen Collection [online]. Available from: http://mith.umd.edu/larsen/ (Accessed 8 December 2017).

The New River. Falco, E. (ed.) [online]. Available from: http://www.cddc.vt.edu/journals/newriver/ (Accessed 1 March 2018).

The Trope Tank [online]. Available from: http://nickm.com/trope_tank/ (Accessed 8 December 2017).

Index

Index

Index

Index